Whitman in Washington

Whitman in Washington

Becoming the National Poet in the Federal City

KENNETH M. PRICE

UNIVERSITY PRESS

Great Clarendon Street, Oxford, OX2 6DP,
United Kingdom

Oxford University Press is a department of the University of Oxford.
It furthers the University's objective of excellence in research, scholarship,
and education by publishing worldwide. Oxford is a registered trade mark of
Oxford University Press in the UK and in certain other countries

© Kenneth M. Price 2020

The moral rights of the author have been asserted

First Edition published in 2020

Impression: 1

All rights reserved. No part of this publication may be reproduced, stored in
a retrieval system, or transmitted, in any form or by any means, without the
prior permission in writing of Oxford University Press, or as expressly permitted
by law, by licence or under terms agreed with the appropriate reprographics
rights organization. Enquiries concerning reproduction outside the scope of the
above should be sent to the Rights Department, Oxford University Press, at the
address above

You must not circulate this work in any other form
and you must impose this same condition on any acquirer

Published in the United States of America by Oxford University Press
198 Madison Avenue, New York, NY 10016, United States of America

British Library Cataloguing in Publication Data
Data available

Library of Congress Control Number: 2020943441

ISBN 978–0–19–884093–0

Printed and bound by
CPI Group (UK) Ltd, Croydon, CR0 4YY

Links to third party websites are provided by Oxford in good faith and
for information only. Oxford disclaims any responsibility for the materials
contained in any third party website referenced in this work.

Preface

During Walt Whitman's decade in Washington, DC, 1863–73, he labored intensely, at times seeming to have three lives at once. He wrote the most distinguished journalism of his career; came into his own as a writer of letters; crafted memorable Civil War poetry, *Drum-Taps* and *Sequel to Drum-Taps* (1865) and later folded it into heavily revised and expanded versions of *Leaves of Grass* in 1867 and 1871; and produced his searching but also flawed critique of American culture, *Democratic Vistas*. Whitman's work through the first three editions of *Leaves* (1855, 1856, 1860–61) often receives the highest praise, yet his writing in the Washington years is exceptional, too, by any reckoning—and is all the more remarkable given that he also cared for thousands of wounded and sick soldiers in Washington hospitals, serving as an attentive visitor. In addition, he served as a government clerk in various positions, most notably in the attorney general's office when much was accomplished on the road toward a multi-racial democracy, including efforts to suppress the Ku Klux Klan, and much was also missed (both by the attorney general's office and by Whitman) in the efforts to advance a more just and vibrant union. This book analyzes Whitman's integrated life, writings, and government work in his urban context to reevaluate the writer and the nation's capital in a time of transformation.

The crisis of war remade both Whitman and Washington, DC. The city more than tripled in size from 63,000 to 200,000 inhabitants and was transformed from a slave-holding city wedged between two slave states into the nation's first emancipated city. In 1862 Washington became the only place in the nation ever to carry out compensated emancipation. The importance of this change cannot be over-emphasized. Prior to the outbreak of civil war, as Frederick Douglass noted, the "District of Columbia [was] the very citadel of slavery, the place most zealously watched and guarded by the slave power, and where humane tendencies were most speedily detected and sternly opposed."[1] By the time Whitman settled in Washington, however,

---

[1] Quoted in Ellen M. O'Connor, *Myrtilla Miner: A Memoir* (Boston, MA: Houghton, Mifflin, 1885), 21.

both types of emancipation—compensated emancipation and the more sweeping Emancipation Proclamation—had gone into effect; his treatment of race in a new era of legal liberation and continuing social discrimination is a recurrent issue across the chapters of this study.

During the war years, Washington, DC, once a relatively quiet town with a busy political season, absorbed a new and year-round population of foreign mercenaries, doctors, diplomats, philanthropists, prostitutes, adventure-seekers, undertakers, nurses, and fugitive slaves. During the War, 40,000 fugitive slaves, known as "contrabands," fled to the nation's capital: they often resided in camps run by the government and charitable organizations and many worked on military projects.[2] Daily life in the city was often interrupted by military drills and the fear or rumor of imminent Confederate attacks. From the First Battle of Bull Run, Confederate armies continually threatened Washington as part of General Robert E. Lee's strategy of taking the war to the north. Lee's offensives of 1862 and 1863, leading to key battles at Antietam and Gettysburg, were meant to threaten Washington, to encourage the numerous Southern sympathizers in the North, and to challenge President Lincoln's administrative authority. In response, Lincoln ordered the creation of a thirty-seven-mile ring of forts and batteries, effectively transforming the nation's capital into a citadel.[3]

This study situates Whitman in the streets, wards, boarding houses, trams, and government buildings of a city being remade. In these settings, Whitman wrote his letters and poems and inscribed notebooks and memoranda. These writings were at times collaborative, perhaps most memorably when Whitman and Civil War soldiers braided their words and experiences of civil war in prose, verse, and letters home. After the war, Whitman refashioned his literary efforts in keeping with profoundly altered local circumstances, continued to visit hospitals where soldiers convalesced long after the end of hostilities, and served as an active participant in the attorney general's office where advice and directives were given as the government was reconstituted.

The chapters that follow pursue guiding concepts, frequently marked by a key word. The opening chapter considers *convulsiveness*, a term Whitman relied on to emphasize the massive economic, political, and personal

---

[2] The term "contraband of war," used by General Benjamin Butler in 1861 to refer to formerly enslaved people who reached Union lines, became widely adopted thereafter.

[3] Kenneth J. Winkle, *Lincoln's Citadel: The Civil War in Washington, DC* (New York: W. W. Norton, 2013), xii.

disruption caused by the war. The next chapter focuses on Whitman as a paradoxical *missionary* to the wounded, as he figured it, a type of evangelist of brotherhood. I follow with an exploration of *pastoralism*, a term that has been regularly employed to denigrate Whitman's war writing as conservatively reinstating a traditional status quo. For Whitman, pastoralism and anti-pastoralism went hand-in-hand—thus we need to have a more complex and nuanced understanding of his remaking of pastoral motifs and conventions. The fourth chapter considers Whitman in light of a new *pensiveness* that manifests itself in the war years, a term with a literary pedigree to Milton that cast an unusually pessimistic shadow over his thought during Reconstruction. The concluding chapter analyzes the *vistas* available and unavailable to Whitman as he worked in the attorney general's office, gazed out his window from his work station, and drafted *Democratic Vistas*, his 1871 analysis of the condition and prospects of the United States.

Whitman in Washington benefits from newly available correspondence, journalism, and nearly 3,000 documents I identified in the National Archives as being in the hand of Whitman. These scribal documents from his work as a clerk in the attorney general's office allow us to pinpoint to the exact day when he encountered certain issues during the early years of Reconstruction. Some documents in his hand concern routine administrative matters, while others treat civil rights, war crimes, treason, western expansion, the rise of white vigilantism, and a host of international incidents. He treated closely related matters while revising *Leaves of Grass* and drafting *Democratic Vistas*. Whitman's cultural critique was informed by the in-depth knowledge he gained in the attorney general's office. This study underscores the significance of the scribal documents and establishes connections between his life in bureaucracy and his poetry of democracy. Whitman thrived in divergent roles as both clerk and cosmos—he was a functionary and simultaneously a visionary poet.

In *Re-Scripting Walt Whitman*, Ed Folsom and I emphasized Whitman's "scripted life," the manuscript origins of his work that tell us much about his motivations, ideas, and thinking processes.[4] We also investigated his "life in press," the ways that his training and experience as a printer and typesetter affected his evolving belief that he could literally transfer his identity to the printed page, embody himself in books. In this study, I go further to consider his life as a scribe, a writer who gave voice or form to others. As a scribe, he

---

[4] Ed Folsom and Kenneth M. Price, *Re-Scripting Walt Whitman: An Introduction to His Life and Work* (Malden, MA: Blackwell, 2005).

drafted letters home for injured soldiers, drafted routine reports and correspondence in governmental offices, and also wrote poetry about the Civil War in *Drum-Taps*. He gained life experience as a ventriloquist of sorts—throwing his voice to become the soldiers themselves as he wrote as and through them to their friends and loved ones, just as he regularly assumed the identity of others as he conducted his work as a government clerk. These experiences of inhabiting another's view—always part of Whitman's poetry, of course, but now acted out quite literally in life—accelerated his developing tendency to write from the perspective of various personae. Mysteriously but also unmistakably in these years he achieved the most unlikely exchange of all, managing to transfer his identity to the nation—and the nation's to himself.

In the vast amount of commentary on Whitman, there is almost no consideration of what it meant for Whitman to become a clerk, how he regarded clerks prior to moving to Washington, and how being a clerk affected him as a person and a writer. Many of his close friends despised being clerks, finding the work stultifying.[5] Whitman, too, had little good to say about clerks prior to moving to Washington, expected to dislike the work, and could only bring himself to look for a clerkship in a "listless sort of way."[6] Once he became a clerk, however, he was surprised to find it suited him. His fellow clerks became his key intellectual network and his sustaining friends during his Washington years. To a large extent, they served to replace the bohemian comrades he had enjoyed at Pfaff's beer hall in New York.

The various dimensions of Whitman's life in Washington have received uneven treatment in the scholarly literature, and the significance of his government work and of Washington—as a place, symbol, vantage point, literary home, and experiment in multi-racial life and governance—has been neglected. Thanks to two extensive online resources I have helped create,

---

[5] See the Letter from W. W. Thayer to Walt Whitman, August 31, 1862:
"Since the failure of T&E [Thayer & Eldridge publishing house], I was out of business five months & then obtained a clerkship in the Boston Post Office where I have worked very hard, and suffered much mentally incapacitating me for writing reading or thinking." Available on *The Walt Whitman Archive* (hereafter abbreviated as WWA).

For more on clerks, see also Ruth L. Bohan, "*Vanity Fair*, Whitman, and the Counter Jumper," *Word & Image* 33 no. 1 (2017), 57–69 and Thomas Augst, *The Clerk's Tale: Young Men and Moral Life in Nineteenth-Century America* (Chicago, IL: University of Chicago Press, 2003).

[6] Letter from Walt Whitman to Nathaniel Bloom and John F. S. Gray, March 19-20, 1863 (*WWA*).

The Walt Whitman Archive and *Civil War Washington*, we have the opportunity to analyze Whitman with the advantages of a much more complete textual record and a more multi-dimensional understanding of the city, grounding his poetry, journalism, hospital work, and government labor in the muddy and sometimes tawdry streets of a city with grand aspirations and vistas.

By studying the mid-career Whitman in his urban context, I address what Wayne Franklin and Michael Steiner called a "spatial amnesia" in American and cultural studies.[7] Whitman's own concern with geo-temporal specificity is clear even in the title of *Memoranda During the War* and especially its subtitle: *Written on the Spot in 1863–'65*. Whitman's insistence on his positioning underscores his awareness of how people make and are made by place. In Whitman's prose, place often appears as a specific locale—a boarding house, a streetcar, a hospital ward, for example. At other times, Whitman encountered sites already heavily weighted with symbolic import such as the Washington monument or the statue of freedom atop the Capitol dome. Whitman's experience of Washington as a place was of course not limited to these immediate and actual places. He also encountered an urban landscape with the mythic and literary space of the pastoral very much in mind, as is evident in his overhauling of pastoral conventions.

Whitman's opinion of Washington, DC, evolved, gradually warming as he explained to Nathaniel Bloom and Fred Gray, former companions at Pffaf's:

> Washington and its points I find bear a second and a third perusal, and doubtless indeed many. My first impressions, architectural, &c. were not favorable; but upon the whole, the city, the spaces, buildings, &c make no unfit emblem of our country, so far, so broadly planned, every thing in plenty, money & materials staggering with plenty, but the fruit of the plans, the knit, the combination yet wanting—Determined to express ourselves greatly in a capital but no fit capital yet here—(time, associations, wanting, I suppose)—many a hiatus yet—many a thing to be taken down and done over again yet—perhaps an entire change of base—may-be a succession of changes.

---

[7] Wayne Franklin and Michael Steiner, *Mapping American Culture* (Iowa City, IA: University of Iowa Press, 1992), 8.

The city's monuments were of special interest to a poet who longed to be the national bard and who saw his work as organically tied to the American Revolution's political ideals.[8] The Washington monument was a mere stump at this time and, as Kirk Savage has shown, funding for its completion and decisions about its ultimate design had been held hostage, prior to the war, to the conflict between northern and southern politicians, hinging on slavery.[9] (In fact, mistakes were made in setting up the original funding for it, both because contributions were limited to "white inhabitants" and capped at $1 as being most democratic.) During the war years, the stunted condition of the monument seemed to testify to bold plans gone bust. Interestingly, as a symbol, George Washington was equally vital to the rebellion and the union defense; his image adorned both the Confederate seal and the federal dollar. Propagandists on both sides claimed him—for the north he was a "defender of union and critic of slavery and [for the south] a slaveholding planter and leader of rebellion."[10] Whitman, like many others, tends to repress the Washington of slave ownership. Yet the legacy of slavery haunted his city. Arlington House, part of Whitman's prospect, on a hillside rising above the Potomac and overlooking Washington, DC, was intended as a living memorial to George Washington while it also served as the home of Confederate General Robert E. Lee and his wife (granddaughter through her first marriage of George Washington's wife). After the war began, the Union army seized this land and it became a graveyard and ultimately Arlington National Cemetery, underlining the lethal effects of slavery within a political system devoted to liberty and democracy. The stakes could not have been higher then for Americans with regard to the meaning of George Washington—both how he was understood and remembered.

Despite the failings of the capital and this troubling vista of a graveyard, Whitman came to admire his adopted city, as he made clear in 1863 when he wrote "Letter from Washington" for the *New-York Times*. He doubted

---

[8] David Haven Blake, "The American Revolution" in *Walt Whitman: An Encyclopedia*, ed. J.R. LeMaster and Donald D. Kummings (New York: Garland Publishing, 1998). Available on WWA.

[9] Savage, "The Self-Made Monument: George Washington and the Fight to Erect a National Memorial," *Winterthur Portfolio*, 22, No. 4 (Winter, 1987), 225–42.

[10] Savage, 231. Starting at age eleven, Washington was a slave-holder and remained one for more than fifty years. A wealthy man, he possessed more than 800 slaves in his life. His misgivings about the institution were deep, and at the end of his life, he freed his slaves in his will, alone amongst slave-holding founding fathers.

"whether justice has been done.... We all know the chorus: Washington, dusty, muddy, tiresome Washington is the most awful place, political and other; is the rendezvous of the national universal axe-grinding, caucusing... and windy bawlers from every quarter far and near." If the "high-life attractions" of other capitals were lacking, Whitman did not miss them: "What themes, what fields this national city affords, this hour, for eyes of live heads, and for souls fit to feed upon them!"[11] In this article, Whitman also reflects on the unfinished Capitol and the sculpture to sit atop the dome, the Genius of Liberty: "A few days ago, poking about there, eastern side, I found the Genius, all dismembered, scattered on the ground, by the basement front—I suppose preparatory to being hoisted."[12] Like so many soldiers who had endured amputations, the Genius of the country had been cut in pieces. It would later be soldered back together in a way that Whitman, in caring for soldiers, could not match despite his best efforts to supply arms and legs for men who had lost them, to embrace the wounded and somehow make them whole again. The scene at the Capitol was indeed one of future potential for reassembling the meaning of liberty, for Whitman saw a huge derrick surmounting the dome and he began to wonder if this "rude and mighty derrick" should remain atop the Capitol as the most fit emblem of the nation and age. Washington and the nation, he realized, would always be under construction.

Daniel Aaron argued four decades ago that the Civil War was "unwritten,"[13] contending that American writers failed to produce texts commensurate with the magnitude of the sacrifice, suffering, and import of this time of national crisis and redefinition. In recent years, scholars have questioned this conclusion: Alice Fahs, Kathleen Diffley, Faith Barrett, Cristanne Miller, Eliza Richards, Randall Fuller, and a host of others have analyzed writings, particularly by women and African Americans, that have enriched our understanding of the range, quality, and importance of the literary response to the war.[14] Aaron's idea about the unwritten war may have been prompted

---

[11] Whitman, "Letter from Washington," *New-York Times*, October 4, 1863: 2 (*WWA*).
[12] Whitman, "Letter from Washington," 2.
[13] Aaron, *The Unwritten War: American writers and the Civil War* (New York: Knopf, 1973).
[14] Alice, Fahs, *The Imagined Civil War: Popular Literature of the North & South, 1861–1865* (Chapel Hill, NC: University of North Carolina Press, 2001); Faith Barrett, *To Fight Aloud is Very Brave: American Poetry and the Civil War* (Amherst, MA: University of Massachusetts Press, 2012); Cristanne Miller, *Reading in Time: Emily Dickinson in the Nineteenth Century* (Amherst, MA: University of Massachusetts Press, 2012); *"Words for the hour": A New Anthology of American Civil War Poetry*, ed. Faith Barrett and Cristanne Miller (Amherst: University of Massachusetts Press, 2005); Randall Fuller, *From Battlefields Rising: How the Civil War Transformed American Literature* (New York: Oxford University Press, 2011).

by—and gained reinforcement from—Whitman's insistence on the war's ineffable quality: "Future years will never know the seething hell and the black infernal background of countless minor scenes and interiors, (not the official surface-courteousness of the Generals, not the few great battles) of the Secession war; and it is best they should not—the real war will never get in the books."[15] Whitman knew that commentators would focus on famous battles, officers, and political leaders and would thereby obscure what he thought was most important and moving: the endurance, stoicism, bravery, and mingled strength and tenderness of ordinary soldiers. He was also convinced that the war—both in its chaotic quality and in its "practicality, minutia of deeds and passions"—would defy efforts to adequately represent it. An honest account could at best offer a "glimpse" of the war's "convulsiveness." Ironically, Whitman's own notebooks, poems, and journalism challenged the claim that the war could not be written, and he succeeded as well as anyone in getting at the "marrow" of the conflict.

In fact, Reconstruction is far more "unwritten" and less studied than the Civil War. This is regrettable because Reconstruction, ultimately a tragic story, is key to understanding ongoing racial disparities and conflict in the United States. As a testing ground for reforms, Washington was always a special place. Prior to and during the war, abolitionists saw it as key to their efforts, and Frederick Douglass, in particular, recognized that the fate of Washington, DC, foretold the trajectory of national history.[16] Free of state-level control and under Congressional jurisdiction, with a sizable African American population larger than most northern cities, Washington, DC, offered a unique opportunity for experimentation, first for abolitionists and later for those aiming to develop new legal and social relations across races and classes. What happened after the war, as citizenship, voting rights, and social equality were at issue, is part of the compelling, frequently painful story of opportunities missed, of Reconstruction gone awry. In the attorney general's office, Whitman was part of a rapidly expanding bureaucracy engaged in reframing the relationship between the nation and its defeated region, the failed attempt to develop a Confederate nation. Just as importantly the self-understanding of the United States was at issue as it worked

---

[15] *Memoranda During the War*, 5.
[16] Cf. Philip Ethington's remark that "Los Angeles has become metonymic for the entire course of human history" in "Los Angeles and the Problem of Urban Historical Knowledge" (2000). Online at http://lapuhk.usc.edu/

toward what Eric Foner has called its "unfinished revolution."[17] The legal and social relations across classes, races, and regions had been disrupted and would remain contentious. The effort to achieve a vibrant and diverse community, so central to Whitman's early work, seemed to be often within grasp as the Civil War gave way to Reconstruction, only to remain elusive.

---

[17] Eric Foner, *Reconstruction Updated Edition: America's Unfinished Revolution* (New York: Harper Perennial, 2014).

Acknowledgments

Many people have helped in the creation of this book, especially my friends and co-workers at *The Walt Whitman Archive* who have been a source of discovery, inspiration, and sustaining friendship. Nearly everyone who has worked for the *Whitman Archive* in the last decade has assisted in some way small or large. Those deserving special thanks include my co-director, Ed Folsom, and other editors, associates and graduate students: Brett Barney, Caterina Bernardini, Matt Cohen, Said Fallaha, Nicole Gray, Caitlin Henry, Christy Hyman, Elizabeth Lorang, Kevin McMullen, Yelizaveta Renfro, Beverley Rilett, Jason Stacy, Vanessa Steinroetter, and Ashlyn Stewart.

Successive department chairs at the University of Nebraska-Lincoln, Susan Belasco and Marco Abel, helped advance my research, and to them I express my sincere thanks. The Center for Digital Research in the Humanities at Nebraska, co-directed by my colleague Katherine Walter, has also been vital, particularly through support of a digital project, *Civil War Washington*. My work on that project with co-principal investigators Susan Lawrence, Elizabeth Lorang, and Kenneth Winkle added significantly to my knowledge of Washington City in Whitman's time. A faculty development leave from the University of Nebraska-Lincoln enabled me to focus on the book at a key stage in its evolution.

Jacqueline Norton, my editor at Oxford University Press, expressed enthusiasm for this project from the start in a manner that was much appreciated. I am grateful to the editors of various journals for permission to reprint in revised form material now appearing in Chapter 1 (*Leviathan*) and Chapter 4 (*Huntington Library Quarterly* and *Textual Studies*).

Matt Cohen, Ed Folsom, Ezra Greenspan, and Vivian Pollak have provided insightful readings of some or all of the chapters. Others offered commentary on at least one chapter including Stephanie Browner, Amanda Gailey, Martin Murray, Amy Nestor, Sean Pears, and Lindsay Tuggle. Jackie Budell, at the National Archives, helped me navigate that repository and was resourceful in finding information about soldiers Whitman befriended, and Jessica Ziparo shared her extensive knowledge of women in the civil service.

My wife, Wendy Katz, is my best reader.

Table of Contents

List of Figures — xix
List of Abbreviations of Whitman's Works — xxiii

1. Whitman, Washington, and the Convulsiveness of Civil War — 1
2. Whitman as a Paradoxical "Missionary to the Wounded" — 23
3. *Strayed* Cattle: Anti-Pastoralism in Whitman's War Writings — 57
4. Social Calamity, Personal Perturbations, and Office Decorum: How *Leaves of Grass* Grew Pensive — 104
5. Multi-racial Democracy and Black Democratic Vistas — 146

Works Cited — 175
Index — 185

List of Figures

1.1. Photograph of Whitman by Alexander Gardner, ca. 1864. Courtesy Clifton Waller Barrett Library of American Literature, Albert and Shirley Small Special Collections Library, University of Virginia.   5

1.2. Interior of a ward in Armory Square Hospital, sometime between 1862 and 1865. Photographer unknown. Courtesy Library of Congress Prints and Photographs Division, Washington, DC.   6

1.3. Courtesy Thomas Biggs Harned Collection of Walt Whitman Papers, 1842–1937, Library of Congress, Washington, DC.   11

2.1. In center is Sanitary Commission President Henry Whitney Bellows. Library of Congress Prints and Photographs Division, Washington, DC.   25

2.2. Group before office of US Christian Commission, 8th and H Sts. Nw. Library of Congress Prints and Photographs Division, Washington, DC.   26

2.3. Envelope from Walt Whitman Papers in the Charles E. Feinberg Collection, 1763–1985, Library of Congress, Washington, DC.   29

2.4. Courtesy Walt Whitman Papers in the Charles E. Feinberg Collection, 1763–1985, Library of Congress, Washington, DC.   30

2.5. Courtesy Walt Whitman Papers in the Charles E. Feinberg Collection, 1763–1985, Library of Congress, Washington, DC.   32

2.6. Courtesy Thomas Biggs Harned Collection of Walt Whitman Papers, 1842–1937, Library of Congress, Washington, DC.   33

2.7. Courtesy Walt Whitman Papers in the Charles E. Feinberg Collection, 1763–1985, Library of Congress, Washington, DC.   35

3.1. *Concert Champêtre*, attributed to Titian or Giorgione. Louvre Museum.   61

3.2. Thomas Eakins, *Arcadia*, Metropolitan Museum of Art, New York. Public domain image.   62

3.3. "Of this broad and majestic." This manuscript contributed to various works, including "Come Up from the Fields Father." Reproduced courtesy of the Berg collection, the New York Public Library.   69

3.4. Cattle on the mall, Washington, DC. Reproduced courtesy of the Library of Congress.   80

3.5. *Harper's Weekly*, January 17, 1863, p. 48.   86

LIST OF FIGURES

3.6. David Hunter Strother, *Osman, Harper's New Monthly Magazine*, 13, no. 76 (September 1856), 452.   89

3.7. Unknown artist, in *Harper's Weekly* (June 14, 1862), 373.   91

3.8. Unknown artist, "Is All Dem Yankees Dat's Passing?" in *Harper's Weekly* (January 7, 1865), 16.   92

3.9. Winslow Homer, *Near Andersonville* (1865–1866; previously known by other titles). Newark Museum.   96

3.10. Eastman Johnson, *Union Soldiers Accepting a Drink* (ca. 1865). Carnegie Museum of Art, Pittsburgh.   97

3.11. Courtesy Walt Whitman Papers in the Charles E. Feinberg Collection, 1763–1985, Library of Congress.   102

4.1. Public domain image from *Vanity Fair*, March 17, 1860, 183.   109

4.2. Detail of letter from J. Goldsborough Bruff to Francis Markoe, August 14, 1843. This public domain image was obtained from the Smithsonian Institution.   114

4.3. Letter from M. T. Pleasants to James A. Morgan, July 14, 1868, inscribed by Walt Whitman. Courtesy National Archives and Records Administration, Washington, DC.   123

4.4. This fairly typical page from the Blue Book gives a sense of the intensity of Whitman's efforts at revision. Photo courtesy of the New York Public Library, Oscar Lion collection.   128

4.5. Letter to Attorney General James Speed, August 1865, with the word *Sodomy* emphasized through underscoring. Courtesy Walt Whitman Papers in the Charles E. Feinberg Collection, 1763–1985, Library of Congress, Washington, DC.   134

4.6. Envelope with Whitman's annotations. Courtesy Walt Whitman Papers in the Charles E. Feinberg Collection, 1763–1985, Library of Congress, Washington, DC.   135

4.7. Inscribed and reinscribed page from a notebook "After an Extract from Heine's Diary." Courtesy Thomas Biggs Harned Collection of Walt Whitman Papers, 1842–1937, Library of Congress, Washington, DC.   137

4.8. Detail of page 27 of the Blue Book. Reproduced with the permission of the New York Public Library.   142

4.9. Whitman's comment on the flyleaf of his copy of *Milton, Young, Gray, Beattie, and Collins* (Philadelphia, 1841). This particular volume is now held in the Bryn Mawr College Special Collections Library. The image of the flyleaf is reproduced with permission.   144

5.1. *Harper's Weekly*, June 22, 1867, p. 397. 150
5.2. William Douglas O'Connor carte de visite. Courtesy Walt Whitman Papers in the Charles E. Feinberg Collection, 1763–1985, Library of Congress, Washington, DC. 154
5.3. Courtesy Thomas Biggs Harned Collection of Walt Whitman Papers, 1842–1937, Library of Congress, Washington, DC. 157

List of Abbreviations of Whitman's Works

D-T and Sequel	*Drum-Taps* (New York: 1865) and *Sequel to Drum-Taps* (Washington: 1865–6).
LG (1855)	*Leaves of Grass* (Brooklyn, NY: 1855).
LG (1860–61)	*Leaves of Grass* (Boston, MA: Thayer and Eldridge, 1860–1).
LG (1871–72)	*Leaves of Grass* (Washington, DC, 1871–2).
LG (1891–92)	*Leaves of Grass* (Philadelphia, PA: David McKay, 1891–2).
MDW	*Memoranda During the War* (Camden: Author's Publication), 1875–6.
NUPM	*Notebooks and Unpublished Prose Manuscripts,* 6 vols., ed. Edward F. Grier (New York: New York University Press, 1984).
PW	*Prose Works 1892,* 2 vols., ed. Floyd Stovall (New York: New York University Press, 1963–4).
WWA	*Walt Whitman Archive* (www.whitmanarchive.org), ed. Ed Folsom and Kenneth M. Price, (1995—).
WWWC	*With Walt Whitman in Camden,* by Horace Traubel, 9 vols. (various publishers, 1906–96).

1
Whitman, Washington, and the Convulsiveness of Civil War

In the Civil War, more wounded soldiers were treated in Washington, DC, than in any other city, and Whitman, a visitor to dozens of hospitals, gravitated toward the epicenter of suffering. He returned repeatedly to Armory Square Hospital, which hosted the worst cases and had the highest death rate. At a time of unprecedented maiming and killing, Whitman engaged in the work of healing. *Leaves of Grass*, his poetic masterpiece, intertwined the physical bodies of men and women and the symbolic body of the nation and saw in both a capacity to embrace contradictions and diversity while still remaining united and whole. Both the nation and Whitman's poetic project were at risk as he confronted innumerable broken and battered bodies. In this new context, he reassessed the possibilities for poetry, the future of democracy, and even the efficacy of affection, a quality that he had always believed sustained civil society. Faced with massive destruction, in what ways did Whitman succeed and fail in making meaning of it, in finding reasons for hope?

Prior to coming to Washington, Whitman had experienced a life far removed from armed conflict. He had spent the pre-war years in the New York area where he had worked as a printer, school teacher, journalist, occasional politician and stump speaker, and a successful builder of homes. He was a remarkably competent and effective contractor: he sold homes for profit, established his mother and the extended family under her care in a dwelling he constructed in Brooklyn, and arrested the family's economic decline.[1] He also mastered the lingo of building with its grounding in concrete particularity, and this approach to language informed his breakthrough book of poetry, *Leaves of Grass*, published in 1855: he wanted his style to be as stout as a plank, as sturdy as a crossbeam. Yet if Whitman's

---

[1] Robert Roper, *Now the Drum of War: Walt Whitman and his Brothers in the Civil War* (New York: Walker, 2008), 54–66.

language was often concrete—even earthy—it could also reach to the stars. Or as Ralph Waldo Emerson explained, Whitman's writing was a "remarkable mixture of the Bhagvat Ghita and the New York Herald."[2]

Writing with great resourcefulness across verbal registers, Whitman established himself as a poet who could see immense value and potential in the ordinary. His opening poem in the first *Leaves of Grass* (ultimately known as "Song of Myself") was like no verse before or since in its brash experimentation, its exuberant hopefulness, its embrace of what others might find homely or rank. Moreover, he brought the body into American literature in new ways. Recently the poet Alicia Ostriker explained what Whitman meant to her as a teenager growing up: "Like some improbably open-minded parent, he would permit everything.... That was the primary thing I noticed. The degree and quantity and variety of love in Whitman are simply astonishing."[3] He has been a liberating force for men and women, gays and straights, blacks, whites, and other hues of humankind. Writing before words like gay and homosexual were in use, Whitman developed his own language of manly attachment and comradeship, articulated most fully in his section of poems called "Calamus." On the eve of a war in which men would kill more than 750,000 of their fellow Americans, he sought ways to deepen and extend love between them.

As is well-known, Whitman's candor about sexuality outraged nineteenth-century reviewers: one called the book an explosion in a sewer, another suggested that Whitman should be publicly whipped, another urged him to commit suicide. His descriptions and language are not in themselves shockingly literal, but his voice was intimate. Whitman wanted to "pass": from poet to reader, from one identity to another, from his time to later generations, and he reimagines the very act of reading, making it a bodily, at times even erotic, experience:

> This is no book,
> Who touches this, touches a man,
> (Is it night? Are we here alone?)
> It is I you hold, and who holds you,
> I spring from the pages into your arms—.[4]

---

[2] Franklin Benjamin Sanborn, "Reminiscent of Whitman," in *Whitman in His Own Time*, ed. Joel Myerson (Iowa City, IA: Univeristy of Iowa Press, 2000), 144.

[3] Ostriker, "Loving Walt Whitman and the Problem of America," in *Walt Whitman: The Measure of his Song*, ed. Jim Perlman, Ed Folsom, and Dan Campion (Rev. ed.). Duluth, MN: Holy Cow! Press, 1998), 457–58.

[4] *LG* (1860–61), 455.

And yet in other moods Whitman was less confident about his ability to convey personal presence. In lines published in the first edition of *Leaves of Grass* but later deleted, he declared:

> This is unfinished business with me.... how is it with you?
> I was chilled with the cold types and cylinder and wet paper between us.
> I pass so poorly with paper and types.... I must pass with the contact of bodies and souls.[5]

This need for personal presence, this desire for contact and connection, would later guide his approach to healing in the hospitals.

Frustrated by political events in the early 1850s, Whitman developed a vision of democracy that involved the remaking of the inner life of people as a necessary response to the looming national crisis. Some of his early lines are as unconventional in poetic style as they are in thought:

> I am the poet of slaves and of the masters of slaves
> I am the poet of the body
> And I am
>
> I am the poet of the body
> And I am the poet of the soul
> I go with the slaves of the earth equally with the masters
> And I will stand between the masters and the slaves,
> Entering into both so that both shall understand me alike.[6]

For Whitman to be sufficiently large (or to "dilate" as he said elsewhere) to encompass seemingly irreconcilable views was a precondition for writing breakthrough poetry and for attempting to heal a nation fracturing before his eyes. In Whitman's manuscript notes toward the first edition of *Leaves of Grass*, it is clear that he once planned to close the book with a poem that pivots on the selling of a slave at auction, the work ultimately called "I sing the Body Electric." Had he done so, he would have further emphasized the painful paradox of slavery in a democracy devoted to freedom. Slavery itself lent urgency to his pre-war poetry and probably intensified his interest in writing about physical bodies then and later. This abbreviated account of Whitman's pre-war thinking may help us appreciate how he developed during the war when he confronted the pressures of a newly emancipated

---

[5] *LG* (1855), 57.   [6] Whitman, "albot Wilson," *NUPM*, 67.

population in Washington, DC, and the bodies of innumerable wounded soldiers.

In the late 1850s, as he drafted the second and third editions of *Leaves of Grass*, Whitman expanded his repertoire, writing powerful love poetry focused on the bonds between men. Even as the nation careened toward its bloodiest war, Whitman sought to bring men together through a kind of love that he often called (borrowing the term from phrenology) adhesiveness. He was emboldened in his exploration of this new terrain through his developing friendships at Pfaff's beer hall on Broadway in New York, a bohemian hangout. Here Whitman found a sustaining network of friends— a variety of workingmen, writers, clerks, actors, and others—who offered opportunities for sociability, good humor, intellectual stimulation, publishing ventures, and sexual exploration. In an 1863 letter to a friend, Nathaniel Bloom, we hear Whitman's fond recollection of a lost life of camaraderie even as he is at pains to remake it, in vastly different circumstances, in the Washington hospitals:

> dear friend, how long it is since we have seen each other, since those pleasant meetings & those hot spiced rums & suppers & our dear friends Gray & Chauncey, & Russell, & Fritschy too, (who for a while at first used to sit so silent,) & Perkins & our friend Raymond—how long it seems— how much I enjoyed it all. What a difference it is with me here—I tell you, Nat, my evenings are frequently spent in scenes that make a terrible difference—for I am still a hospital visitor, there has not passed a day for months (or at least not more than two) that I have not been among the sick & wounded, either in hospitals or down in camp—occasionally here I spend the evenings in hospital—the experience is a profound one, beyond all else, & touches me personally, egotistically, in unprecedented ways—I mean the way often the amputated, sick, sometimes dying soldiers cling & cleave to me as it were as a man overboard to a plank, & the perfect content they have if I will remain with them, sit on the side of the cot awhile, some youngsters often, & caress them &c.—It is delicious to be the object of so much love & reliance, & to do them such good, soothe & pacify torments of wounds &c—You will doubtless see in what I have said the reason I continue so long in this kind of life—.[7]

---

[7] Walt Whitman to Nathaniel Bloom, September 5, 1863, available at the *WWA*.

Figure 1.1. Photograph of Whitman by Alexander Gardner, ca. 1864. Courtesy Clifton Waller Barrett Library of American Literature, Albert and Shirley Small Special Collections Library, University of Virginia.

The experience was mutually beneficial, as Whitman acknowledges, or as he elsewhere said more succinctly: these were "terrible, beautiful days" (see Figures 1.1 and 1.2).[8]

How did he find himself in these Washington hospitals? In December 1862, Whitman left Brooklyn for Virginia to search for his brother George, who had been wounded at the battle of Fredericksburg. Once assured of his brother's safety, Whitman assisted more badly wounded soldiers, accompanying them on their trip to Washington and its hospitals. He then settled in the city, making it his home for the next ten years.

Washington was a booming place because of the war, and there were chronic housing shortages. In a city of increasing wealth, Whitman lived simply, with notable economy. What little money he had often went to help

---

[8] *WWWC*, 1: 115.

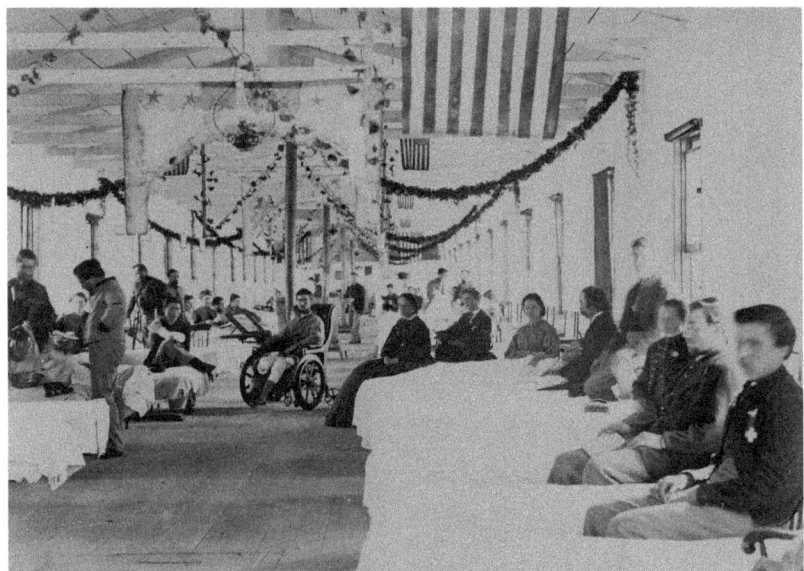

Figure 1.2. Interior of a ward in Armory Square Hospital, sometime between 1862 and 1865. Photographer unknown. Courtesy Library of Congress Prints and Photographs Division, Washington, DC.

support his mother; he routinely enclosed a dollar or two in his letters to her, at a time when a dollar meant something. He moved more than once a year during his time in Washington. He economized by moving out when he went home to Brooklyn for a visit, saving a bit of rent, and finding a new place on his return. He lived without paying board for the first six months or so with a friend he had met through their reliance on a common book publisher, William Douglas O'Connor, and his wife Ellen or "Nelly." As Nelly O'Connor recalled about her home at 394 L street North:

> Washington had no general system of water supply or drainage, and a pump at the corner of our street was reputed to be of very pure water... fed from a spring at Rock Creek. To this pump every morning Walt would go for a pitcher for our table, and he was especially fond of taking a long draught...[9]

---

[9] Ellen M. Calder, "Personal Recollections of Walt Whitman," *The Atlantic Monthly*, 99 (June 1907): 828.

Whitman met some of the children of the city on his morning outings for water, on his way to work at the Army Paymaster's office (where he first found work as a copyist), and on his way to the hospitals. Interestingly, despite the weight of concerns he felt for wounded soldiers, for his often troubled family back in Brooklyn, and for his multifaceted literary life—he found time for casual play with children on Washington streets. In a letter of reminiscence dated March 8, 1891, Mary Jordan[10] asked Whitman:

> Do you remember when you lived near the corner of 12th and M streets in Washington, D.C., some little children who lived on the other corner? Probably you do not, nor that you used to be very good to them, playing "tag," and marbles with them—now and then letting them drink out of your brown water jug... —a great honor. It happens that I was one of those children—my father was Solicitor of the Treasury Edward Jordan. Now I am teaching English rhetoric in this college for girls and am even more indebted to you for pleasure and help than I used to be in the old days.[11]

It is not surprising that Whitman would be memorable to a child since he was often seen walking the streets, looking a bit like St Nicholas on his way to the hospitals, haversack and pockets full to bulging with the candy, oranges, tobacco, stationary, and small gifts of all kinds he would distribute, along with copious amounts of love, to the wounded soldiers.

Only a few blocks away the poet also encountered black children. In what is apparently a draft piece of journalism dated 8.30 a.m., April 1, 1863, Whitman wrote:

Washington Sight / for instance

You see ^for instance such a sight as the following as you walk out for ten minutes before breakfast. Over the muddy crossing, ^ half past 8, morning of April 1st, '63 at 14th and L street, came a stout young wench wheeling a wheelbarrow—the wench perhaps 15 years old, black and jolly and strong as a horse; —in the wheelbarrow, cuddled up, a child-wench, of six or seven years, equally black, shiny black and jolly with an old quilt around her, ^

---

[10] Mary Jordan's sister, Emily, became Emily Jordan Folger, the co-founder with Henry Clay Folger of the Folger Shakespeare library, the world's largest collection of Shakespeare material, a collection that now also includes some Whitman manuscripts.

[11] The Charles E. Feinberg Collection of Walt Whitman, Manuscripts Division, The Library of Congress.

sitting plump back, riding backwards, partially holding on, a little fearful ~~of being tumbled out~~, and trying to hold in her arms a ^ full grown young lapdog, curly, ^ beautiful white as silver, with ^ sparkling peering, round black ~~bright~~ eyes—the child-wench bareheaded; —and, all, ~~with~~ the dog, ~~and~~ the stout-armed negress, firmly holding the handles, and pushing on through the mud—the heads of the ~~beautiful~~ pretty silver dog, and the pictorial black ~~child the~~ e round and young & with alert eyes, as she turned half way around, ^ twisting her neck anxious to see what prospect, (having probably been overturned in the mud on some previous occasion)—the gait of the big girl, ^ ~~strong~~ so sturdy and so graceful with her short petticoats her legs stepping, plashing steadily along through [deleted word, illegible] obstructions—the shiny-curl'd dog, standing up in the hold of the little one, —she huddled in the barrow, riding backwards with the patch-work quilt around her, sitting down, her feet visible poking straight out in front [?]—made a passing group which as I stopt to look at it, you may if you choose stop and imagine.[12]

These negresses may have been among the many African Americans who flooded into the nation's capital during the War. In any event, they were at Whitman's doorstep, right outside the boarding house where he and the O'Connors lived when he first arrived in the city. The negresses were also on the route Abraham Lincoln would take that summer as he made his way, with Whitman often watching, to and from the White House and the Soldiers' Home where the summer nights were cooler. About ten blocks north of where Whitman encountered his "Washington sight" was a contraband camp on 12th Street, near Boundary (today's Florida Avenue). By the end of the War there were approximately 40,000 contrabands scattered throughout the District.

The time, 8.30 a.m., April 1, 1863, was the beginning of a new day in several senses, but it was unclear what that day was to bring. Slavery had been abolished in the District a year before, on April 16, 1862. A progressive community of African Americans played a vital role in abolishing slavery in Washington, despite regularly encountering hostility and resistance from white residents and soldiers. The Compensated Emancipation Act of April

---

[12] This transcription is drawn from my essay "The Lost Negress of 'Song of Myself' and the Jolly Young Wenches of Civil War Washington" in *Leaves of Grass: The Sesquicentennial Essays*, ed. Susan Belasco, Ed Folsom, and Kenneth M. Price (Lincoln, NE: University of Nebraska Press, 2007), 231–32.

1862 ordered all 3,000 slaves in the District of Columbia to be freed, marking the first time the US government had officially liberated any group of slaves. The city led the way, then, in the liberation of slaves eight months before Abraham Lincoln signed the Emancipation Proclamation on January 1, 1863, extending freedom much further across the land, though not everywhere, since slaves in loyal border states remained in bondage. This particular day was, then, the four-month anniversary of African American freedom—or, more precisely, nominal freedom for those enslaved persons who happened to live in states hostile to the Union, since with the Emancipation Proclamation Lincoln freed all the slaves in states he couldn't control and left slavery intact in states he could somewhat control (slave-possessing border states that remained loyal). African Americans could not entirely relax about the Fugitive Slave Law since it remained on the books *after* the Emancipation Proclamation, though it was rarely enforced after 1863 (the law would not be repealed until June 1864).[13]

Beginnings teem with possibilities—this is early in the day and in the month and in the season of hope and renewal; it is early in the lives of the young "negresses" and the "young lap-dog"; and it is early in the history of emancipation. And yet despite all this earliness, Whitman avoids projecting his thoughts forward to the future (or backward to the past). The young African American women Whitman observed might have been free people all their lives, they might have been newly emancipated, or they might have been fugitive slaves. These differences were hugely significant, but they don't factor into Whitman's account, which focuses on the present and the visual probably because of Whitman's uncertainty about his argument. The postemancipation negresses leave him puzzled. Whitman can paint, describe, or record them, but he can't fit them easily into an argument. Convinced before emancipation of the necessity of African American freedom, Whitman was unclear about the consequences of that freedom after emancipation. As Ed Folsom has succinctly remarked: "It is fair to say that [Whitman] was more supportive of blacks during the period when the issue was slavery than during the period after emancipation, when the issue became the access of free blacks to the basic rights of citizenship, including the right to vote."[14]

---

[13] Kate Masur, *An Example for All the Land: Emancipation and the Struggle Over Equality in Washington, D.C.* (Chapel Hill, NC: University of North Carolina Press, 2010), 29–30.

[14] Ed Folsom, "Lucifer and Ethiopia: Whitman, Race, and Poetics before the Civil War and After," in *A Historical Guide to Walt Whitman*, ed. David S. Reynolds (New York: Oxford University Press, 2000), 46. Over the course of his career, Whitman held a variety of views on racial characteristics. Especially early in his career, Whitman resisted arguments for white

The calendar day we have been considering has a further implication. Mark Twain famously said, "April 1. This is the day upon which we are reminded of what we are on the other three-hundred and sixty-four."[15] April Fool's Day is of course a day of pranks and jokes that has its origin in the shift to the new Gregorian calendar. The day carries with it a carnivalesque tradition of an overturned social order and new possibilities for the underclass, all of which is implied in Whitman's description of these half-amusing, half-unnerving, young women. In a year of monumental change, April 1, 1863 is another marker of new beginnings and transformations that Whitman greets with mixed feelings.

Whitman depicts these young women as "black and jolly." Given that *both* are described in these terms—even the one who is fearful—that part of the account is formulaic, as if Whitman is seeing via cultural stereotypes rather than with the clearer and more independent insights he achieved in 1855 in the poems eventually titled "Song of Myself," "The Sleepers," "To Think of Time," and "I Sing the Body Electric." The idea of being jolly while pushing a wheelbarrow through "obstructions" or being jolly while fearing that one will be "overturned in the mud [as] on some previous occasion" rings false.

And what about this mud? At this time, the streets of Washington, DC, were unpaved (except for Pennsylvania Avenue), and they were strewn with refuse. The District was notable for disorder and for its "defective sewage system."[16] Whitman's stress on the "pretty" and "pictorial" quality of this scene challenges ordinary aesthetic assumptions and attempts to remake our perceptions so that we appreciate how the older girl could be "so sturdy and graceful" while "pushing through the mud." Whitman probably had urban street-urchin genre paintings in mind, as is suggested by language from the visual arts: "prospect" and "group." He struggled to find a generic mode— comic? street-urchin painting?—that would account for the spectacle and its impact on his senses. He tries different methods to portray the girls, shifting

---

superiority. He marked an article on "The Slavonians and Eastern Europe" which argued that there are "three variety of human beings" and that "up to the present moment, the destinies of the species appear to have been carried forward almost exclusively by its Caucasian variety." Whitman responded in the margin: "? yes of late centuries, but how about 5 or 10, or twenty thousand years ago?" See *Dear Brother Walt: The Letters of Thomas Jefferson Whitman*, ed. Dennis Berthold and Kenneth M. Price (Kent, OH: Kent State University Press, 1984), 92n.

[15] Twain, *Pudd'nhead Wilson and Those Extraordinary Twins* (New York: Norton, 1980), 105.

[16] Margaret Leech, *Reveille in Washington* (New York: Harper and Brothers, 1941), 77.

frames and modes, and if there is incoherence in Whitman's method, it results in part from being drawn to that from which he retracts himself.

Mud, dirt, earthiness, sexuality—these things have long been associated with each other. Given the mention of "petticoats" and "wench" and "sturdy legs," the sexual aspect of the scene is apparent. *Daybooks and Notebooks* records a clipping Whitman preserved that says: "The word *Wench*, formerly, was not used in the low and vulgar acceptation that it is at present."[17] One of Whitman's own manuscripts indicates that he believed the word *wench*, like *Indian*, was a "great mistake" (see Figure 1.3). It is not entirely clear why he thought the word was a mistake, though it may be significant that in the nineteenth century the word *wench* could be used to refer to a black servant, and it was also connected to a "vulgar acceptation" and had a strong association with women of ill repute. It is a notable feature of Whitman's lexicon that he reserved the word *wench* for black women and appears never to have applied it to white women. For Whitman, the word mainly had class and racial implications, though it inevitably carried sexual connotations as well. There is a charged and discomforting aura conveyed by terms such as "wench" and "child-wench," especially in light of the reference to the short petticoats. *Child-wench*—a term Whitman applies

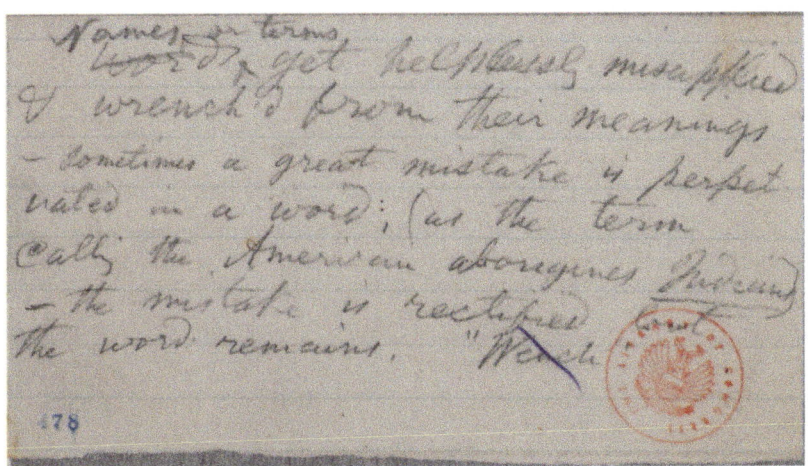

Figure 1.3. Courtesy Thomas Biggs Harned Collection of Walt Whitman Papers, 1842–1937, Library of Congress, Washington, DC.

---

[17] Whitman, *Daybooks and Notebooks*, ed. William White (New York: New York University Press, 1978), 3:694.

here to the six- or seven-year-old—hovers uneasily in its suggestiveness between child-servant and child-as-eroticized being.

The younger "child-wench" is peering with "alert eyes"; the dog is peering with "bright eyes"; and Whitman, too, is peering with eyes that don't get described. All of this gazing might lead to love, as it does so often in Whitman: we recall the twenty-ninth bather who "saw [the men] and loved them" just as he says of the black drayman: "I behold the picturesque giant and love him." In *Memoranda During the War* Whitman recounts several exchanges in which eyes lock and love and sympathy are inspired. When he encounters the negresses, however, no gazes meet. If the young black women glanced at Whitman, they perhaps found the old greybeard even more pictorial, unfathomable, and vaguely threatening than he found them.

Because of the real possibility of a tumble into the mud, the scene edges toward physical humor and is suggestive of the tumbles and turns Whitman would have seen in the theatre (not to mention blackface shows). By projecting onto the scene "jollity," by refusing seriousness, by invoking the almost-comic, Whitman registers a discomfort with black female sexuality. Is black female fecundity both threatening and funny, verging on the comic because it is threatening—and especially when turned toward a black democratic vista that Whitman regards with some trepidation?[18] (As we will see, Whitman's discomfort with the involvement of African Americans in the electoral process becomes clear in subsequent years, especially in *Democratic Vistas* where he offers an evasive answer to Thomas Carlyle's racist diatribe "Shooting Niagara.")[19] Whitman provides himself with a distancing device that limits sympathy and disables the compassionate gaze he so often bestowed at this time on soldiers. Whitman's nervous attempts to be amused or amusing surface elsewhere in his wartime and immediate post-War commentary on blacks: he explained to his mother on October 20, 1863, that in his new lodgings he had a "good big bed, I sleep first rate—there is a young wench of 12 or 13, Lucy, (the niggers here are the best & most amusing creatures you ever see)—she comes & goes, gets water &c., she is pretty much the only one I see."[20] We also recall his quip about

---

[18] My reading of this passage is indebted to conversation and email exchanges with Amy R. Nestor. I wish also to thank Brett Barney, Amanda Gailey, and Lisa Renfro for incisive comments on this chapter.
[19] See Folsom's discussion in "Lucifer and Ethiopia," 77–80.
[20] Whitman, *The Correspondence*, ed. Edwin Haviland Miller (New York: New York University Press, 1961), 1:168.

Washington, DC, in 1867: the city is "filled with *darkies*," he said, "the men & children & wenches swarm in all directions—(I am not sure but the North is like the man that won the elephant in a raffle)."²¹ By turning the wheelbarrow scene into a humorous spectacle rather than a heart-engaging specimen, he restricted his emotional involvement and circumscribed the seriousness and potential of these negresses. In contrast, with Civil War white soldiers—whom he treats with the same attention to detail—we don't find beings whose meaning is limited by bleak circumstances. His soldier boys are invested with great significance despite their often diseased or disfigured bodies.

As far as we know, neither one of these black children ever wrote to Whitman, unlike Mary Jordan discussed above. (No doubt it would have been difficult for them to do so because public schooling for black children in the District had barely begun; what progress had been made was owed to what Frederick Douglass called "the zeal, the faith, and the courage of Myrtilla Miner," a pioneer educator and friend of Whitman's close associate Ellen O'Connor.²²) Nonetheless, the two accounts of Whitman's interactions with children—one written by him and one written to him—shed light on Whitman and race. A key difference between the two accounts is that he engages directly in play with the white children while remaining more detached, more of an observer with the blacks. The proximity of black and white children on the streets of Washington was not a surprise. The 1860 census of Washington indicates that a very high proportion of the African American community was thoroughly integrated, after a fashion, with the white community. That is, they frequently lived in white homes as enslaved people or servants or nearby in Washington's alleys.²³ What is new in the scene Whitman depicts is the "prospect" for the black children in a time of fundamental change. It was a prospect that few people, including Whitman, could adequately imagine.

In the scene with the two young black girls, Whitman provides exact spatial and temporal coordinates. The place, 14th and L streets, Washington, DC, sets the scene at the heart of a democratic experiment that was

---

²¹ *Correspondence*, 1:323.
²² Quoted in Ellen M. O'Connor, *Myrtilla Miner: A Memoir* (Boston, MA: Houghton, Mifflin, 1885), 21.
²³ See Rob Shepard, "Historical Geography, GIS and Civil War Washington," in *Civil War Washington: The City and the Site*, ed. Susan Lawrence (Lincoln, NE: University of Nebraska Press, 2015), 51–52. For an earlier study, see James Borchert, *Alley Life in Washington: Family, Community, Religion, and Folklife in the City, 1850–1970* (Urbana, IL: University of Illinois Press, 1980).

imperiled because of its failure to realize the implications of its own founding principles. Interestingly, 14th Street is the location Whitman associated with the Washington monument.[24]

The lack of a proper water system noted by Nelly O'Connor reminds us how much Washington was a city under construction at this time. Prostitution flourished, and there were hundreds of brothels in operation. A fetid canal ran from the Anacostia River to the Potomac, passing behind the Executive Mansion or what is now called the White House. At times dead livestock were left to rot there, and the canal functioned in the war years primarily as a sewer and storm drain system. It was a genuine health hazard and probably caused the death, from typhoid fever, of Lincoln's son Willie. The only paved street was Pennsylvania Avenue, where mud seeped through the bricks. Whitman saw all the muck and problems but also recognized the potential of Washington as a work in progress: "the fruit of the plans, the knit, the combination, yet wanting."[25] Human possibility was yet to be fully etched and imagined. The possibilities for African American life were unresolved at this time, as were the possibilities for male friendship and love in a pre-Freudian age.

Famously, Whitman had a remarkable capacity to reach out to white soldiers, but he sometimes lacked a corresponding capacity to sympathize with or "imagine" African Americans. He wrote to his mother:

> there are camps here of every thing—I went once or twice to the Contraband Camp, to the Hospital, &c. but I could not bring myself to go again—when I meet black men or boys among my own hospitals, I use them kindly, give them something, &c.—I believe I told you that I do the same to the wounded rebels, too—but as there is a limit to one's sinews & endurance & sympathies, &c. I have got in the way after going lightly as it were all through the wards of a hospital, & trying to give a word of cheer, if nothing else, to every one, then confining my special attentions to the few where the investment seems to tell best, & who want it most.[26]

Skin color seems to be the key to what makes some hospitals Whitman's "own" and others not. Yet given Whitman's poetic commitments to fluidity,

---

[24] http://www.whitmanarchive.org/manuscripts/figures/loc_jc.01406.jpg
[25] Walt Whitman to Nathaniel Bloom and John F. S. Gray, March 19–20, 1863, available at the *WWA*.
[26] Walt Whitman to Louisa Van Velsor Whitman, July 7, 1863, available at the *WWA*.

crossing, and wide-ranging sympathy, skin color seems an odd basis for identification or non-identification. The limitations in Whitman's sympathy give pause precisely because of his claims, variously articulated, to be "of every hue and trade and rank" and to "resist anything better than my own diversity."[27] In 1860, in "Calamus 19" (ultimately titled "Behold this Swarthy Face") he described himself as dark-skinned:

> Behold this swarthy and unrefined face—these gray eyes,
> This beard—the white wool, unclipt upon my neck,
> My brown hands, and the silent manner of me, without charm;
> Yet comes one, a Manhattanese, and ever at parting, kisses me lightly on the lips with robust love.[28]

If Whitman considered white soldiers his "own" concern (despite his imaginative crossings of the color line), it was not for any lack of fascination with blacks during the War. He focused on the growing enlistment of black troops after the Emancipation Proclamation and followed the developments closely in the spring and summer of 1863 (he kept a list of seventeen clippings on black troops).[29] He noted that some of the best pilots of US ships in the attack on Charleston were blacks.[30] (The black engineers, brave troops, and skilled pilots constituted a challenge to a view he sometimes entertained, that blacks lacked resolve and needed protection: when he considered writing "Poem of the Black person" he reminded himself to "infuse the sentiment of a sweeping, surrounding, shielding protection of the blacks—their passiveness."[31]) He rode out to see the 1st US Colored Infantry on July 11, 1863 and found black troops whose "determin'd bravery...compell'd the plaudits of the thoughtful and thoughtless soldiery."[32] He was especially interested in the way that black people went by some of the most distinguished names of the country: Washington, Adams, Webster, Madison, for example. Elsewhere in the army black soldiers had the names Thomas Jefferson and Andrew Jackson as well (currently the national registry of Civil War soldiers lists 311 black soldiers named Andrew Jackson and 86 named Thomas Jefferson). Andrew Jackson, Thomas

---

[27] *LG* (1855), 24.   [28] *LG* (1860–61), 364.
[29] *NUPM*, 2:635, and Charles I. Glicksberg, ed., *Walt Whitman and the Civil War* (1933; rpt. New York: Barnes, 1963), 187 n.21.
[30] *NUPM*, 2:635.   [31] *NUPM*, 4:1346.   [32] *Prose Works 1892*, 2:587–89.

Jefferson, and George Washington—these were names that were now shared by American presidents, black soldiers, and Whitman's own biological brothers. The poet felt a kinship with white soldiers that he didn't feel with blacks, though the shared names challenged the wall of separation his sentiments imposed.

Despite his sustained interest in black soldiers, Whitman didn't include significant treatment of African Americans in his Civil War poems written while the conflict was underway. We find instead a remarkable avoidance of certain key issues in his published poetry, including African American citizenship and the African American role in the War. Whitman only includes blacks belatedly when he depicts an older black woman in "Ethiopia Saluting the Colors" (1870), a poem that didn't enter the "Drum-Taps" cluster of *Leaves of Grass* until 1881. The perspective of the poem is that of one of Sherman's soldiers who regards the black woman as "hardly human." She is desexualized like other aged black women Whitman approved of as nurses for soldiers. This poem has made many white critics uncomfortable over recent decades, yet it has resonance and complexity that African American poets and composers seem to have been best able to appreciate (for further discussion, see Chapter 3).

The desexualized old black woman in "Ethiopia Saluting the Colors" contrasts with the highly sexualized "swart" old man that Whitman imagined himself being in order to compose "Children of Adam." (*Swart* is a proto-Germanic word in its origins meaning *black*.) The association of darkness with sexuality, in a masculine context, served to liberate the poet's imagination. He uses blackness, especially male blackness, strategically as suggestive of the realized natural sexual self.[33]

> Full of animal-fire, tender, loving, the tremulous ache, delicious, yet such a torment,
> The swelling and elate and vehement, that will not be denied
> ...
> Presenting a vivid picture... of a fully-complete, well-developed old man eld, bearded, swart, fiery.[34]

---

[33] A poem such as "O Tan-Faced Prairie-Boy" comes to mind.
[34] Manuscript in the Trent Collection, William R. Perkins Library, Duke University. Also quoted in *Leaves of Grass*, Comprehensive Reader's Edition (New York: New York University Press, 1965), 90n. Whitman elsewhere used the word *swart* to refer to the racial other. See his poem "A Broadway Pageant" about envoys from Japan who had come to the US to negotiate treaty arrangements between Japan and the United States.

Whitman was convinced before the war of the necessity of African American freedom, but he was unclear about the consequences of that freedom after emancipation. At the beginning of the war, both Lincoln and Whitman saw the conflict as being about the preservation of the union. But Whitman, unlike Lincoln, did not evolve in his thinking. By the time of the Second Inaugural address, Lincoln was ready to state unmistakably that "One eighth of the whole population were colored slaves, not distributed generally over the Union, but localized in the Southern part of it. These slaves constituted a peculiar and powerful interest. All knew that this interest was, somehow, the cause of the war."[35] Whitman, in contrast, rarely saw the war as fundamentally about slavery and so he was deprived of a positive resolution to his war narrative. The arc of his narrative did not reach toward liberation, and so he could not argue that the terrible toll of suffering was offset by an extraordinary achievement: the liberation of four million people.

In *Memoranda* and in *Drum-Taps*, his book of war poems, Whitman says very little about famous battles or key officers in part because he had little experience near the front lines, but more importantly because he was convinced that a top-down approach was distorting. To write an account of masterful men was to guarantee that the "real war will never get in the books."[36] He argued that the gulf between the great body of the men and the individual officers must be removed entirely or our "whole American theory is a big wind-bag."[37] Thus his poems do not treat major historical events. One looks in vain for mentions of Gettysburg, Shiloh, and Manassas, nor can we find Grant, Lee, and Stonewall Jackson in his poems (a rare and significant exception is the reference to Sherman in "Ethiopia Saluting the Colors"). Unlike Herman Melville, Whitman avoids naming places, events, and people in his Civil War poems. Melville's *Battle-Pieces* mentions specific engagements and key leaders as his volume progresses from the execution of

> Over the Western sea hither from Niphon come,
> Courteous, the swart-cheek'd two-sworded envoys,
> Leaning back in their open barouches, bare-headed, impassive,
> Ride to-day through Manhattan. (*LG* 1892, 193)

Whitman is described as "swart" in at least one review as well. "Walt Whitman," *Chambers's Journal of Popular Literature, Science, and Art* 45 (July 4, 1868), 420–25. And *swart* is associated with manliness (and eroticism?) in "Some Diary Notes at Random," *PW*, 2:583.

[35] Lincoln, "Second Inaugural Address" in *The Collected Works of Abraham Lincoln*, ed. Roy P. Basler (New Brunswick: Rutgers University Press, 1953), 8:332.
[36] *SD*, 116.   [37] "Confession to Make," in *NUPM*, 2: 662.

John Brown through major battles to the surrender at Appomattox and the martyrdom of Lincoln. Whitman in *Drum-Taps* perceived a chaotic war, and he refused to impose on events a single narrative line.

Instead, Whitman strives to capture the felt experience of common soldiers. "Vigil Strange I Kept on the Field One Night" illustrates his approach:

> VIGIL strange I kept on the field one night,
> When you, my son and my comrade, dropt at my side that day,
> One look I but gave, which your dear eyes return'd, with a look I shall never forget;
> One touch of your hand to mine, O boy, reach'd up as you lay on the ground;
> Then onward I sped in the battle, the even-contested battle;
> Till late in the night reliev'd, to the place at last again I made my way;
> Found you in death so cold, dear comrade—found your body, son of responding kisses, (never again on earth responding;)
> Bared your face in the starlight—curious the scene—cool blew the moderate night-wind;
> Long there and then in vigil I stood, dimly around me the battle-field spreading;
> Vigil wondrous and vigil sweet, there in the fragrant silent night;
> But not a tear fell, not even a long-drawn sigh—Long, long I gazed;
> Then on the earth partially reclining, sat by your side, leaning my chin in my hands;
> Passing sweet hours, immortal and mystic hours with you, dearest comrade—Not a tear, not a word;
> Vigil of silence, love and death—vigil for you, my son and my soldier,
> As onward silently stars aloft, eastward new ones upward stole;
> Vigil final for you, brave boy, (I could not save you, swift was your death,
> I faithfully loved you and cared for you living—I think we shall surely meet again;)

> Till at latest lingering of the night, indeed just as the dawn appear'd,
> My comrade I wrapt in his blanket, envelop'd well his form,
> Folded the blanket well, tucking it carefully over head, and carefully under feet;
> And there and then, and bathed by the rising sun, my son in his grave, in his rude-dug grave I deposited;
> Ending my vigil strange with that—vigil of night and battle-field dim;
> Vigil for boy of responding kisses, (never again on earth responding;)
> Vigil for comrade swiftly slain—vigil I never forget, how as day brighten'd,
> I rose from the chill ground, and folded my soldier well in his blanket,
> And buried him where he fell.[38]

This poem captures the intensity of loss through figuring comradeship as a familial bond. The bond between the men is what matters here rather than the location of the battle (omitted) or its place in the strategic movements of an army (ignored). The vigil, "wondrous" and "sweet" serves, if anything, to intensify the loss and suffering in this last moment of earthly connectedness and first of ongoing remembrance, the "vigil I never forget." In this passage, the foreshortened final line, by far the briefest in the poem, signals a life abruptly cut off. Elegant in its simplicity, the final line is made up of nickel words—nothing fancy. The only word of more than one syllable is the one that counts: buried.

Whitman perceived Lincoln, too, to be a paradoxical commoner, one of the "divine average": "I think well of the President. He has a face like a hoosier Michael Angelo, so awful ugly it becomes beautiful, with its strange mouth, its deep cut, criss-cross lines, and its doughnut complexion. My notion is, too, that underneath his outside smutched mannerism, and stories from third-class county bar-rooms... Mr. Lincoln keeps a fountain of first-class practical telling wisdom."[39] Whitman saw Lincoln regularly, at times daily, as the President commuted between the executive mansion and the Soldiers' Home (where Lincoln and his family escaped the heat and intensity

---

[38] *D-T*, 42–43.
[39] Walt Whitman to Nathaniel Bloom and John F. S. Gray, March 19–20, 1863 (*WWA*).

of downtown Washington). Nodding to the President and being acknowledged in turn by him were recurrent wartime experiences for Whitman. In the death of Lincoln, recounted in his famous elegy "When Lilacs Last in the Dooryard Bloom'd," Whitman reaches beyond the President to encompass and mourn all those lost in the war:

> And I saw askant the armies,
> I saw as in noiseless dreams hundreds of battle-flags,
> Borne through the smoke of the battles and pierc'd with missiles I saw them,
> And carried hither and yon through the smoke, and torn and bloody,
> And at last but a few shreds left on the staffs, (and all in silence,)
> And the staffs all splinter'd and broken.
> I saw battle-corpses, myriads of them,
> And the white skeletons of young men, I saw them,
> I saw the debris and debris of all the slain soldiers of the war,
> But I saw they were not as was thought,
> They themselves were fully at rest, they suffer'd not,
> The living remain'd and suffer'd, the mother suffer'd,
> And the wife and the child and the musing comrade suffer'd,
> And the armies that remain'd suffer'd.[40]

No one had literally seen the "debris of all the slain soldiers of the war," but Whitman saw an enormous amount in the hospitals. In this extrapolated vision of the totality of destruction, the poet comprehends the magnitude of mass death. "Fully at rest," the soldiers have perhaps found some comfort in peace and freedom from pain. In the "white skeletons" Whitman sees, it is unclear if he is lamenting the passing of white soldiers, or—as would be fitting in a poem about Lincoln—all soldiers white and black, now reduced to bones and indistinguishable by color and race.

"Lilacs" may be Whitman's greatest Civil War poem, but current residents of the city, or at least users of the Dupont Circle metro stop, are more frequently reminded of "The Wound-Dresser." Part of that poem is inscribed on a frieze at the station, and the lines relate directly to Whitman's hospital experiences:

---

[40] *LG* (1891–92), 261.

> Thus in silence in dreams' projections,
> Returning, resuming, I thread my way through the hospitals;
> The hurt and wounded I pacify with soothing hand,
> I sit by the restless all dark night—some are so young;
> Some suffer so much—I recall the experience sweet and sad.

One commentator in an online discussion board wrote: "Damn, that's a depressing inscription to have to view every time I ascend from the Dupont station."[41] I do not think Whitman saw it as so thoroughly depressing: it was "sweet and sad," reminiscent of the "terrible, beautiful" days mentioned earlier. For him, the war validated the fortitude and heroism of everyday individuals and reconfirmed his faith in the ordinary people so vital to the democratic experiment. Two key lines—the last lines of the poem—have been omitted from the Dupont Circle inscription: "(Many a soldier's loving arms about this neck have cross'd and rested, / Many a soldier's kiss dwells on these bearded lips.)" Whitman found in the hospitals a place where male affection could be openly and freely expressed. He saw its beneficial power when he assisted by inscribing letters for soldiers too ill to write to loved ones, or when he simply stayed by a soldier's side through an amputation and the long night that followed, or when he held the hand of soldiers facing imminent death. Whitman no doubt yearned for many of the needy and often dying men he soothed, but he also handled himself with dignity and discipline. As Robert Roper has noted, his efforts were met with "near universal gratitude" from the soldiers, many of whom credited him with saving their lives.[42]

With an ordinary man's vantage point on the War and an extraordinary artist's sensibility, Whitman, living in the nation's past and future capital, focused on what often escaped attention: the war experiences of the common soldier, the stoicism and heroism of otherwise average individuals, and—above all—the suffering, dignity, and enormous courage he saw in his hospital visits to thousands of wounded men, Northerners and Southerners alike. After his experience of the War, Whitman's poetic voice would never be the same. He had seen too much to remain the exuberant Whitman of the antebellum years. His new poetry modulated in keeping with the grief, hardship, loss, endurance, courage, and sacrifice he

---

[41] "Dupont Metro Gets Poetry" (http://dcist.com/2007/06/dupont_metro_ge.php) Web. December 15, 2013.

[42] Roper, 225.

witnessed and experienced. Extending his range without abandoning his earlier poetry, his writings became richer. Soldiers from every region of the country came to the Washington hospitals, and through them, in ways terrible and beautiful, he sacrificed the best years of his writing life and became the national poet.

2
Whitman as a Paradoxical "Missionary to the Wounded"

> I think Swedenborg was right when he said there was a close connection—a very close connection—between the state we call religious ecstacy and the desire to copulate. I find Swedenborg confirmed in all my experience. It is a peculiar discovery.[1]

In his visits to the men in the Civil War hospitals Whitman had the most terrible and most rewarding experiences of his life. Out of them he penned his most eloquent and moving letters; helped invent the genre of war reporting; filled notebooks with scraps of raw information, idle doodles, stories from soldiers, and early drafts of compelling war poetry and prose. Within the hospitals he also became a self-described "missionary to the wounded." As Drew Gilpin Faust has noted, "religion defined the values and assumptions of most mid-nineteenth-century Americans," and it profoundly shaped commentary on the war.[2] At a time when appeals to God for victory in battle were pervasive, when fallen soldiers were routinely depicted as martyrs, Whitman attributed sacred importance to healing, caring, grieving, loving, and restoring. Still, there is something odd about Whitman calling himself a *missionary*, a striking term. More than a passing conceit, the term *missionary* provides an important frame of reference for his hospital work and can be used not only to gloss his Civil War service but also to illuminate some of the largest ambitions he entertained as a poet and cultural theorist.

One way to think about this term is how it gave Whitman entrée to the hospitals. Many organizations arose to aid wounded soldiers but the two most prominent were the United States Sanitary Commission and the

---

[1] *WWWC*, 5:376.
[2] Faust, *This Republic of Suffering: Death and the American Civil War* (New York: Vintage, 2008), 172.

Christian Commission. The Sanitary Commission, by far the larger and more studied of these two, emerged in the summer of 1861, and was modelled on the British Sanitary Commission, an organization that helped minimize loss of life in the Indian and Crimean wars. The US Sanitary Commission, involving scientists and others concerned with public health, strove to safeguard Civil War soldiers by developing and enforcing hygienic practices.[3] The Sanitary Commission represented a type of "bureaucratic and professional approach that would dominate postwar American society."[4] Its male administrative leaders came from the elite ranks of society, while much of the daily work of the Commission was carried out by middle-class white women. Louisa May Alcott, in her six weeks in the hospitals, for example, worked for the Sanitary Commission. Although the Sanitary Commission saved many lives during the conflict, evangelical Christians worried that it neglected the spiritual needs of the soldiers and sailors; they sensed an opportunity to build their own ranks; and they thus formed the United States Christian Commission.

Ministers were involved in both the Sanitary Commission and the Christian Commission, but they were men of different theological outlooks. The president of the Sanitary Commission was Henry W. Bellows, a well-regarded Unitarian minister[5] (see Figure 2.1). Under his leadership, the Sanitary Commission was practical: it was interested in systematized approaches to aiding up to half a million soldiers. The Christian Commission, in contrast, was under evangelical auspices and so put spiritual welfare of individuals first, which contributed to friction between the two groups, as did rivalry for funds and prominence (see Figure 2.2).

The development of the Christian Commission was related to the rise of the Young Men's Christian Association (YMCA). The founding convention of the Christian Commission, held in New York City, November 14–15, 1861, featured "veterans of missionary, Bible and Tract, temperance, Sunday School, and Y.M.C.A. work."[6] The YMCA, begun in Britain in 1844 and in the United States in 1851, arose partly as a response to fears of the corrupting influences of city life and aimed to "save both the young men's souls for

---

[3] Theresa R. McDevitt, "Fighting for the Soul of America: A History of the United States Christian Commission," PhD dissertation Kent State University (1997), 61, 79–80.
[4] James A. Tidei, "Healing the Wounded: The United States Christian Commission During the Civil War," MA thesis University of Nebraska-Kearney, 2015, p. iii.
[5] James O. Henry, "History of the United States Christian Commission," PhD dissertation University of Maryland, 1959, 291.
[6] McDevitt, 109–10 and 7.

Figure 2.1. In center is Sanitary Commission President Henry Whitney Bellows. Library of Congress Prints and Photographs Division, Washington, DC.

God and their minds and bodies for productive enterprises."[7] The evangelical mission of the YMCA, in Whitman's New York, included a solid anti-slavery stance (furor erupted when the YMCA libraries refused to subscribe to pro-slavery papers such as *The Express*). The YMCA was also notable for male-male bonding. As Susan K. Cahn has noted:

---

[7] The quotation is from McDevitt, 44. For the starting dates of the YMCA in Britain and the US, see John Donald Gustav-Wrathall, *Take the Young Stranger by the Hand: Same-Sex Relations and the YMCA* (Chicago, IL: University of Chicago Press, 1998), 10. See also C. Howard Hopkins, *History of the YMCA in North America* (New York: Association Press, 1951) for a reliable and comprehensive history.

Figure 2.2. Group before office of US Christian Commission, 8th and H Sts. Nw. Library of Congress Prints and Photographs Division, Washington, DC.

Members understood the binding force of the organization to rest in men's love for each other; through passionate attachments, young men would strengthen their characters, adhere to a religious and virtuous life, and prepare themselves for lives as the heads of businesses and families. Led by paid "general secretaries" who typically married late in life or not at all, the YMCA fostered an intensely homosocial world that provided an alternative to Victorian norms of heterosexual marriage, even as it upheld marriage and family as proper duties of Christian manhood.... Physical beauty and "magnetic" love sublimated in intensely spiritual friendships produced a charged environment that balanced "homoerotic attraction against the virtues of self-control."[8]

---

[8] Susan K. Cahn review of John Donald Gustav-Wrathall, *Take the Young Stranger by the Hand: Same-Sex Relations and the YMCA* in *American Historical Review* 104, no. 5 (December 1999), 1706.

It is not coincidental that Whitman composed his tract "Manly Health and Training," appearing in a cheap Sunday paper, the *New York Atlas*, at about the time of the rise of the YMCA: Whitman and the YMCA were trying to build the bodies, minds, and souls of young men, to equip them for urban life. There were differences, too: the YMCA was geared to raise an upwardly mobile generation of clerks, whereas Whitman imagined a wider range of employment for his readers. The common ground of male homosociality may illuminate Whitman's decision to become an agent of the YMCA-shaped Christian Commission rather than the Sanitary Commission. It is important to remember, however, that Whitman ultimately developed deep doubts about Christianity and in particular its version of genteel masculinity, a masculinity that seemed to him too dandified, too European, and too hamstrung by narrow rules. In conversations with his biographer Horace Traubel in his final years we learn that Whitman "laughed outright and heartily" at the notion of a "Christian gentleman"! "He is an unknown quantity, almost!... [I]n fact, we do not know what a Christian gentleman is, 'Christian gentlemen' have been rare indeed!—and fortunately for us, too!"[9]

Whitman had changing views of religion over time. Gay Wilson Allen once estimated that "nearly three times as many 'specific allusions' to the Bible are found in Whitman's early and juvenile writings as in his later poetry and prose." Allen observed that "as Whitman's mind and art matured, the biblical influence became deeper, more abstract, and more difficult to identify precisely."[10] Whitman evolved from a relatively conventional view of Christianity to strikingly unconventional views. In the early 1850s he held in uneasy balance competing notions. On the one hand he befriended Jesse Talbot, a painter who was also an agent for an evangelical society. Whitman owned an oil painting by Talbot of *Christian at the Cross* that he described as "an original of marked beauty & value."[11] Whitman also placed a review of Talbot in *The American Phrenological Journal*.[12] As late as the early 1850s, when Whitman promoted Talbot, he was sympathetic to the millennialist idea of a golden age being possible. In the 1850s he came under the influence of Swedenborg (phrenology and Swedenborg often went hand-in-hand, as did a kind of reform-minded liberalism), contributing to his growing interest in eroticized mysticism. Both Floyd Stovall and David

---

[9] *WWWC*, 5:306.
[10] Gay Wilson Allen, "Biblical Echoes in Whitman's Works," *American Literature*, 6 (November 1934), 303.
[11] Walt Whitman to William D. O'Connor, September 28, 1869 (*WWA*).
[12] Whitman, "Talbot's Pictures," *The American Phrenological Journal* (February 1853), 45.

Reynolds believe that in the "long foreground" prior to *Leaves of Grass* Whitman attended the independent Christian church of Thomas Lake Harris, a self-educated man whose beliefs had affinities with Swedenborg and could be said to anticipate *Leaves*.[13] By 1855 Whitman was ambivalent at best about religion, regarding it as a vital necessity while also lamenting how religion had manifested itself historically and in his own time. In one revealing manuscript draft he noted modern scientific and technical advances, "steamboats and vaccination, gunpowder and spinning-jennies," yet he asked: "are our people half as peaceable and happy as were the Peruvians and Mexicans, ere the Spanish navigators introduced to them the blessings of artificial science and of the true faith?"[14]

Whitman's ambivalent outlook is even more evident in a paradoxical 1857 notebook entry, "Founding a new American / Religion (? No Religion)." He sometimes foresaw and tried to bring into existence a religion without dogma and little or no ceremony.[15] In the 1855 Preface to *Leaves of Grass* Whitman announced that "[t]here will soon be no more priests" to mediate the relationship of the human and the divine, but he quickly qualifies this claim by adding, "A new order shall arise" and "take ... [the priests'] place": "they shall be the priests of man, and every man shall be his own priest."[16] Whitman held that sacred functions could be achieved without the negative consequences of institutionalization and their undemocratic hierarchies.[17] He had always been impatient with intermediaries, as an early notebook indicates: "We will ascend to that tribunal of last resort—we will not waste words with messengers and secretarys.—We will ... stand face to face with the chief of the supreme bench. We will speak with the soul.—"[18] This non-sectarian religious or spiritual impulse in Whitman was often emphasized by nineteenth- and early twentieth-century commentators, but modern critics have instead stressed Whitman's literary and political achievements and his contributions to understandings of gender and sexuality. Yet nineteenth-century religious ferment like Whitman's desire for every man to be his own priest was congruent with the social and sexual

---

[13] Stovall, *The Foreground of* Leaves of Grass (Charlottesville, VA: University Press of Virginia, 1974), 247–48; David Reynolds, *Walt Whitman's America: A Cultural Biography* (New York: Knopf, 1995), 266. Interestingly, Stovall and Reynolds differ on the dates Harris's church operated in New York.
[14] *NUPM*, 1: 177.
[15] *NUPM*, 6: 2046; W. C. Harris, "Whitman's *Leaves of Grass* and the Writing of a New American Bible," *Walt Whitman Quarterly Review* 16 (Winter 1999/Spring 1999), 174–75.
[16] *LG* (1855), xi.   [17] Harris, 174.
[18] See Whitman's notebook "In his presence" available at the *WWA*.

experiments of the Latter Day Saints, the Shakers, and various free love groups. Even the YMCA, tied as it was to the development of the Christian Commission, was key in developing a space for what one historian calls an "unstigmatized same-sex love that included eroticism."[19]

On January 20, 1863, roughly three weeks after arriving in Washington, Whitman was appointed as a delegate of the Christian Commission (see Figures 2.3 and 2.4), thus beginning the first of what would be numerous affiliations with governmental or quasi-governmental bureaucracies (the Christian Commission gained approval to operate during the Civil War from Abraham Lincoln). Whitman may have been encouraged to take this step of joining the Christian Commission for the access to the hospitals provided by delegate status.

We might be inclined to think that the Christian Commission, with its evangelical purposes, made for an odd host for Whitman. As an adult, Whitman did not attend church services, and yet good standing in an evangelical church was touted as a necessary qualification of a Christian Commission delegate. How Whitman evaded this requirement or why it was waived in his case is not known. While there are a few mysteries here, in some ways his association with this group—as opposed to the larger and more famous US Sanitary Commission—made sense. Whitman preferred the Christian Commission because it was less elite than the Sanitary Commission, and because the Christian Commission encouraged direct

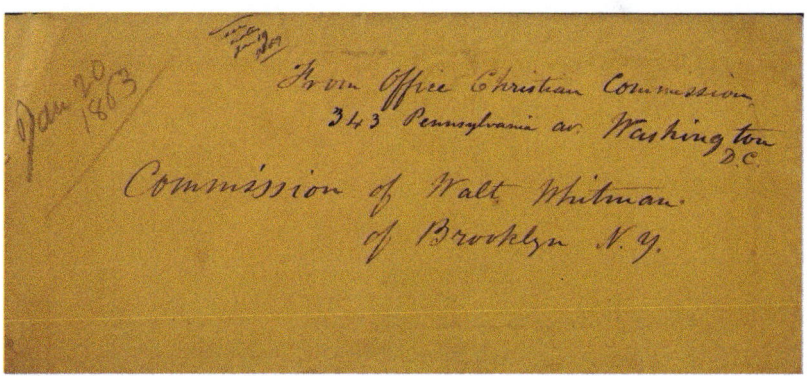

Figure 2.3. Envelope from Walt Whitman Papers in the Charles E. Feinberg Collection, 1763–1985, Library of Congress, Washington, DC.

---

[19] Cahn, 1706.

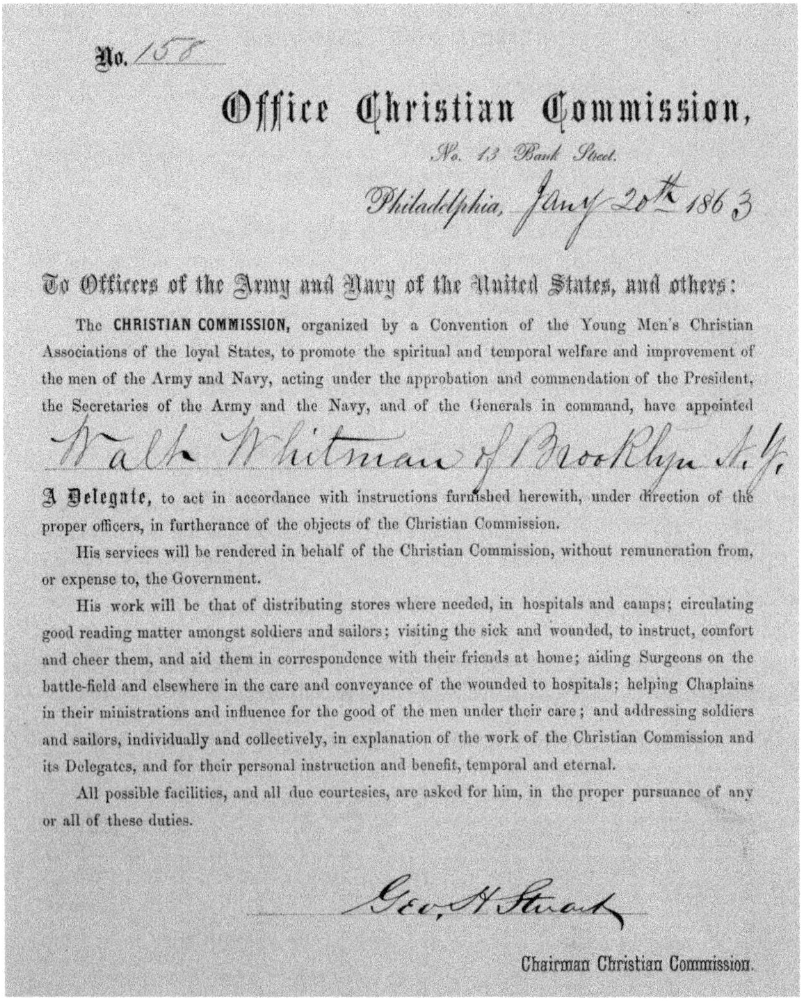

> **No.** 158
>
> ## Office Christian Commission,
> *No. 13 Bank Street.*
>
> *Philadelphia,* Jany 20th 1863
>
> **To Officers of the Army and Navy of the United States, and others:**
>
> The **CHRISTIAN COMMISSION**, organized by a Convention of the Young Men's Christian Associations of the loyal States, to promote the spiritual and temporal welfare and improvement of the men of the Army and Navy, acting under the approbation and commendation of the President, the Secretaries of the Army and the Navy, and of the Generals in command, have appointed
>
> *Walt Whitman of Brooklyn N.Y.*
>
> **A Delegate**, to act in accordance with instructions furnished herewith, under direction of the proper officers, in furtherance of the objects of the Christian Commission.
>
> His services will be rendered in behalf of the Christian Commission, without remuneration from, or expense to, the Government.
>
> His work will be that of distributing stores where needed, in hospitals and camps; circulating good reading matter amongst soldiers and sailors; visiting the sick and wounded, to instruct, comfort and cheer them, and aid them in correspondence with their friends at home; aiding Surgeons on the battle-field and elsewhere in the care and conveyance of the wounded to hospitals; helping Chaplains in their ministrations and influence for the good of the men under their care; and addressing soldiers and sailors, individually and collectively, in explanation of the work of the Christian Commission and its Delegates, and for their personal instruction and benefit, temporal and eternal.
>
> All possible facilities, and all due courtesies, are asked for him, in the proper pursuance of any or all of these duties.
>
> *Geo. H. Stuart*
>
> Chairman Christian Commission.

Figure 2.4. Courtesy Walt Whitman Papers in the Charles E. Feinberg Collection, 1763–1985, Library of Congress, Washington, DC.

interaction with the troops (many in the Sanitary Commission preferred to distribute goods through medical professionals). Whitman was deeply suspicious of Sanitary agents:

> As to the Sanitary Commissions & the like, I am sick of them all, & would not accept any of their berths—you ought to see the way the men as they lie helpless in bed turn away their faces from the sight of these...foxes &

wolves)—they get well paid, & are always incompetent & disagreeable—As I told you before the only good fellows I have met are the Christian Commissioners—they go everywhere & receive no pay.[20]

The Christian Commission was also less bureaucratic than the Sanitary Commission, though perhaps Whitman chafed even against their loose guidelines.[21]

Still, many of the famous aspects of Whitman's hospital work—his haversack, work as an amanuensis, gift-giving, reading to wounded soldiers, and making a record of visits in his notebooks—had their roots in or were reinforced by Christian Commission policy and practices. A Whitman notebook, stamped "Christian Commission" on its cover (see Figure 2.5), was probably one of the handbooks given to Christian Commission delegates so that they, as instructed, could "use them freely in noting facts, names, incidents, dates, and everything of interest." Each delegate was also supplied with a haversack and with "paper, pen, ink, envelopes and stamps, for his own use as well as to give to those who need them."[22] Whitman did this and more, all the while recording poignant details and distinctive traits of innumerable wounded and sick men. On the inside of his Christian Commission notebook he made note of his newly conceived role: "Walt Whitman Soldier's Missionary to Hospital, Camp, & Battle Ground (Young Men's Christian Commission 343 Pennsylvania av. Washington D. C.)"[23] (see Figure 2.6). Interestingly, the possessive here makes him beholden not to the Commission but to the soldiers.

The description of the obligations of a Christian Commission delegate aligned with Whitman's own approach to hospital visits, and perhaps shaped his approach. A Christian Commission delegate was to distribute "stores" where needed in the hospitals, circulate "good reading matter," and visit the sick and wounded to "instruct, comfort, and cheer them." Delegates were also charged with assisting in "correspondence with friends at home" and aiding "Surgeons on the battle-field and elsewhere" in the treatment and conveyance of the wounded to the hospitals. What constituted "good reading

[20] Walt Whitman to Louisa Van Velsor Whitman, June 22, 1863, available at the *WWA*. Whitman agreed when Traubel used the phrase "hireling minister" (*WWWC*, 2:274).
[21] On the more elite nature of the US Sanitary Commission, see McDevitt, 224.
[22] See "Instructions to Delegates of the Christian Commission," printed matter that is available in Whitman's notebook with the title Christian Commission on the cover. Thomas Biggs Harned Collection of Walt Whitman, Library of Congress.
[23] Ted Genoways, "'Memoranda of a year (1863)': Whitman in Washington, D.C.," *Mickle Street Review* 17–18 (2005), <micklestreet.rutgers.edu>. See also *NUPM*, 2: 602.

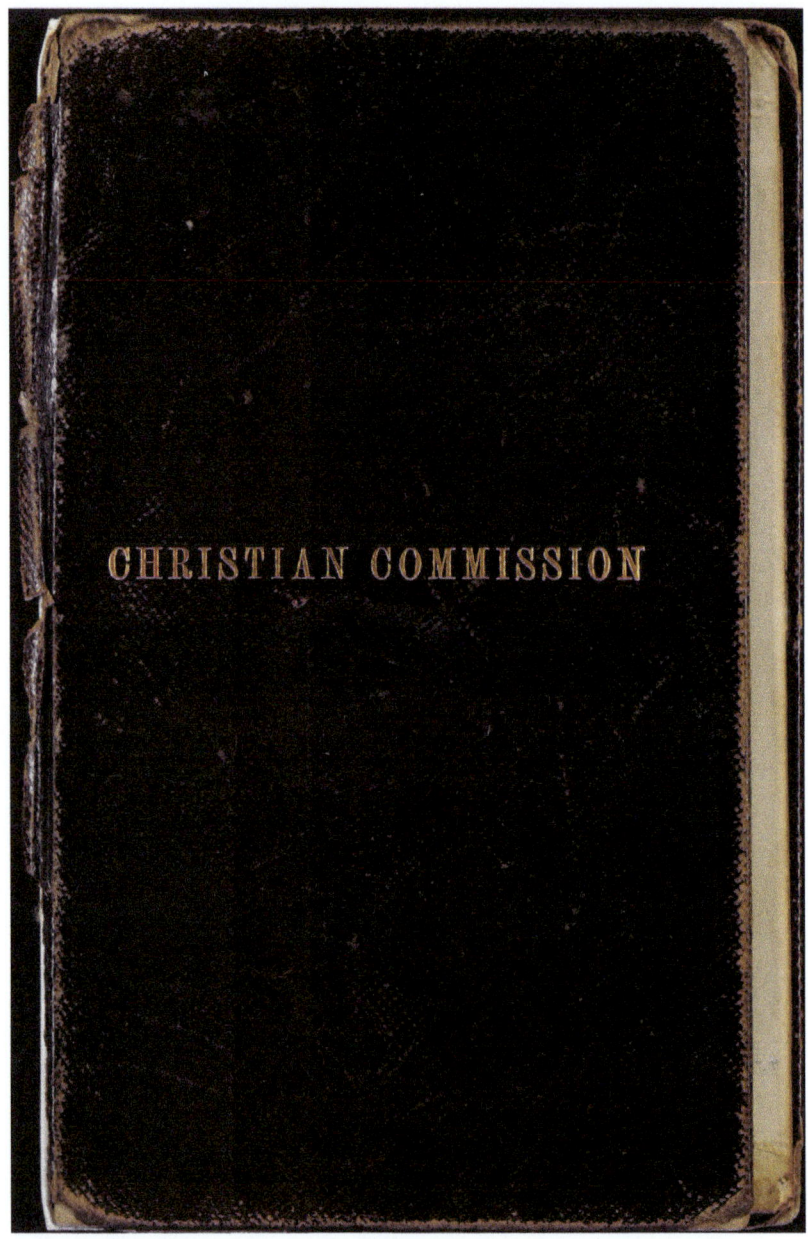

Figure 2.5. Courtesy Walt Whitman Papers in the Charles E. Feinberg Collection, 1763–1985, Library of Congress, Washington, DC.

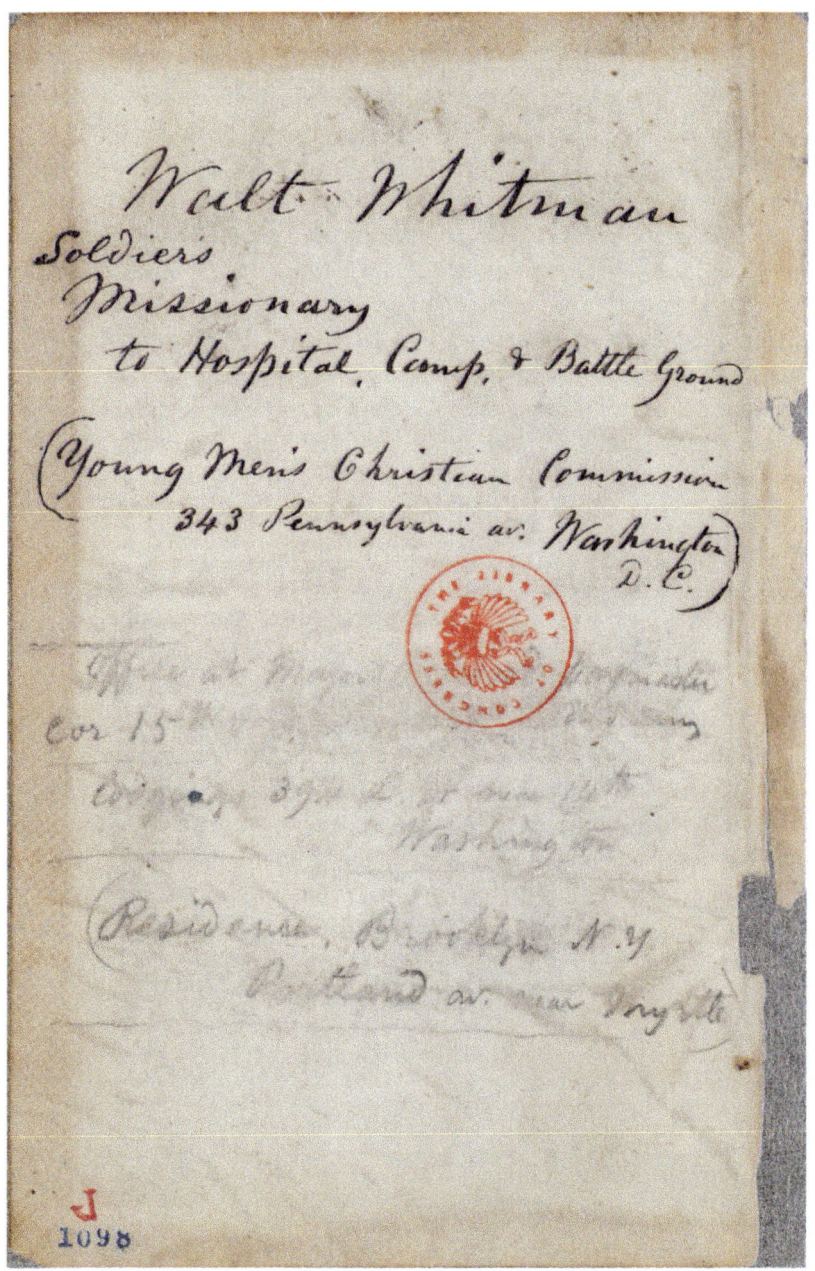

Figure 2.6. Courtesy Thomas Biggs Harned Collection of Walt Whitman Papers, 1842–1937, Library of Congress, Washington, DC.

matter" of "high moral and religious tone" was not clarified, but since Whitman rarely if ever read *Leaves of Grass* to his soldier friends, he did not run afoul of authorities in that regard.[24] Whitman's goals perhaps did not even skew away from the Christian Commission in their final purposes: "helping Chaplains...for the good of the men...temporal and eternal," though the conventionally pious among them might have thought so. Far from doctrinaire about religion, Whitman did not gear his efforts toward conversion in any ordinary sense: he had said in *Leaves of Grass*, "I will write the evangel-poem of comrades and of love."[25] But he *was* on a mission.

That mission was shared by some of Whitman's abolitionist friends. For example, Whitman drafted a letter to the journalist, anti-slavery activist, and publisher James Redpath on the back of a Christian Commission information sheet (see Figure 2.7), with surface and substance inextricably joined in his messaging. The final copy was probably also written on the same type of stationery. Redpath deduced that the poet was working in association with the Christian Commission. Redpath said: "I wrote to Mr. Emerson to get him to interest some of his friends (he has several rich ones who give away large sums to various good causes) in your Christian Commission Agency." Although he wished to help Whitman, Redpath was not above needling him, too, addressing him as "Dear Evangelist" in one letter. For Redpath, it was not religiosity but sympathy that mattered when aiding soldiers. Writing for the Boston *Commonwealth*, Redpath declared that "Dying of homesickness is no figure of speech, but a reality of weekly occurrence in our army. To such invalids the religious tract, or the mechanical consolations of theology, give no relief; not musty manna from the church wilderness, but living waters of sympathy from the warm heart of man who loves them is what they need to save them. And this they get from the rough singer of Brooklyn."[26] Redpath nonetheless found fundraising for Whitman

---

[24] "Instructions to Delegates of the Christian Commission." John Townsend Trowbridge reported that Whitman "took me two or three times to the great Armory Square Hospital, where I observed his methods of work. I was surprised to learn that he never read to the patients any of his own compositions, and that not one of those I talked with knew him for a poet, or for anybody but plain 'Mr. Whitman.' I cannot help speaking of one poor fellow, who had asked to see me because Whitman had told him I was the author of one of the pieces he liked to hear read, and who talked to me with tears in his eyes of the comfort Whitman's visits had given him. The pathos of the situation was impressed upon me by the circumstance that his foot was to be amputated within an hour." See "Reminiscences of Walt Whitman," *Atlantic Monthly* 89 (February 1902), 169.
[25] *LG* (1860–61), 11.
[26] Redpath, *Commonwealth*, April 10, 1863; quoted in Martin Buinicki, "The 'need of means additional': Walt Whitman's Civil War Fundraising," *Walt Whitman Quarterly Review* 31 (Spring 2014), 145.

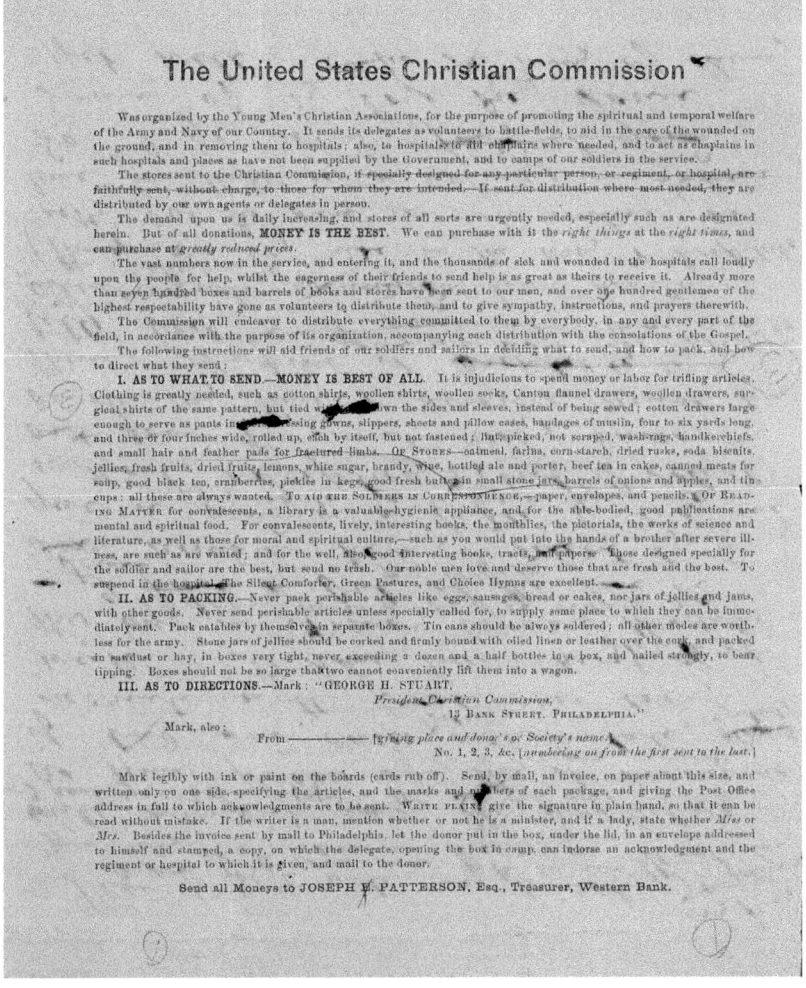

Figure 2.7. Courtesy Walt Whitman Papers in the Charles E. Feinberg Collection, 1763–1985, Library of Congress, Washington, DC.

challenging: he explained that there was reluctance in Emerson's circle to support the poet's hospital work because "It is believed that you are not ashamed of your reproductive organs, and, somehow, it wd seem to be the result of their logic—that eunuchs only are fit for nurses."[27] Redpath's wry

---

[27] James Redpath to Walt Whitman, 10 March 1863 and 5 May 1863 (*WWA*).

note and gentle mocking of Whitman highlighted how the poet of sex and the body might seem an odd fit in an organization emphasizing Christian piety. Some New Englanders, including Thomas Wentworth Higginson, were convinced that nursing was not sufficiently "manly," a view that Redpath echoes.[28] In any event, Redpath's remarks may have clarified for Whitman how his association with the Christian Commission could be perceived as incongruous, thus leading him to distance himself from the Commission. He would assert repeatedly and publicly that he was in the hospitals "on my own hook," though he relied on the affiliation when it was useful.[29] In *Memoranda During the War* he notes that "Mrs. G., lady nurse, Ward F., wants a bottle of brandy—has two patients imperatively requiring stimulus—low with wounds and exhaustion. (I supplied her with a bottle of first-rate brandy, from the Christian Commission rooms.)"[30]

Later descriptions of the Christian Commission emphasize not the brandy but the soul saving and may indicate what led Whitman to distance himself from the organization. On May 20, 1863, an account by George Stuart, the man who signed Whitman's Christian Commission papers, speaks of the "great benefit which the soldiers had derived from the operations of the Christian Commission, and told of many instances in which dying soldiers, through the instrumentality of the missionaries sent by the Christian Commission, had been converted to the Lord."[31] This zeal of the Christian Commission sometimes drew criticism. Frederick Law Olmsted, the landscape architect and anti-slavery writer who had taken leave as director of New York's Central Park to work as Executive Secretary of the Sanitary Commission, argued that every soldier was entitled to proper care and should not have to endure religious appeals in order to gain assistance.[32]

---

[28] Robert K. Nelson and Kenneth M. Price, "Debating Manliness: Thomas Wentworth Higginson, William Sloane Kennedy, and the Question of Whitman," *American Literature*, 73.3 (2001), 498.
[29] Walt Whitman to Hugo Fritsch, October 8, 1863 (*WWA*).
[30] *MDW*, 37. McDevitt notes that "distribution of Christian Commission stores was also far less controlled. The delegates attempted to be judicious in their direct distribution of goods to soldiers and to supply materials fairly and to those most in need. There were no specific rules for the distribution of materials that might give their work the appearance of system" (235). However, unwritten rules of gender discrimination were widespread and quite consistently enforced: Mrs. G. was not able to get the brandy herself because the Christian Commission did not ordinarily allow women to act as delegates, relegating them to work in kitchens.
[31] See "Anniversary of the Young Men's Christian Association," *Brooklyn Daily Eagle*, May 20, 1863, p. 2. In this same article, Stuart described Christian Commission delegates as "co-laborers in the great army of King Jesus, battling against the great rebellion that had commenced in the garden of Eden."
[32] McDevitt, 256.

Others asserted bluntly that "this fooling away of money on tracts and broken down preachers is all humbug" and a "waste of real blood and muscle." One editorial argued that "tracts will do after the war" and reminded readers that "if a man has his leg shot off, tracts won't bind it."[33] Within a Christian Commission context of caregiving there were indeed some who acted on narrow views and so diverged sharply from Whitman's approach. For example, Dwight Moody, the preacher, evangelist, and publisher, gave his primary attention to soldiers on the battlefield who were *not* saved. If he found a man who was wounded or dying but already saved, he moved on to someone else, because he considered the mortal body as less important than the immortal soul.[34] Christian Commission policy, however, did *not* support Moody's choice.[35] In fact, a publication from 1863 stated that on the battlefield, relief to the body should come before spiritual comforts.[36]

There is no evidence that the Christian Commission ever dismissed Whitman (though they did dismiss some delegates) nor have I found any evidence that Whitman ever formally severed ties with them.[37] However, a mere month after joining the Christian Commission he was already emphasizing his independence. In the February 26, 1863, *New-York Times* article headlined, "The Great Army of the Sick," Whitman states, "Upon a few of these hospitals I have been almost daily calling as a missionary, on my own account, for the sustenance and consolation of some of the most needy cases of sick and dying men, for the last two months."[38] Whitman accordingly preferred to be seen, and to act, as an independent agent, even if this meant shouldering the new burden of fund raising, as a letter to his mother on June 9, 1863, makes clear:

---

[33] Quoted in McDevitt, 257.
[34] J. Wilbur Chapman, *Life and Work of Dwight Moody* (London: James Nisbet, 1900), 177.
[35] McDevitt notes that the policy of "relief before moral suasion was reflected in Christian Commission documents that again and again instructed delegates to assist the soldier and provide any kindnesses they could before they attempted to do spiritual work. For example, in the *Annals*, Moss wrote that the Christian who did not do what he could for his fellow man in need was not only guilty of inhumanity, but also missing a valuable selling point to the furtherance of the work of God and the Commission" (153).
[36] United States Christian Commission, *Facts, Principles, and Progress* (Philadelphia, PA: William S. and Alfred Martien, 1864), 17–18.
[37] See Roy Morris, Jr., *The Better Angel: Walt Whitman in the Civil War* (New York: Oxford University Press, 2000), 108–10. Morris thinks Whitman did break with the Christian Commission, though he doesn't cite any evidence to support such a conclusion.
[38] Walt Whitman, "The Great Army of the Sick," *The New-York Times*, February 26, 1863, 2.

Mother, I think something of commencing a series of lectures & readings &c. through different cities of the north, to supply myself with funds for my Hospital & Soldiers visits—as I do not like to be beholden to the medium of others—I need a pretty large supply of money &c. to do the good I would like to.[39]

His experiences in the hospitals led Whitman (like the Sanitary Commission) to perceive just what a giant undertaking it was even to support one person's charitable efforts—in short, he gained a realistic sense of what his independence would have to rest on in terms of income.[40] In conjunction with his low-level governmental work at the time—he started in the Army paymaster's office and would later move on to clerkships in the Bureau of Indian Affairs and in the office of the Attorney General—Whitman came to recognize, despite his inclination to operate as a loner, the overlapping and increasingly bureaucratic ways that governmental, philanthropic, and religious systems could serve the public.

If Whitman's affiliation with the Christian Commission was fleeting—the record is unclear—his use of the term "missionary" was not.[41] Paradoxically, he positioned himself both in opposition to and in agreement with the religiosity that was central to the Christian Commission's purpose. Even if he found narrow, unnecessary, and off-putting the Commission's heavy emphasis on winning a soul to Christ, he himself appropriated a specific and charged religious language. In fulfilling and revising missionary approaches and purposes, queering them and in an odd way fundamentalizing them—by which I mean he sought an original purity of motive by radically reimagining what religiously-oriented assistance might be—he made male-male adhesiveness central to his missionary effort.

There are striking continuities between the religiously charged language of the third edition of *Leaves of Grass* and Whitman's hospital work. Whitman aspired to write a *new* American Bible with the 1860 edition of *Leaves* brought out by the abolitionist publishers Thayer and Eldridge.[42] In drafting the third edition of *Leaves of Grass*, he spoke of the New Bible as

---

[39] Walt Whitman to Louisa Van Velsor Whitman, June 9, 1863 (*WWA*).

[40] Martin Buinicki, "The 'need of means additional': Walt Whitman's Civil War Fundraising," *Walt Whitman Quarterly Review* 31 (Spring 2014), 135–57.

[41] Approximately 5,000 delegates made up the Christian Commission. Whitman was delegate number 158, but all numbers from 156 to 159 are missing from the official history.

[42] W. C. Harris notes that "critics have tended to minimize Whitman's reference to a 'New Bible.'" See his "Whitman's *Leaves of Grass* and the Writing of a New American Bible," 172.

"the principal object—the main life work"; once he moved to Washington, he treated the mission to the soldiers with comparable devotion. Whitman's compassionate hospital work and the writing of *Leaves of Grass* were of a piece. He wanted "to found a new, scripturally based social formation."[43] Whitman was fully aware of the various institutional causes in which theology had been enlisted, "the ~~paraphernalia~~? of modern worship, [the] sects, churches, creeds, pews, sermons, [and] observances... [that] have nothing to do with real religion."[44] His idea of a social formation was *not* a church. His desire to address ultimate questions can also be seen in his plan—never realized directly—to "Write a new burial service. A book of new things."[45] Although a liturgical volume never came to fruition, Adam Bradford notes that *Drum-Taps* itself serves to "mediate grief and foster successful mourning through a book that... not only represented the deceased, but allowed readers to imagine themselves reconnected to them through its pages."[46] Moreover, individual poems drafted in response to the war such as "Ashes of Roses" (discussed more fully below) reflect on life and death, loss and renewal in a landscape given over to ashes but far from bereft of hope.

Although Whitman was neither evangelical nor religious in a conventional sense, he long believed that those who relished work in hospitals were driven by an inner light and put into action values of compassion and self-sacrifice. Prior to the Civil War he visited in New York hospitals ailing omnibus drivers whom he knew, and in a manuscript from 1854 he asserted: "If you have in you that which makes you realize the delicious-{ness} of visiting the sick in hospitals and the poor—if you have those sublime moments released from all cares and soaring to the idea of God, rapt, sublime—if elate with immortality, realizing the divine of man, then you have the curious something, the crown of life and being, the lumine of the soul."[47] These comments, with their emphasis on inner light, may stem from Whitman's longstanding interest in Quaker thought.

Early in life Whitman committed himself to a purposeful poverty as an ethical choice.[48] In the passage above, Whitman fittingly mentions the "poor" because, in the antebellum US, hospitals were places where the

---

[43] Harris, 173.   [44] *NUPM* 6: 2091–2092.   [45] *NUPM*, 4: 1313.
[46] Adam C. Bradford, "Embodying the Book: Mourning for the Masses in Walt Whitman's *Drum-Taps*," *Mickle Street Review* no. 21 (Spring 2016), micklestreet.rutgers.edu.
[47] *NUPM*, 6: 2042.
[48] Whitman, *Daybooks and Notebooks*, 3 vols., ed. William White (New York: New York University Press, 1978), 3:767.

indigent went to die. Decades later, after the war, and after hundreds of additional hospital visits, he asserted

> it never occurred to me... that I had any right or call to abandon my work: it was a religion with me. A religion? Well—every man has a religion: has something in heaven or earth which he will give up everything else for—something which absorbs him, possesses itself of him, makes him over into its image: something: it may be something regarded by others as being very paltry, inadequate, useless: yet it is his dream, it is his lodestar, it is his master. That, whatever it is, seized upon me, made me its servant,... induced me to set aside the other ambitions: a trail of glory in the heavens, which I followed, followed, with a full heart.[49]

Whitman as servant of his lodestar is a very different nurse than Florence Nightingale and Clara Barton—both of whom can be usefully compared to Whitman, and both of whom did important nursing. Their most significant contributions were organizational, with Nightingale working within the Sanitary Commission model and Barton working independently of it. In contrast, Whitman's greatest contributions were at the side of the individual soldier. Whitman became a "sustainer of spirit and body in some degree, in time of need."[50] He provided companionship, someone to talk to, healing touch, and a concern for the individual at a time when many soldiers perceived coldness and corruption in the military establishment.[51] His approach was idiosyncratic and provided no template for others to follow. Whitman's highly personalized approach could have been criticized by those like Bellows of the Sanitary Commission, who were understandably suspicious of "careless charity" and the irregularity of those outside an established system. But Whitman's approach yielded important results. D. Willard Bliss, the chief surgeon of Armory Square, the hospital with the highest mortality rate and where Whitman spent most of his time, asserted: "From my personal knowledge of Mr. Whitman's labors in Armory Square and other hospitals, I am of [the] opinion that no one person who assisted in the hospitals during the war accomplished so much good to the soldier and for the Government as Mr. Whitman."[52]

---

[49] *WWWC*, 3: 581–82.
[50] "'Tis But Ten Years Since," *New York Weekly Graphic*, March 7, 1874: 46.
[51] McDevitt, 336.
[52] Thomas Donaldson, *Walt Whitman the Man* (New York: Francis P. Harper, 1896), 169.

In teasing out the implications of *Leaves of Grass* as an "evangel-poem of love and comrades," it is useful to consider more closely the implications the name *missionary* had for Whitman. In his early years as a journalist, Whitman had expressed skepticism about missionaries. In a July 27, 1846, newspaper piece on "Rev. Mr. Jacobus's Church.—Foreign Missions" in the *Brooklyn Daily Eagle*, after a long article on missionaries, Whitman appended an editor's note: "*Note by Ed. Eagle*— ... Instead of 'the [missionary] operations of the British in India,' being 'a means adopted by God,' to spread Christianity, we think these operations a bitter *insult* to Christianity, and prompted more by the Devil than a God of love."[53] On September 8, 1846, again in the *Eagle*, Whitman quoted with approval a *Globe* article that celebrates the aid missionaries provided to the "heathen" but wonders "how many there are who subscribe large sums...who would scorn from their presence a poor little barefooted boy." The article scolded those who "do not reflect that they are surrounded by persons more miserable...than any people of any heathen country on the globe." In short, Whitman held views akin to Charles Dickens who, in *Bleak House,* would criticize Mrs. Jellyby for her commitment to missionary work in Africa while neglecting her parental duties at home. For Dickens, missionaries were "perfect nuisances who leave every place worse than they find it."[54] In fact, the early Whitman held views similar to Herman Melville in *Typee,* who criticized missionaries and recognized that the effort to remake belief systems was destructive, an attack on other people's cultures.

In his final years, in conversations with Traubel, Whitman could be as dismissive of missionaries as he had been as a journalist in the 1840s, highlighting again his somewhat curious adoption of the role during the Civil War. In 1888, he said of Robert Pearsall Smith, one of his Quaker friends, that he was "once a missionary or something or other of that useless sort."[55] At times, though, Whitman praised missionaries in his final years, as when he discussed the work of Father Damien, known as "the Apostle of the Lepers," on Molokai island: "These things take you back to the early days of Christianity—the early days of anything, everything—days of purity.... [T]his man was very broad—steeped in humanities, liberalities!"[56]

---

[53] "Rev. Mr. Jacobus's Church.—Foreign Missions," in Walt Whitman, *The Journalism: 1834–1846,* ed. Herbert Bergman, Douglas A. Noverr, and Edward Recchia (New York: Peter Lang, 1998), 1: 480–81.
[54] Quoted in Patrick Brantlinger, *Rule of Darkness: British Literature and Imperialism, 1830–1914* (Ithaca, NY: Cornell University Press, 1988), 178.
[55] *WWWC*, 1: 172.   [56] *WWWC*, 5: 436.

We may now think of missionaries largely in terms of evangelism, but missionaries themselves often framed their work in terms of benevolence and charity. In the September 8, 1846, article, both Whitman and the *Globe* start by lauding missionaries before they critique them, with the poet acknowledging "truly noble motives and heroic disinterestedness." In wartime, when Whitman used the word *missionary* to characterize his own efforts, it was meant to denote an extraordinary commitment to self-sacrificing good works, a commitment so profound as to resemble religious devotion. Others often saw his work this way, too: Whitelaw Reid, a long-time editor of the New York *Tribune*, first met Whitman in the hospitals and noted that "No one could fail [during the War] to admire his zeal and devotion."[57] Whereas most missionaries were middle-class evangelicals, driven by the spirit of the Second Great Awakening and linked reform movements, who found political support from the Whigs, the article Whitman quoted from the Democratic *Globe* specifically imagines the suffering (and neglected) American as a working-class, probably white, boy, a little "Brother Jonathan."[58] He would later see many of the soldiers he tended in these terms.

Whitman's approach to missionary work was atypical: instead of going to a strange land to convert people of color, he went to the nation's capital to treat primarily fellow whites. Instead of working to destroy a culture viewed as alien, he attempted to help realize a culture lurching fitfully toward an inclusive democracy. If most missionary work occurred on the imperial frontier, Whitman's took place on medical, psychic, social, and sexual frontiers. If the ordinary missionary aimed to convert and to save souls, Whitman held that humans were already quasi-divine, and thus he focused on assisting in this life. He cared deeply about souls but not in a conventional way. For Whitman, bodies and souls were entangled, mutually constitutive: souls were inextricable from bodies, and bodies were divinized. Perfect or damaged, bodies mattered enormously, and he adored them even when mangled, weakened with disease, or disfigured because of wounds or amputations. It is not surprising that he responded positively to Father Damien, even at a stage of life when he was prone to dismiss other missionaries.

---

[57] See Charles N. Elliot, *Walt Whitman as Man, Poet and Friend* (Boston, MA: R. G. Badger, Gorham Press, 1915), 213, and *Studies in Bibliography*, 8 (1956), 242–49.

[58] Whitman would later join the Republican party which, in a rapidly shifting political landscape, captured the lion's share of the evangelical vote in 1860, despite Lincoln's own unconventional religious thought.

Missionary work was also critiqued in the nineteenth century as risking not just cultural imperialism, but economic exploitation advanced under the veneer of religious conversion.[59] Whitman's own awareness of these issues was influenced through reading Constantin Volney's *The Ruins, or Meditation on the Revolutions of Empires*. The book had been one of his father's favorites, and Whitman told Traubel that it was one of the "books on which I may be said to have been raised."[60] The poet remained fascinated by Volney even at the end of his life, as an annotated copy of an 1890 reprinting of *Ruins* makes clear. Volney held that human suffering stemmed from "the ignorance of the weak and the greed of the strong, abetted by organized religion and tyrannical governments." Volney tempered this with hope that through the study of "nature and enlightened self-love mankind might devise a truly natural religion and thereby reach moral 'perfection.'"[61]

Accordingly, at the very time when Whitman adopted the language of "missionary" work, he seemed to some people refreshingly irreligious. Richard Hinton, a Union Colonel and former associate of John Brown in Kansas, wrote of Whitman:

> When this old heathen came and gave me a pipe and tobacco, it was about the most joyous moment of my life.... There were plenty of [other visitors] I assure you. The little bay at the head of my cot was full of tracts and testaments, and every Sunday there were half a dozen old roosters who would come into my ward and preach and pray and sing to us, while we were swearing to ourselves all the time, and wishing the blamed fools would go away. Walt Whitman's funny stories, and his pipes and tobacco were worth more than all the preachers and tracts in Christendom. A wounded soldier don't like to be reminded of his God more than twenty times a day. Walt Whitman didn't bring any tracts or Bibles; he didn't ask if you loved the Lord, and didn't seem to care whether you did or not.[62]

---

[59] For two insightful critiques of missionary work from different angles, see Jose Rabasa, *Writing Violence on the Northern Frontier* (Durham, NC: Duke University Press, 2000) and George E. Tinker, *Missionary Conquest: The Gospel and Native American Cultural Genocide* (Minneapolis, MN: Fortress Press, 1993).

[60] *WWWC*, 2:445.

[61] Sherwood Smith, "Volney, Constantin (1757–1820)," *Walt Whitman Encyclopedia*, ed. J. R. LeMaster and Donald D. Kummings (New York: Garland, 1998), 755.

[62] H. J. R. [Richard Hinton], "A Reminiscence," *Cincinnati Commercial*, August 26, 1871, 2.

Hinton was not alone in being annoyed by the evangelical blending of religious exhortation and medical aid. Whitman's heathen persona deliberately perverted the usual meaning of missionary.

Like Volney, he sought a more democratic and natural morality. He had articulated his own unorthodox creed in the 1855 Preface to *Leaves of Grass*:

> This is what you shall do: Love the earth and sun and the animals, despise riches, give alms to every one that asks, stand up for the stupid and crazy, devote your income and labor to others, hate tyrants, argue not concerning God, have patience and indulgence toward the people, take off your hat to nothing known or unknown or to any man or number of men, go freely with powerful uneducated persons and with the young and with the mothers of families...re examine all you have been told at school or church or in any book, dismiss whatever insults your own soul, and your very flesh shall be a great poem.

Whitman's decision to "argue not concerning God" guided his work in the hospitals. There he operated within the bounds of what he called "True religion," a concept he would explain after the war to his young friend Harry Stafford. Whitman had given Stafford a book to read by Robert Green Ingersoll, "a notorious atheist" and the eulogist at Whitman's funeral. After Stafford discussed the book with his minister (who let him know he was "risking his soul by even reading such trash"), Stafford wrote in distress to Whitman. In his response, the poet offered a definition of the "good life" as "steady trying to do fair." This required "a sunny disposition," a non-judgmental "inclusiveness," and a key third component:

> True religion (*the most beautiful thing in the whole world*, & the best part of any man's or woman's, or boy's character) consists in *what one does* square and kind & generous & honorable all days, *all the time* – & especially with his own folks & associates & with the poor & illiterate & in devout meditation, & silent thoughts of God, & death—& not at all in what he says nor in Sunday or prayer meeting gas.[63]

So when Oscar F. Wilber, suffering from "chronic diarrhoea, and a bad wound also," asked Whitman to read him a chapter from the New

---

[63] Walt Whitman to Harry Stafford, January 27 [1881] (*WWA*).

Testament, he "readily complied." Oscar was pleased to hear one of the "chapters describing the latter hours of Christ, and the scenes at the crucifixion." Oscar then asked if Whitman enjoyed religion, prompting this exchange: "I said: 'Perhaps not, my dear, in the way you mean, and yet, may-be, it is the same thing.' He said: 'It is my chief reliance.' He talk'd of death, and said he did not fear it. I said: 'Why, Oscar, don't you think you will get well?' He said: 'I may, but it is not probable.'... He died a few days after the one just described." This near-death exchange illustrates the principle that "each case requires some peculiar adaptation to itself."[64] Recognizing that Wilber was devout, Whitman had no interest in arguments about God, if they risked compromising his ability to bond with the soldier.

The account of Wilber's death is almost immediately followed in *Memoranda During the War* by the singing of "Shining Shores" by the women nurses. Here Whitman nods toward, without affirming or denying, widespread belief in a heavenly destiny. Whitman seems to value the beauty and consolation provided by the song. For himself, however, Whitman was ready to abandon conventional notions of heaven and hell as he made clear in the 1865 poem "As I Lay with my Head in your Lap, Camerado": "And the threat of what is call'd hell is little or nothing to me; / And the lure of what is call'd heaven is little or nothing to me."[65]

Whitman was first someone who shunned conventional religion, only later to embrace the possibility of remaking it. Responding to the looming crisis of the union, he imagined reconstituting human relations to establish a new community, a new politics, a new set of loving relations based on bonds between men. Jason Stacy has noted that "In many ways, the new American bible that Whitman had labored so hard to bring to fruition [in 1860] was quickly outmoded once the war began," and he argues that the book itself was a victim of the war.[66] Arguably, though, Whitman shifted his focus from thought to action, implementing ideas articulated in *Leaves of Grass*, his new bible, in the Washington hospitals, where he found a deeply consequential testing ground.

Like Emily Dickinson, Whitman "could not entirely swallow the candied placebo of a family reunion in heaven."[67] If Whitman worried about the

---

[64] "Our Wounded and Sick Soldiers," *New-York Times*, December 11, 1864, [1]–2.
[65] *D-T*, 19.
[66] Jason Stacy, "Introduction," Leaves of Grass, *1860: The 150th Anniversary Facsimile Edition* (Iowa City, IA: University of Iowa Press, 2009), xlvii.
[67] Barton Levi St. Armand, *Emily Dickinson and Her Culture: The Soul's Society* (Cambridge: Cambridge University Press, 1986), 48.

afterlife of soldiers, he rarely says so. In *Memoranda* and in *Drum-Taps* he does not invite readers to ponder the supernatural dimensions of the fate of souls—rather, as in "As I Lay My Head in Your Lap Camerado," he tends to dismiss the issue. His focus instead is on overcoming the soldiers' pangs of loneliness and a family's fear that a loved one will die alone.

Whitman's poem "A March in the Ranks Hard Prest and the Road Unknown" dramatizes these issues. The poem emerged from a conversation with a Maine soldier, Milton Roberts, who had had his left leg amputated. He told Whitman of a "scene in the woods... after the battle of White Oaks church, on the retreat, the march at night—the scene between 12 & 2 o'clock that night at the church in the woods, ... the wounded brought in—previous the silent stealthy march through the woods, at times stumbling over the bodies of dead men in the road...." From Roberts' account, recorded in Whitman's notebook, the poet seized and reworked many horrific details. It "was a pretty good sized old church used impromptu for a hospital for the wounded of the battles of the day thereabout—with these it was filled, all varieties, horrible beyond description—the darkness dimly lit with candles, lamps, torches, moving about, but dark but plenty of darkness & half darkness.—the crowds of wounded, bloody & pale, the surgeons operating—the yards outside also filled—."

> We come to an open space in the woods, and halt by the dim-lighted building;
> 'Tis a large old church, at the crossing roads—'tis now an impromptu hospital;
> —Entering but for a minute, I see a sight beyond all the pictures and poems ever made:
> Shadows of deepest, deepest black, just lit by moving candles and lamps,
> And by one great pitchy torch, stationary, with wild red flame, and clouds of smoke.[68]

Alice Fahs notes that southern and northern writers were equally confident that God was on their side, with each asserting the righteousness of the war and giving it the veneer of divine sanction.[69] However, Whitman rarely

---

[68] *D-T*, 44.
[69] Alice Fahs, *The Imagined Civil War: Popular Literature of the North & South, 1861–1865* (Chapel Hill, NC: University of North Carolina Press, 2001), 79.

provides such veneer: this scene—despite the church setting—is more hellish than divinely sanctioned. Whitman highlights the incongruity of a place of worship becoming a vault for the detritus of war. If this repurposing of a church seems jarring, it was also remarkably common in the Civil War: in the Washington, DC, area, where Whitman experienced the war, nearly one quarter of the churches—eighteen out of seventy-nine—were turned into hospitals.[70]

Whitman inserted a vital element lacking in Roberts' account of his experience: a desperately wounded young soldier who captures the narrator's attention and who, by his presence, alters the overall tenor of the previously ghoulish scene:[71]

> By these, crowds, groups of forms, vaguely I see, on the floor, some in the pews laid down;
> At my feet more distinctly, a soldier, a mere lad, in danger of bleeding to death, (he is shot in the abdomen;)
> I staunch the blood temporarily, (the youngster's face is white as a lily;)
> Then before I depart I sweep my eyes o'er the scene, fain to absorb it all;
> Faces, varieties, postures beyond description, most in obscurity, some of them dead;
> Surgeons operating, attendants holding lights, the smell of ether, the odor of blood;
> The crowd, O the crowd of the bloody forms of soldiers — the yard outside also fill'd;
> Some on the bare ground, some on planks or stretchers, some in the death-spasm sweating;
> An occasional scream or cry, the doctor's shouted orders or calls;
> The glisten of the little steel instruments catching the glint of the torches;
> These I resume as I chant—I see again the forms, I smell the odor;

---

[70] Susan C. Lawrence, "Military Hospitals in the Department of Washington" in *Civil War Washington: History, Place, and Digital Scholarship*, ed. Susan C. Lawrence (Lincoln, NE: University of Nebraska Press, 2015), 107.

[71] Ed Folsom, from commentary on Civil War MOOC.

> Then hear outside the orders given, Fall in, my men, Fall in;
> But first I bend to the dying lad—his eyes open—a half-smile gives he me;
> Then the eyes close, calmly close, and I speed forth to the darkness,
> Resuming, marching, as ever in darkness marching, on in the ranks,
> The unknown road still marching.[72]

This soldier only gradually comes into focus—"more distinctly a soldier"—and the soldier and narrator only briefly interact. Yet the intensity of the connection is striking. Just as the church has become an "impromptu" hospital, this unforeseen, unsought, and unmistakable love is "impromptu." As brief as it is intense, as valuable as it is fleeting, the connection is marked from the start by mortality. Two parentheticals are used in the three lines about the soldier, serving to slow down the relentless surge of this single-sentence poem. The first is a blunt, unflinching statement: "(he is shot in the abdomen)." The narrator recognizes that the boy is in grave danger both from infection and from "bleeding to death." The speaker's only option is to "staunch the blood temporarily," gaining a respite. The multi-syllable word "temporarily" slows the poem down, extending a charged moment, as the boy rests on the border between time and eternity.

As the narrator hears the order to prepare to march, he thinks of that final moment before death: "his eyes open, a half-smile gives he me." Ed Folsom notes that the tenderness of this moment is given added emphasis by an unusual inversion: "gives he me." The "he me" exact rhyme highlights this perfect pairing established in a moment of crisis. The narrator, called now to march yet again, goes onward with the memory of that gifted smile, the physical manifestation of their profound connection. There is a reciprocity here with caregiver and wounded affecting one another. With regard to the dying soldier, there is no conversion, no concern that a soul is saved: instead Whitman offers an evangel poem of love and comradeship. He puts the emphasis again on being a "sustainer of spirit and body in some degree, in time of need." The lily needs no further purification.

As a missionary, instead of finding people to correct, alter, or improve, Whitman found people to affirm, sustain, revere, and celebrate. It was

---

[72] *D-T*, 44–45.

precisely as a lover of men that he performed his version of missionary work. As he explained: "Even in a medical point of view, it is one of the greatest things; and, in a surgical point of view the same. I can testify that friendship has literally cured a fever, and the medicine of daily affection, a bad wound. In these sayings are the final secret of carrying out well the role of an hospital missionary for our soldiers, which I tell for those who will understand them."[73]

The Missionary and Trans*mission*: Scribal Writing and Fluid Identity

In striving to act on religious impulse during the war, to achieve a life of "steady trying to do fair," Whitman acted on his strength: writing, and specifically helping others with correspondence. In a discussion with Traubel that interwove consideration of *Leaves of Grass* and his hospital work, he said: "We were just talking of personal things—of the Leaves—the complete book: we insist upon the personal: well, you have it in these letters too: they, too, demonstrate me—my theory, philosophy, what I am after: they too. If you want to know what I mean watch what I do."[74] A complement to his *Leaves*, letter writing was also in keeping with the work of a missionary. The word *missionary* dates to the seventeenth century and derives from the Latin *missionarius*. The Latin *missionem*, indicating "act of sending," is found in biblical usage. In one Latin translation of the Bible, Christ applies the word to disciples sent to preach in his name.[75] As a missionary to the wounded, Whitman assisted in the trans*mission* of letters. As he remarked in *Memoranda During the War*, "When eligible, I encourage the men to write, and myself, when call'd upon, write all sorts of letters for them, (including love letters, very tender ones)."[76] If Whitman showed little interest in the idea of a family reunion in heaven, he was keen to reunite families in this life, connecting them through letters, and also deeply interested in establishing alternative families with soldiers with whom he became mother, father, uncle, brother, as circumstances warranted. At other times, always protean, he became the intimate friend or lover.

---

[73] "The Great Washington Hospitals," *Brooklyn Daily Eagle*, March 19, 1863: [2].
[74] *WWWC*, 3:577.
[75] Charles R. Tabor, "Editorial Essay: Mission, Missions, Missionary—The Words We Use," *Leaven*, 7 (1999), 4.
[76] *MDW*, 9.

Whitman sometimes wrote letters as soldiers, sometimes in his own voice, and sometimes as a blend of both. He was often engaged in the most difficult of tasks: helping soldiers undergo amputations or maintain self-worth while enduring dignity-destroying wounds or while in the throes of diarrhea, a deadly killer during the war. Too often he had to help soldiers prepare for death and to help families accept loss. A letter inscribed by Whitman on behalf of Albion Hubbard, a twenty-one year old Massachusetts soldier, who would die eight days later, highlights how Whitman gained the confidence of those who entrusted him with what Lindsay Tuggle calls the "peculiar intimacies" of proxy letter writing:[77]

> As I have a favorable opportunity, by means of a visitor to the hospital, who is now sitting by the side of my bed, I write you again, making the second time this week, to let you know that I am tolerably comfortable, have good care & medical attendance, & hope to be up before long—have been up & moving around the ward both this forenoon & afternoon though I move around pretty slow as I am weak yet—A member of the Massachusetts Relief society has called upon me & given me a few trifles——- Dear friend, I wish you would say to Mrs. Rice I send her my best love & respects—I send my love to Horace, also to Charles & Mrs Clare—I would like so much to see the face of a friend, —I wish you would write me a good long letter, some of you my dear friends, as a letter from home is very acceptable in hospital——— My diarrhea is still somewhat troublesome yet I feel in pretty good spirits—I send you an envelope with my address on— Keep a copy of it & this one you please put a stamp on & write to me—Please give my love to the friends in the village & tell them I should like to hear from them, & give them my direction here in hospital—Good bye for the present
>
> Albion F. Hubbard
written by Walt Whitman, a friend.

Whitman incorporates and conveys the voice of a soldier in this letter as he does periodically in his notebooks and recurrently in *Drum-Taps*. He expands and nuances his voice in helping others find theirs. The very simplicity of language in the hybrid Hubbard/Whitman document contributes to its emotional impact. This communicative act connects in fundamental ways with Whitman's poetic ambitions. Before the war in an

---

[77] Lindsay Tuggle, *The Afterlives of Specimens: Science Mourning, and Whitman's Civil War* (Iowa City, IA: University of Iowa Press, 2017), 96.

unpublished manuscript drafted while preparing *Leaves of Grass*, the poet considered how he might "transpose my...spirit": "It is you talking—I am your voice—It was tied in you—In me it begins to be loosened.... I am the voice of another man."[78] As with Milton Roberts, as we saw in "A March in the Ranks," Whitman renders the soldier's account, channeling another's voice, even as he enriches it. This type of sympathetic identification and extension is crucial to Whitman's Civil War acts of generosity and compassion, even as it enriched his literary expression.[79]

Whitman's wide-ranging effort to aid soldiers through his pen extended to anti-slavery efforts in his proxy writing for Samuel Frayer.[80] Commenting on the Frayer letter, Whitman explained to Traubel that he "wrote hundreds of such, similar, letters for the boys: letters for their friends—for their folks: fathers, mothers, sweethearts: they were too sick to write, or not sure of themselves, or something: why, I even said their prayers for them—some of them."[81] A young New Yorker from Albany, a former stage driver, Frayer resembled other men to whom Whitman was strongly attracted. Little is known of their relationship other than a letter Whitman inscribed for him indicating that Frayer wished to attain an officer's position leading black troops.[82]

Fort Bennett,
~~Washington~~
July 21st 1863
Adjutant General Thomas,

---

[78] See the manuscript "myself to celebrate" in the Trent Collection of Whitmaniana, Duke University, Durham, North Carolina. An image of this manuscript is available on the WWA as duk.00787 in the integrated finding guide to Whitman's manuscripts.

[79] By chance, the person who recently unearthed this letter from family records is herself a midwife. Without prompting, she commented in an email on similarities between her own role as a midwife and Whitman's Civil War ministrations: "It is a very powerful dynamic to lend companionship and bear witness to suffering—both for the witness and the receiver. Walt Whitman is bearing witness to their lives, their suffering, and their strength. Not everyone (man or woman) can do this kind of work, and it is generally a rare characteristic in western men. In a sense, it is what we do when there is nothing else we can do, and we hope that our mere presence—and acts of nurturance—will give hope and strength. In the case of these young men, this bearing witness no doubt lent strength—strength to live, strength to heal, or strength to die. For Whitman, I expect he found in bearing witness, a peaceful and positive way to contribute and to cope." Abbie L. Kleppa email to Kenneth Price, April 7, 2016.

[80] This letter is quoted in Walter Lowenfels, *Walt Whitman's Civil War* (New York: Knopf, 1960), 171 and in *WWWC*, 3: 577–78, though both give the name erroneously as Freyer.

[81] Traubel, *WWWC*, 3:577–78

[82] Samuel Frayer's compiled military service record contains numerous letters from Frayer to his parents, though these letters were written in a variety of hands, probably because he could not write for himself. Whitman's own role in writing a letter on Frayer's behalf is consistent with this pattern.

General: I have the honor to forward this my application for an officer's position in one of the Colored Regiments now forming in the District of Columbia.

I have been in the military service of the government as a private since the beginning of the War—enlisted first in the 8th New York Militia 19th April 1861, for three months—subsequently on the 25th August 1862, in the 2nd New York Artillery for three years—& am still in the regiment. I was born in the state of New York, am in ~~perfect~~ sound health, and 26 years of age.

Herewith please see testimonials from my officers—
I have the honor General to remain &c
Samuel S. Frayer, Co E 2nd New York Vol. Artillery.

Whitman's work on behalf of Frayer came at the height of his own interest in black troops, a time when the poet collected newspaper articles on their valor in battle. Just ten days before inscribing the letter for Frayer, on July 11, Whitman accompanied Major Lyman Hapgood when he issued payments to black troops on Analostan Island, an outing discussed in the previous chapter. Whitman helped both white and black soldiers during the war. He remarked in *Memoranda During the War*: "Among the black soldiers, wounded or sick, and in the contraband camps, I also took my way whenever in their neighborhood, and did what I could for them."[83] A visit to contraband camps was dangerous because of the widespread disease that afflicted them. Whitman's efforts on behalf of blacks, in both contraband camps and hospitals, was warmly appreciated in some quarters. In the account of his seventieth birthday celebration in *With Walt Whitman in Camden*, Horace Traubel mentions a "negro cook" who rushed to "embrace and shake hands" with Whitman.[84] When asked about this encounter later, Whitman recalled going "frequently" to a "hospital for negroes...at Culpepper."[85] As Frayer's wish to lead black troops indicates, he and Whitman probably shared what were by this time Republican sympathies, with both men welcoming the role of African Americans in the military. African Americans, in fighting for the Union, underlined that the war had become a fight for liberation and freedom. Through military service, albeit under white officers, African Americans seized the opportunity to secure their own rights. Nonetheless, Frayer's ambition to lead colored troops went

---

[83] *MDW*, 56.   [84] *WWWC*, 5: 250.   [85] *WWWC*, 5: 299.

unfulfilled, and he remained with his New York artillery unit until just days before the end of the war, when he died from a bullet wound to the head.[86]

Sacred Bereavement and the Complexities of Remembering and Forgetting

Frederick Douglass said the Civil War was not a struggle of mere "sectional character," but a "war of ideas, a battle of principles." It was "a war between the old and the new, slavery and freedom, barbarism and civilization... and in dead earnest for something beyond the battlefield."[87] Whitman, too, came to see the war as about liberation: it was "the great struggle between the Nation and the Slave power" that concluded with the "free areas around and ahead of us assured and certain."[88] In retrospect, of course, that prediction sounds too pat and too optimistic in light of Jim Crow laws, extra-legal violence, and the convict lease system that combined in many places to recreate conditions tantamount to slavery itself. Regrettably, Whitman's focus on "free areas" rather than "free people" is evasive, too, a habit characteristic of his handling of racial issues in the post-war years. In Whitman's conception of the war's dead, he once more becomes a missionary, with the mixed baggage that implies. The question of how to remember the dead—of how to *think* the war, of how to process and make meaning of such carnage not just for the white working man central to Whitman's thought but for all Americans—was of paramount importance in Whitman's time and in our own. What ultimately became known as Memorial Day took on the trappings of a secular religious festival. Memorial Day was important to blacks and whites alike, to ordinary and notable figures, including Redpath, Whitman, and Frederick Douglass. After the war, Decoration Day (as it was first known) was begun by African Americans as a "ritual of remembrance and consecration." David Blight notes that African Americans saw the war as a "triumph of their emancipation over a slaveholders' republic, and not about state rights, defense of

---

[86] The information on Frayer is drawn from the Widow's certificate files in the National Archives (WC #128738). Frayer's file, including more than sixty images and at least a half-dozen letters from Frayer to his parents, has been digitized and is available on Fold3. Frayer was hospitalized in 1864 and perhaps earlier as well.

[87] David Blight, "Forgetting Why We Remember," *New York Times*, May 29, 2011. Available online.

[88] *Two Rivulets* (Camden: Author's Edition, 1876), 9 and 14.

home, nor merely soldiers' valor and sacrifice." Memorial Days were initially occasions of "sacred bereavement," but they soon became co-opted by whites in the early twentieth century who used these occasions to help "forge national reconciliation around soldierly sacrifice, regardless of cause. In North and South, orators and participants frequently called Memorial Day an 'American All Saints Day,' likening it to the European Catholic tradition of whole towns marching to churchyards to honor dead loved ones."[89]

The contrast between the writings of Frederick Douglass and Whitman on Decoration Day highlights the complexity of remembering and forgetting and the dangers of both. Whitman, like so many whites, and in keeping with his missionary role, works toward reconciliation and forgiveness for both sides whereas Douglass celebrates the "loyal dead" of the North. In "The Unknown Loyal Dead," a speech Douglass delivered at Arlington National Cemetery on Decoration Day, May 30, 1871, he honors "the loyal soldiers who imperiled all for country and freedom." He bestows flowers on those who reached "that last highest point of nobleness.... They died for their country." He knows what was at stake in this "fearful struggle," and he refuses to "remember with equal admiration those who struck at the nation's life and those who struck to save it, those who fought for slavery and those who fought for liberty and justice." Without being a "minister of malice," he insists: "We must never forget that victory to the rebellion meant death to the republic. We must never forget that the loyal soldiers who rest beneath this sod flung themselves between the nation and the nation's destroyers."[90] Douglass makes a powerful argument. Nonetheless, if there is no forgetting can there be any reconciling?

The contrast with Whitman is striking. In the face of massive death and ruination, the former missionary to the wounded thinks in religious terms, though it is a religion of nature and elemental life forces. In a manuscript draft of "Ashes of Roses," probably drafted between 1868 and 1871, Whitman contemplated burial and reunification of the country:

Decoration Day May 30.
——— ☐
Ashes of Roses

---

[89] Blight, "Forgetting Why We Remember."
[90] Frederick Douglass, "The Unknown Loyal Dead," in *Frederick Douglass: Selected Speeches and Writings*, ed. Philip S. Foner; abridged and adapted by Yuval Taylor (Chicago, IL: Lawrence Hill Books, 1999), 609–10.

The dust & debris below, in all the cemeteries not only in Virginia & Tennessee but all through the land

The names of the flowers.
lilacs
roses
early lilies
the colors,
purple & white
& red & yellow
& red—
—the graves—
Ashes of Armies
The Unknown 🕮
? Army-Ashes
The dust of each mingling fused all with in the dust of each—(i.e. the rebel & the Union)
Are we to have a National Hy[mn by Cen]tennial time?
? Ashes of Roses
☐
Dust of the dead—
ashes of blue & gray,
—ashes of battle-pits,

solemn & strange cement—

not a field crop grows hence in the field, of north or south
—Not Nor moisture of the river, nor falling rain

Ashes of blue and gray—the colors of uniforms—serve to erase skin color. We have no black here either because of a failed inclusiveness or (if read generously) because Whitman hoped that white and black were both submerged in union blue. "Ashes of Roses" could be thought of as his new "burial service." The many fires of the war led him to his repetitive concern with ashes, suggesting an ashes-to-ashes meditation. Fire can destroy but it also can purify, and it can transform different substances into a single one—ashes. Whitman wants both sides cleansed, with both purified through a baptismal flow of river or falling rain. What was new was also as old as time: the renewal of flowers. And the "solemn & strange cement"—the mixing of bodies, rock, and sand and water becomes an adhering force needed to get sworn enemies to adhere to one another. Whitman was looking for and was perhaps himself trying to make the national hymn—a religious song emphasizing the unity—of reunited states and reconciled races.

3
Strayed Cattle
Anti-Pastoralism in Whitman's War Writings

Walt Whitman's life and writings were shaped by the actual places he experienced in Washington from 1863–73, yet his life and writings "on the spot" were also filtered through the imagined space of the pastoral. We can trace the interplay of place and space, the actual and the imaginary, by examining how he wrote with an awareness of pastoral conventions—and also how he has been read with pastoralism in mind both in his own time and in ours. For example, Edward Dowden analyzed Whitman and pastoralism in an extended discussion in 1871, and in recent years influential critics have repeatedly invoked pastoralism.[1] Timothy Sweet, Faith Barrett, and Eliza Richards among others have asserted that pastoralism leaves Whitman's Civil War writing compromised. They contend that he draws a "pastoral or picturesque frame around the war," thereby "legitimating its violence"; that the "pastoral mode becomes an essential part of the poet's strategy for reuniting the nation," with the poems insisting on "moral certainties which the recuperative force of the pastoral provides"; or that he "naturalizes Civil War violence through pastoral rhetoric."[2] These recent critics see Whitman's "pastoral" as a retreat from social progressivism and poetic experimentation to a more traditional outlook shaped by nostalgia,

---

[1] For a discussion of Whitman and pastoralism in his own time, see Edward Dowden, "The Poetry of Democracy: Walt Whitman," *The Westminster Review* 96 (July 1871), 33–68 (*WWA*). Dowden drew a contrast between Whitman's reverence for ordinary people in his "poetry of democracy" and the "literature of an aristocracy." The latter features those who "play at pastoral," if the "shepherds and shepherdesses are permitted to choose graceful classical names, if the crooks are dainty, and the duties of the penfold not severe" (39).

[2] See Timothy Sweet, *Traces of War: Poetry, Photography, and the Crisis of the Union* (Baltimore, MA: Johns Hopkins University Press, 1990), 7; Faith Barrett, "Addresses to a Divided Nation: Images of War in Emily Dickinson and Walt Whitman," *Arizona Quarterly* 61, No. 4, (Winter 2005), 79; Eliza Richards, "Weathering the News in US Civil War Poetry," in *The Cambridge Companion to Nineteenth-Century American Poetry*, ed. Kerry Larson (Cambridge: Cambridge University Press, 2011), 133. It is worth noting that Barrett's analysis of Whitman and pastoralism is the most nuanced of the three, particularly in her analysis of "Come up from the Fields Father."

escapism, and support of conventional Republican ideology. In fact, however, Whitman's work is distorted by the claim that he renders Civil War violence normal, fitting, or right. Both in prose and poetry he typically treats war as disturbing without trying to frame it within a larger pastoral order. Instead, he repeatedly invokes pastoral conventions to disrupt them, often to reach anti-pastoral ends. His *Memoranda During the War* (1875), a work largely drafted during the war, is especially jarring and powerful when it highlights the incongruity between scenes of natural beauty and the horror and convulsiveness of war. By reassessing the connections between Whitman and pastoralism we can sharpen our understanding of his wartime writings and see how his love of cities, including the often-maligned capital, and his yearning for a more egalitarian social structure, steered him away from pastoral goals for American life.

The history and development of pastoralism was very much alive in the minds of writers during the Civil War, a time of cataclysmic upheaval. Pastoralism originated in the writings of Theocritus, the Greek traditionally credited with the *Idylls*—though some of these poems are no longer attributed to him—and *Bucolica*. Adapting Theocritus, Virgil wrote *Eclogues* and *Georgics*, with the former focusing on leisure and the latter on work. For both Theocritus and Virgil, the care of livestock was an important dimension of pastoralism because it suggested parallels between natural harmony and a particular view of social harmony: as the shepherd tends his flock, so the patriarch guides his family, and so a leader governs the people (late in life, Whitman was criticized by some of his allies for a poem describing Emperor Wilhelm I of Germany as a "shepherd" and patriot in commemorating his death).[3] Virgil wrote at a time of civil war and depicted herdsmen in rural settings who had been dispossessed of their own lands, who experienced revolutionary change, work, and the vagaries of love. As Sarah Wagner-McCoy has recently emphasized, some of the herdsmen Virgil depicted were slaves, so pastoral writing engaged servitude and exploitation from the beginning.[4] These intertwined issues—comradeship, slavery, and the rightful ownership and use of land—preoccupied Whitman, too.

The American poet had a longstanding interest in the classics, and at a pivotal time—just before and during the war—he wrote with Virgil in mind.

---

[3] Whitman's poem sparked criticism from Benjamin R. Tucker, a Boston publisher and bookseller. See *WWWC*, 1: 22.

[4] See Sarah Wagner-McCoy, "Virgilian Chesnutt: Eclogues of Slavery and Georgics of Reconstruction," *ELH*, 80, no. 1 (2013), 199–20 and Keith Bradley, *Slavery and Society at Rome* (New York: Cambridge University Press, 1994).

In a manuscript note dated "Oct & Nov. '57," Whitman records that he was "reading Virgil's Bucolics, Eclogues, & the Æneid." He did not much admire *The Æneid* ("it seems to me well enough, except for the fatal defect of being an imitation, a second-hand article"), but he held that "the Bucolics and Georgics are finely expressed—they are first rate."[5] In fact, he owned two copies of *The Works of Virgil: Literally Translated into English Prose with Notes by [Joseph] Davidson.*[6] Widely used in the United States, the Davidson translation was literal, closer to the original than John Dryden's poetic rendering of Virgil. Late in life, Whitman annotated one of his copies of the Davidson translation: "had this Vol. with me in NY.—Washington—and in Camden—1862-1889—(the edge stains are from breaking a bottle of Virginia wine in a trunk with it on a journey during the war there)— WW."[7] This story—inscribed twice in this volume and also discussed in conversation with Horace Traubel—seems to have been emblematic for Whitman. Perhaps he thought of Jesus and the parable of new wine in old wineskins as he contemplated the classics, Virginia, and the stains and shatterings of Civil War. Even at the end of his life, Whitman felt Virgil's magnetism, as noted by his close friend Traubel who included Virgil in a list of books the poet regularly consulted.[8]

Whitman's interest may have been piqued by Virgil's treatment of same-sex love, his privileging of male-male bonding in Corydon's attachment to the beautiful young man Alexis (*Eclogue* 2). In discussions of this amorous dimension of pastoralism some critics see Arcadia (historically an actual place in Greece, but mythically a utopian region of harmony and natural beauty) as a protected space enabling the flourishing of a same-sex love rarely sanctioned outside of Periclean Athens. The homosocial dimensions

---

[5] This manuscript is located at the Albert and Shirley Small Special Collections Library, University of Virginia.

[6] One of Whitman's copies of *The Works of Virgil: Literally Translated into English Prose A New Edition, Revised, with Additional Notes, by Theodore Alois Buckley of Christ Church* (New York: Harper & Brothers, 1857) is now held at the Library of Congress and one at the New York Public Library.

[7] New York Public Library copy of Virgil owned by Whitman. On another blank leaf of front matter, perhaps written earlier, Whitman noted the same incident with only slightly different wording and dating: "the stains in edges are f 'm breaking a bottle of Virginia wine in my satchel during a jaunt war-time 1863—Walt Whitman." And in a conversation described by Horace Traubel (October 20, 1891) we are told: "As W. fingered the book he was writing on on my entrance, he explained, laughing, 'This is my old Virgil—you have seen it? It is the book I had in my carpet bag and burst a bottle of wine over in one of my trips to the army in Virginia. I am writing that in the margin here.' I said, 'It makes a history.' 'I suppose it does: it is badly soiled— the wine was good!'" (*WWWC*, 9: 59).

[8] *WWWC*, 8: 581.

of the pastoral have been strikingly depicted in numerous paintings ranging from the famous *Concert Champêtre* (c. 1509; see Figure 3.1), attributed to Giorgione or Titian, to *Arcadia* (1883; see Figure 3.2) by Whitman's friend Thomas Eakins.[9] Another of Whitman's allies, William Douglas O'Connor, may have been thinking of same-sex love when he wrote to Whitman on August 19, 1882: "Much obliged for your interest about the Florio Montaigne.... I have been re-reading him lately. It is immense.... That chapter, 'On Some Verses in Virgil', is tremendous, and backs you greatly."[10] As Todd Reeser has emphasized, Montaigne's essay on Virgil features male-male eroticism within a discussion of conventional marriage.[11] In the Eclogues, poetic-musical competitions occur with shepherds vying to outsing each other. Several poems link same-sex bonding to the dynamic of poetic performance, not just personal beauty. So for Whitman there was a poetic-professional appeal, too.

In the 1860–61 edition of *Leaves of Grass*, Whitman's treatment of calamus—at once a plant, a rustic pipe fashioned from a reed (*calamo permisit agresti* in Virgil), and an image of the pen and penis—stems from classical usage. As noted, comradeship is a key feature of the pastoral in Virgil's limning of male-male harmony. Whitman's famous "Calamus" poems have ties to the pastoral tradition, but we should note that his Blue Book, a copy of *Leaves of Grass* he revised during the war but never brought to publication, proposed to eliminate nearly a quarter of the "Calamus" poems, perhaps suggesting that he saw war and pastoral love poetry as incompatible.[12] I discuss Whitman's misgivings about the "Calamus" poems while at work on the Blue Book in more detail in the next chapter. For now, suffice it to say that Whitman's depiction of love in these poems as

---

[9] *Concert Champêtre* may have been painted by either Giorgione or Titian. Jonathan Unglaub, "The Concert Champêtre: The Crises of History and the Limits of Pastoral," *Arion: A Journal of Humanities and the Classics*, Third Series, 5, No. 1 (Spring–Summer, 1997), 46–91, 93–96. For discussions of Whitman, the pastoral, and same-sex love, see Byrne R. S. Fone, "This Other Eden: Arcadia and the Homosexual Imagination," *The Journal of Homosexuality*, 8, nos. 3–4 (1983), 29–31 and Robert K. Martin, "Conversion and Identity: The 'Calamus' Poems," *Walt Whitman Review*, 25 (June 1979), 59–66. For a contrasting view not treating Whitman directly, see Peter Boag, "Sexuality, Gender, and Identity in Great Plains History and Myth," *Great Plains Quarterly*, 18 (1998), 327–40.

[10] William Douglas O'Connor to Walt Whitman, August 19, 1882 (*WWA*).

[11] Todd W. Reeser, "Queer Energy and the Indeterminate Object of Desire in Montaigne's 'On Some Verses of Virgil,'" *Journal for Early Modern Cultural Studies*, 16, no. 4 (2016), 38–71.

[12] Andrew Miller argues that in the British literary tradition pastoralism and war are antithetical but that in American poetry the pastoral is "in league with war." See "Taking Fire from the Bucolic: The Pastoral Tradition in Seven American War Poems," *Amerikastudien/American Studies*, 58, No. 1 (2013), 101.

Figure 3.1. *Concert Champêtre*, attributed to Titian or Giorgione. Louvre Museum.

set "along the pond-side...far, far in the forest" is not a typically open pastoral scene, but instead something more unconventional, untamed, and furtive.

Whitman's awareness of pastoralism came from many sources beyond Virgil, of course. Another key source for thinking about pastoralism and shepherds is the Bible with its pervasive motif of the shepherd: "The Lord is my shepherd...." In addition, innumerable adaptations of Virgil across European cultures have added an array of related pastoral conventions. In Great Britain, as Raymond Williams notes in *The Country and the City*, the word *pastoral* came into common usage "for shepherds in the fourteenth century, and has an almost contemporary analogical association for priests."[13] The association of the pastoral with herdsmen would continue

---

[13] Raymond Williams, *The Country and the City* (New York: Oxford University Press, 1973), 307.

Figure 3.2. Thomas Eakins, *Arcadia*, Metropolitan Museum of Art, New York. Public domain image.

over the centuries, prompting Leo Marx's pithy formulation, "no shepherd, no pastoral."[14]

Whitman benefitted from multiple strands of a literary heritage—classical, Biblical, and British in particular—he frequently belittled or denied. He had a broad familiarity with pastoral prose and a more detailed knowledge of pastoral poetry. During the Civil War, a volume he regularly consulted—titled *Milton, Young, Gray, Beattie, and Collins*—featured a group of poets strongly linked with pastoral writing.[15] Wordsworth, too, another poet of considerable interest to Whitman, would address the tension between nature and artifice in the pastoral when he wrote: "Dismissing therefore all Arcadian dreams, / All golden fancies of the golden age / . . . /

---

[14] Leo Marx, "Pastoralism in America," in Sacvan Bercovitch and Myra Jehlen, eds., *Ideology and Classic American Literature* (Cambridge: Cambridge University Press, 1986), 45.

[15] Whitman's copy of *Milton, Young, Gray, Beattie, and Collins* (Philadelphia, PA: Grigg & Elliott, 1841) is now held in the Bryn Mawr College Special Collections Library.

Give entrance to the sober truth."[16] Like Wordsworth, Whitman recognized the romantic and imaginary dimension of pastoral, and ultimately this mode is at odds with a realist aesthetic—Whitman's Civil War prose in particular is at pains to adhere to what he called "real things."

The concept of pastoralism, then, can be used in discussing the poet if done advisedly. In applying this word to Whitman's writings, the connection between pastoralism and the clergy should make us pause: on the one hand, Whitman often displayed a marked anti-clerical bent but, on the other, as the previous chapter stressed, he depicted himself as a "missionary to the wounded," highlighting how his war-time secular and charitable efforts were structured like a religious mission. In short, for Whitman there is continuity between missionary efforts and pastoral care.

American Pastoralism

American Studies scholars have linked wilderness in the United States to antebellum visions of the country as "nature's nation," with corresponding implications that ordinary people compose its citizenry. The pastoral implies ordinary people, too, but invokes the Jeffersonian vision of the yeoman farmer and a nation of independent landowners. Literary scholars tend to define pastoralism quite broadly as a celebration of the countryside or nostalgia for rustic life, subjects that feature common people and natural plenitude. Leo Marx's landmark study *The Machine in the Garden* contends that pastoral "has been used to define the meaning of America ever since the age of discovery... with an unspoiled hemisphere in view it seemed that mankind actually might realize [the Arcadian dream that]... had been thought a poetic fantasy."[17] That Arcadian dream offered bountifulness and also implied, as William Empson claims in *Some Versions of Pastoral*, "a beautiful relation between rich and poor."[18] Exceptionalism comes into play because it is American republican institutions that will permit the nation to achieve an idyllic relationship between classes and between people and nature.

---

[16] William Wordsworth, "Home at Grasmere," in *William Wordsworth: The Major Works*, ed. Stephen Gill (Oxford: Oxford University Press, 1984), 194.

[17] Marx, *Machine in the Garden*, 3.

[18] William Empson, *Some Versions of Pastoralism* (1935; rpt: New York: New Directions, 1950), p. 11.

The impact of Empson's work has been profound, with commentators in both Britain and the United States discussing pastoralism largely in terms of class, though recent work has begun to emphasize race as well. Commentators have critiqued both pastoralism and Empson's and Marx's interpretation of it for naturalizing (or mystifying) antebellum social hierarchies that exploited people of color and advanced American policies of western expansion.[19] Still, pastoralism then as now is a complex tradition, with anti-modern and anti-capitalist critique embedded in its very elements, and it can be used for many purposes. As Lawrence Buell notes, it has "ideological multivalence."[20]

Given that pastoralism has sometimes promoted green consciousness and sometimes normalized land appropriation—given, that is, that there is no single or constant politics of American pastoralism—it is important to discuss it with care and nuance when considering individual poets or their works. In its nostalgia for a stable, unchanging social order and its conservative mode, pastoralism poorly describes Whitman's war writings, which do not yearn for an illusory harmonious past but instead focus on the demands of the immediate present.[21] Alive to both class and racial conflicts, his war writings are, if anything, marked by disruptions of pastoralism, despite the strength of the pastoral tradition of same-sex love. To the limited extent that he can be regarded as a pastoral writer, he invokes this mode to show that he *sees through* its conventions—in the sense of both seeing with pastoral conventions in mind, and also resisting, overturning, and highlighting their inadequacy for the Civil War crisis at hand.[22]

The pastoral is typically employed by urbanites to fantasize a rural life in harmony with nature as urban life is not. As David M. Rosenberg notes, the Alexandrian court poet Theocritus had "created an innocent bucolic fiction

---

[19] Sarah Wagner-McCoy, "Introduction" to her "Transatlantic Pastoral and the Realist Novel," PhD dissertation, Harvard University, 2011, 1-15.
[20] Lawrence Buell, *The Environmental Imagination: Thoreau, Nature Writing, and the Formation of American Culture* (Cambridge, MA: Harvard University Press, 1996), 42.
[21] I have modified Lawrence Buell's remark in *The Environmental Imagination* that pastoral "sometimes activated green consciousness, sometimes euphemized land appropriation," 31.
[22] The idea of "seeing through" pastoralism is indebted to Charles Lock who writes: "In the pastoral we are able to see through conventions as in themselves they really and beatifically are: yet 'to see through' in two senses, as seeing the convention for what it is, and despite that, allowing the convention to be that through which we see. At which point we can simply observe that all 'serious' literature must partake of the counter-pastoral, must solicit resistance to its own seductions. Pastoral, we might venture, comes to life—to life as literature, and in literature—only when it fails to seduce: when it is felt to be cold. Better, perhaps: when it is felt to be colluding in the reader's own act of resistance, when it would forbid its readers to ignore or 'see through' its conventions." Quoted in Andrew Miller, "Taking Fire from the Bucolic," 106.

from the ironic perspective of urbane sophistication," and so, too, was Virgil "aware of the discrepancies between simple, innocent Arcadia and complex, worldly Rome."[23] However, as those who knew Whitman best in Washington realized, tamed nature rarely moved him. Instead, as his close friend the naturalist John Burroughs remarked, Whitman celebrated "scenes of power and savagery in nature" (even if the poet had relatively few direct experiences with them, such as his trip on the Mississippi to New Orleans). Real or imagined elemental forces were "more stimulating to him, than the scenes of the pretty and placid, and he cherished the hope that he had put into his 'Leaves' some of the tonic and fortifying quality of Nature in her more grand and primitive aspects"—that is, nature (and morality) prior to being tamed and turned into a productive field or an enticing garden.[24] In short, Whitman's fascination with rough, rugged, even sublime nature was more characteristic than a yearning for pastoral calm. Whitman views the wilderness through the conventions of the frontier myth and the Romantic sublime, imagining it as an escape from human civilization. In his construction of pastoral, however, he follows more complex literary conventions by integrating worldly cares into his lyrical landscape. Pastoral, in his experience and in his poetry, offers no guarantee of idyllic calm. It is *beautiful*, but does not *beautify* the relations of rich and poor, war and peace, slave and free.[25]

From his early days as a journalist Whitman concerned himself with land use and the competing demands of open pastoral grazing versus enclosed plots. In conflicts between the claims of community property versus private property, Whitman typically sided with the latter. For example, in his 1849 journalistic series "Letters from a Travelling Bachelor," he disapproved of devoting land to large grazing areas rather than individual plots for yeoman farmers or individual workers, on the grounds that it was wasteful. He continued to hold the same views more than a decade later, during the Civil War, as is evident from his reprinting of this same passage with only minor changes in "Brooklyniana," a journalistic series he published in the *Brooklyn Standard* just prior to his move to Washington, DC. On September 27, 1862 he argued:

---

[23] David M. Rosenberg, *Oaten Reeds and Trumpets: Pastoral and Epic in Virgil, Spenser, and Milton* (Lewisburg, PA: Bucknell University Press, 1981), 20.
[24] John Burroughs, *Whitman: A Study* (Boston, MA: Houghton Mifflin, 1896), 2.
[25] For this formulation, I am indebted to Sarah Wagner-McCoy (email to the author).

The great obstacle to improvement, all about here, is the monopoly of most of this immense tract of plains, by the town of Hempstead, the people whereof will not sell, nor divide it among themselves even, as was proposed a few years ago. If they *would* consent to sell, the town treasury would be prodigiously the gainer; and, cut up in strips, the land would be cultivated, adding to the looks of that region, to productiveness and human comfort, to the wealth of the town of Hempstead, and consequently decreasing the rate of taxes....

Land monopoly shows one of its beauties most pointedly in this matter. We don't know, indeed, where one could go for a more glaring and unanswerable argument of its evils. Here is good land, capable of administering to the existence and happiness of thousands upon thousands of human beings, all lying unproductive, *within thirty miles of New York city*, because it is monopolized by one principal owner! We know the people save the right of pasturing their cattle, horses and sheep, on the plains—but that privilege, however widely used, does not develop one-twentieth of the resources of the land. Thousands of acres of it are covered with nothing but "kill-calf," and other thousands, where nothing grows, could be redeemed by two or three seasons' cultivation and manuring.[26]

Whitman opposed the concentration of landownership in a single entity, whether it was a wealthy individual or a city government, and he advocated instead turning common property into small plots. His concern was less to advance capitalism than to enable a yeoman to possess a modest farm and— with decent luck and a great deal of hard work—to thrive.

As the Civil War unfolded, Whitman commented repeatedly on land use and labor, north and south alike, and on the relation between city and country. There are poems in *Drum-Taps* lauding rural life, including "A Farm Picture," "Pioneers! O Pioneers!", and "Come Up from the Fields

---

[26] Compare "Letters from a Travelling Bachelor. Number IV," in *New York Sunday Dispatch*, November 4, 1849: [1] to "Brooklyniana; A Series of Local Articles, on Past and Present. No. 36," *Brooklyn Standard*, September 27, 1862: [unknown]. These two items shed light on the vexed question of the dating of "Brooklyniana." That is, rather than confirming Luke Mancuso's view that "Brooklyniana" is an exercise in "nostalgia" during the trauma of war, the reprinting of much earlier work supports the more recent argument of Ted Genoways that "Brooklyniana" draws on content written much earlier despite being published in the war years. See Luke Mancuso, "Civil War," in Donald D. Kummings, ed., *A Companion to Walt Whitman* (Malden, MA: Blackwell, 2006), 293-98 and Ted Genoways, *Walt Whitman and the Civil War: America's Poet during the Lost Years of 1860-1862* (Berkeley, CA: University of California Press, 2009), 108-109 and 164.

Father," though the affirmations of this last poem are sharply undercut, as discussed below. These rural poems are balanced, however, by adulatory city poems such as "First O Songs for a Prelude," "City of Ships," and "A Broadway Pageant." Whitman, an urban denizen, inscribed the war as he knew it not while situated in or seeking a rural retreat but from the vantage points offered by New York and Washington, and his poems do not see urban life as corrupt (or at least no more corrupt than anywhere else), nor do they set it against rural values and an idealized simplicity. In "Give me the Splendid Silent Sun" (1865) he refuses to embrace the country alone, despite its charms, because of the delights of diverse city crowds.[27] Limited to neither city nor country, Whitman's writing moves fluidly between the two. Leo Marx observed that Virgil's "ideal pasture has two vulnerable borders: one separates it from Rome, the other from the encroaching marshland."[28] Yet for Whitman both the city and the swamp possessed interest and provided insights unavailable via a pastoral setting.

The persuasive power of Whitman's writing is greatest when he depicts not the pasture but instead what was beyond its borders at either end—the city or the wilderness. His pastoral imaginings have interest but are less effective (an exception is the passage that ultimately became section 28 of "Song of Myself"). An early manuscript draft, probably written before 1855, shows the poet considering the attractions of a pastoral scene—perhaps as compensation for his own lack of actual land at that time in life. As this manuscript indicates, Whitman occasionally entertained romantic fantasies that partook of a simpler, weaker form of pastoralism. As a poet, he allowed himself to believe, he could rethink the very nature of ownership leading to a non-exploitative, sweat-free possession of productive land. Here he echoes Ralph Waldo Emerson's claim in *Nature* that only the poet "owns the landscape":[29]

> this broad and majestic
> Of ~~all that there is~~
> ~~in the~~ universe, ~~you ca~~
>   all

---

[27] Gary Schmidgall, *Containing Multitudes: Walt Whitman and the British Literary Tradition* (New York: Oxford University Press, 2014), 248–49.
[28] Leo Marx, *The Machine in the Garden*, 22.
[29] Ralph Waldo Emerson, *The Collected Works of Ralph Waldo Emerson*, vol. 1, *Nature, Addresses, and Lectures*, ed. Alfred R. Ferguson (Cambridge, MA: Harvard University Press, 1971), p. 9.

> mention nothing either ^ in
> and much in
> the visible world, ^ or the
> greater world invisible,
> [illegible] what is
> that is not owned by the
> Poet.—He owns the
> solid ground and tills it
> and reaps from every field
> cotton and
> and harvests fr the grain
> the timothy and the clover.
> and grass.— All the woods
> and all the orchards –
> ear and
> the corn with its stalks
> and tassels – the buckwheat
> and   tops
> with its sweet white blossom
> and the that there
> where bees ^ hum ^ all day–

This passage has been scored with a vertical line, a mark Whitman often employed to indicate that the material was *used* rather than to signify deletion. (He did in fact use words and phrases here in a variety of published pieces.[30]) This passage is informative about the relationship of traditional

---

[30] Elements of this manuscript appear in a variety of Whitman publications as is made clear in the "Integrated Catalog of Walt Whitman's Literary Manuscripts" available on the *WWA*: "Two phrases and images from this manuscript appear, slightly altered, in the 1855 edition of *Leaves of Grass*, in the poem that would later be titled 'Song of Myself.' The manuscript was therefore probably written before or early in 1855. In the manuscript Whitman has added the phrase 'the timothy and the clover' to a description of plants growing in a field. On page 18 of the 1855 edition of *Leaves of Grass* Whitman describes jumping from the crossbeams of a barn into the hay and says he will 'seize the clover and timothy.' Later in the manuscript he writes of 'the buckwheat and its white tops and the bees that hum there all day,' and on page 36 of the 1855 *Leaves* he writes of the 'white and brown buckwheat, a hummer and a buzzer there with the rest.' A similar line concerning buckwheat and bees appeared in the poem 'Come Up From the Fields Father,' and a reference to 'clover and timothy' appeared in 'Give Me the Splendid Silent Sun.' Both poems were first published in *Drum-Taps* in 1865. 'Clover and timothy' also appears in the poem 'The Return of the Heroes,' which was first published in the 1881 edition of *Leaves of Grass*. On the reverse of this manuscript (nyp.00085) are poetic lines, one of which appeared in the poem ultimately titled 'I Sing the Body Electric.'"

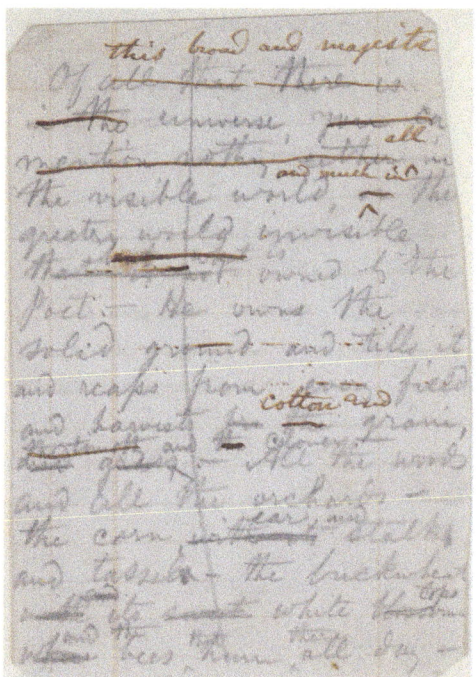

Figure 3.3. "Of this broad and majestic." This manuscript contributed to various works, including "Come Up from the Fields Father." Reproduced courtesy of the Berg collection, the New York Public Library.

pastoral lyrics to property and ownership (see Figure 3.3). The fact that the manuscript never cohered as a literary unit but was only available to him in partial forms is telling of the pastoral's weakness for him. Whitman imagines an ownership more fundamental and sweeping than in any property deed, an ownership of both the visible and invisible worlds. Yet the draft is not fully convincing in its articulation of poetic over economic returns. The poet "tills" the land, merging verse and agriculture in a way reminiscent of Virgil. The gaze and labor of a poet who owns land only in an imaginary sense is necessarily different from the farmhands who actually work the land, even if they are blind to its poetry. In what appears to be a later revision of the manuscript in ink, the poet "harvests cotton"—the most valuable US export of the time—and does so without reliance on racial slavery or the complicity of northern merchants, textile factories, and bankers.

The buckwheat and the bees (Virgil famously wrote about bee-keeping in Book 4 of the *Georgics*) mentioned at the end of this jotting appear together again in "Come Up from the Fields Father," a *Drum-Taps* poem that opens by invoking the pastoral unmistakably, but that invocation is preceded by an ominous letter and a cry to the father:

> Come up from the fields, father, here's a letter from
>   our Pete;
> And come to the front door, mother—here's a letter
>   from thy dear son.
>
> Lo, 'tis autumn;
> Lo, where the trees, deeper green, yellower and redder,
> Cool and sweeten Ohio's villages, with leaves fluttering
>   in the moderate wind;
> Where apples ripe in the orchards hang, and grapes on
>   the trellis'd vines;
> (Smell you the smell of the grapes on the vines?
> Smell you the buckwheat, where the bees were lately
>   buzzing?)
>
> Above all, lo, the sky, so calm, so transparent after
>   the rain, and with wondrous clouds;
> Below, too, all calm, all vital and beautiful—and the
>   farm prospers well.
>
> Down in the fields all prospers well;
> But now from the fields come, father—come at the
>   daughter's call;
> And come to the entry, mother—to the front door come,
>   right away.[31]

In this opening of the poem, we have a tranquil scene of pastoral harmony—the trees "cool and sweeten" Ohio villages and the "farm prospers well." It does so with labor invisible and merely implicit rather than described—perhaps the demands of the land are what keep the summoned father from ever arriving in the poem.

"Come up from the Fields" begins with radiant lines emphasizing lush abundance: "apples ripe in orchards hang," while ripe grapes cover the trellis. The landscape is pleasant and bountiful in every way, even in the

---

[31] *D-T*, 39.

recollected sound of buzzing bees (the only workers described in the poem) and the pleasant odors that Whitman emphasizes through an attention-grabbing inversion of word order:

> (Smell you the smell of the grapes on the vines?
> Smell you the buckwheat, where the bees were lately buzzing?)

The subtlety of the poem begins with the title, which directs attention to the "father," a person who is absent throughout the body of the poem. Instead, the pain of the mother is central and evokes our sympathy. In fact, much of "Come Up from the Fields Father" operates in a similar fashion—through displacement, absence, and indirection. Whitman, the Washington hospital visitor, knew too well what he called without need of embellishment "the odor," the smell of putrefaction and death itself. (In "A March in the Ranks," set in an impromptu church-hospital, the speaker said: "Then before I depart I sweep my eyes o'er the scene fain to absorb it all, / Faces, varieties, postures beyond description, most in obscurity, some of them dead.../ These I resume as I chant, I see again the forms, I smell the odor.") In short, pastoralism as manifested in this poem with its pungent aroma of budding life, its fragrant loveliness, proves to be misleading and almost cruel. All the things that matter most in "Come Up from the Fields"—the father and son labor that would be needed to sustain the farm; the smell of the hospitals rather than the smell of the farm; and the son himself—are only present through their absence.

In this poem, Whitman highlights the reaction of a mother and her family as they absorb fateful news about her son and their brother, news that is understood to be worse than is actually stated. An unidentified scribe, a Whitman-like figure, wrote the letter meant to be reassuring, though it is ultimately understood as family-shattering news. Whitman's own biographical role as a war time amanuensis, as a "strange hand" who assisted soldiers, informs the situation he dramatizes. The letter comes from outside the family and—though it may have conveyed precisely what the soldier wished—is inaccurate in its prediction: "*At present low, but will soon be better*" (italics in the original). Typically, a letter involves at least two people—a sender and a recipient—and two locations—an origination point and a destination. In this poem, the letter is the connecting link that joins two places, one described and one left to our imagination. Whitman enacts an interesting reversal by focalizing the poem through the pastoral family imagining the hospital rather than the dying soldier's nostalgia for his pastoral home. The italicized words above prompt the mother immediately to foresee the death of her "only son," despite the letter's optimistic claim. Whitman must have regularly pondered how his own letters for soldiers would be received, the uncertainty of his best assessments, and the dangers of prognostication.

This poem is directly rooted in history and biography—specifically, in Whitman's admiration for Oscar Cunningham, an Ohio soldier he met in his hospital ministrations. During the war, Whitman misjudged the degree of danger facing his "Ohio boy," and he did not encourage Oscar's sister, Helen, to visit the soldier in Washington. Though the Cunningham family was grateful for Whitman's kindness and care, Helen criticized the poet for discouraging her travel, thus keeping her from seeing her brother a final time. In "Come Up from the Fields," Whitman named the soldier "Pete" (a rare naming of a character in his poetry), and since this coincided with his new relationship with Peter Doyle, the naming suggests the intensity of his emotions as this rural idyll is vacated of hope and happiness.

At the time of Cunningham's death, Whitman regularly encountered bodies suffering horrific decay. In the very letter informing his mother of Cunningham's death, he remarked: "we receive [soldiers] here with their wounds full of worms—some all swelled & inflamed, many of the amputations have to be done over again—one new feature is that many of the poor afflicted young men are crazy."[32] Whitman commented on stench occasionally in the antebellum period, but his poems and letters from Washington emphasize it as a salient war-time experience. In visits to Civil War hospitals his senses were regularly assaulted. Whitman included a cluster in the 1871 *Leaves of Grass* called "Bathed in War's Perfume." His strong emphasis on the lovely smells in the poem is, then, painfully ironic.

In one influential study, Sarah Burns has described the mid-century pastoral as "longings, overt or submerged, to escape from the pressures of the present, to burrow back into an ideal past, to be a child again, to shed the burden of adult responsibility,"[33] yet Whitman invokes such imagery in "Come Up from the Fields" only to avoid fulfilling this expectation through the disappointment and pain conveyed via the letter. This poem is anything but an escapist mystification. The counter-pastoral dimensions of the poem are further highlighted when we read "Come Up from the Fields Father" in

---

[32] Walt Whitman to Louisa Van Velsor Whitman, June 7, 1864 (*WWA*).
[33] Sarah Burns, *Pastoral Inventions: Rural Life in Nineteenth-Century American Art and Culture* (Philadelphia, PA: Temple University Press, 1989), 313.

the context of Whitman's Blue Book. On the back of the only known leaf of surviving fair copy manuscript of "Come Up" Whitman bitterly charged the Confederacy with guilt. The recto and verso of the manuscript are two responses to the war. The front and back of the same leaf are often not connected intellectually in Whitman's manuscripts, though in this case a possible connection is evident. In contrast to the published poem, these other lines are angry, perhaps because of the loss of Oscar Cunningham. The extraordinary concluding lines, a revision of "Chants Democratic 1" (the poem ultimately titled "By Blue Ontario's Shore"), describe an unidentified "Last great Scorner" as "Already a carrion dead, & despised of all the earth – an offal rank / This day to the dunghill maggots spurn'd," a denunciation of the South and Southern institutions that is sharply at odds with the conciliatory approach he had taken in the third edition of *Leaves of Grass* (1860–61).[34] The focus on waste products—carrion, offal, dunghill—could not be further from the golden aura of the pastoral. Yet, for Whitman, they were inseparable. Overall, "Come Up" presents a pastoral, a yeoman farm landscape, depopulated of its male heir. A different form of patriarchy, the southern commitment to a more hierarchical social and economic system built on slavery, has destroyed the son and left a female world stricken with grief.

Death and the patriarchal order are also at issue in Whitman's famous pastoral elegy on the death of Abraham Lincoln, "When Lilacs Last in the Dooryard Bloom'd." R. W. French notes that, like the structure of other pastoral elegies, Whitman makes use of "the funeral procession, the mourning of nature, the placing of flowers upon the coffin, the contrast between nature's cyclical renewal and humanity's mortality, the eulogy, and the final resolution of sorrow."[35] These ritual elements are key to the pastoral's recuperative and harmonizing function. "When Lilacs Last in the Dooryard Bloom'd" mourns the death of Abraham Lincoln and imagines a "burial house" for Lincoln in a pastoral setting, though not to the exclusion of the city visible from afar. Here Whitman engages Virgil's "*Et in Arcadia ego*," the idea that even in Arcadia death is inescapable.

[34] See the verso of the leaf Whitman inserted between pages 114 and 115 in the *Blue Book*. A facsimile reproduction is available as *Walt Whitman's Blue Book: The 1860-61 Leaves of Grass Containing his Manuscript Additions and Revisions, vol. 1, Facsimile of the Unique Copy in the Oscar Lion Collection of the New York Public Library* (New York: The New York Public Library, 1968). Facsimile images of the Blue Book are also available on the WWA.
[35] R. W. French, "When Lilacs Last in the Dooryard Bloom'd" in *Walt Whitman: An Encyclopedia*, ed. J. R. LeMaster and Donald D. Kummings (New York: Garland Publishing, 1998), 771.

> O what shall I hang on the chamber walls?
> And what shall the pictures be that I hang on the walls,
> To adorn the burial-house of him I love?
>
> Pictures of growing spring, and farms, and homes,
> With the Fourth-month eve at sundown, and the gray-smoke lucid and bright,
> With floods of the yellow gold of the gorgeous, indolent, sinking sun, burning, expanding the air;
> With the fresh sweet herbage under foot, and the pale green leaves of the trees prolific;
> In the distance the flowing glaze, the breast of the river, with a wind-dapple here and there;
> With ranging hills on the banks, with many a line against the sky, and shadows;
> And the city at hand, with dwellings so dense, and stacks of chimneys,
> And all the scenes of life, and the workshops, and the workmen homeward returning.[36]

In addition to these idyllic pictures, we encounter the more unexpected aspects of "Lilacs" that work against and complicate pastoralism, especially the emphasis on the swamp and debris. Overall, then, the poem is varied in its use of pastoralism: the debris is anti-pastoral in ways that the gorgeous golden flood of the indolent sunset is not. The poem is uneven in the good sense of being complex and internally conflicted in rich and fascinating ways.

Swamps were common throughout the south including the area around Washington, DC (the western side of the Mall, past the Washington Monument, was still wetlands during the time Whitman lived in DC. In nearby Alexandria, Jones Point was a swamp, and Whitman walked in the area with Peter Doyle and John Burroughs. Slightly further away, there were additional swamps in Prince George's county).[37] Swamps were famous for offering a haven for enslaved people, a protection that was nearly impossible

---

[36] *D-T and Sequel*, 7.
[37] It was only later that the Army Corps of Engineers dredged the Potomac River and expanded the landmass on that end of the city. My thanks to Martin Murray and Kim Roberts for information on swamps in the Washington, DC, area (emails to the author, June 18, and June 20, 2019, respectively).

to find in cultivated regions. Tynes Cowan notes that for enslaved African Americans a swamp could be a "foreboding place, but it also was a space that could be theirs, not the white man's."[38] A swamp could be dangerous because of snakes and other threats. Linked to death even as it was teeming with life, the swamp offered a natural order not necessarily in harmony with the social order. The swamp indeed stood in sharp contrast with cultivated plantation spaces. Whitman said near the end of his life, in praising Alma Johnston (a woman he put on a par with his admired English friend Anne Gilchrist) that Johnston's strength resulted from her willingness to venture "down in the raggedness of society—the shadows, horrors—in marsh, swamp—full of teachableness—from which no man can come the same person as before."[39]

Whitman's turn to the swamp also rejected familiar Christian consolation and its shepherds—the American swamp was instead a "locus for African American magic and spirituality."[40] Lincoln died on Good Friday, so the opportunity to turn the poem to Christian ends was evident.[41] Avoiding religious iconography on the tomb walls, he turns instead to the beauties of the land itself: "With floods of the yellow gold of the gorgeous, indolent, sinking sun, burning, expanding the air... / In the distance the flowing glaze, the breast of the river, with a wind-dapple here and there." Rather than a modern representation of Hades,[42] the swamps Whitman experienced in and around Washington, where African American fugitives could achieve a hard-earned if only partial freedom, were more important for a poem about a fallen President famous for his own freeing of enslaved people through an act that achieved only a partial freedom, too.

In an 1863 letter Whitman remarked: "I believe fully in Lincoln— few know the rocks & quicksands he has to steer through."[43] The sheer difficulty of the metaphoric landscape and actual history Lincoln had to navigate may have contributed to the comfort offered through the wished-for

---

[38] Tynes Cowan, "The Slave in the Swamp: Affects of Uncultivated Regions on Plantation Life," in Grey Gundaker, ed., with the assistance of Tynes Cowan, *Keep Your Head to the Sky: Interpreting African American Home Ground* (Charlottesville, VA: University Press of Virginia, 1998), 195.

[39] *WWWC*, 7:337–38.   [40] Cowan, 205.

[41] Helen Vendler says, for example: "Whitman offers no word placing Lincoln in the context of Christ's passion, Good Friday, or Easter Sunday. He does not put Lincoln in a Judeo-Christian frame at all—even though contemporary commentators such as Bishop Simpson at the Washington funeral compared Lincoln to Moses." See "Poetry and the Mediation of Value: Whitman on Lincoln," in Grethe B. Peterson, ed., *The Tanner Lectures on Human Values*, vol. 22 (Salt Lake City, UT: University of Utah Press, 2001), 144.

[42] Vendler, 153.   [43] Walt Whitman to Abby H. Price, October 11–15, 1863 (*WWA*).

serenity-in-death offered in Whitman's decoration of Lincoln's final "chamber walls." Within the poem, the hermit thrush is secluded in the swamp, a landscape as difficult (for humans) as rocks and quicksand. The swamp, a word then and now associated with Washington, is a marshy locale, a wetland, that is neither quite land nor quite water—worthless in some ways and invaluable in others, including as a human and wildlife refuge. The song of the thrush affirms life despite the death of the president.

Whitman also emphasizes debris in "Lilacs," again focusing on the disorderly, the partial, and the seemingly discarded. He relies on debris to extend mourning beyond the individual death of a (very human) president to include the fragmentary and chaotic remains of all those lost in the war. Sweet believes the poem erases the violent facts of Lincoln's death and the other traumas of Civil War.[44] The circumstances of the assassination are not depicted, but "Lilacs" does show a poet grappling with personal and national trauma without pastoral elision. Whitman reckons with Lincoln's death and looks beyond it to all the dead:

> I saw battle-corpses, myriads of them,
> And the white skeletons of young men—I saw them;
> I saw the debris and debris of all dead soldiers.

Debris defies orderliness and is inconsistent with pastoral harmony. Debris draws attention to what is typically omitted in a pastoral scene: to focus on debris is to adopt a way of seeing that recognizes that no cow pasture is without dung, nor do we have beef cattle without offal. Here and elsewhere in Whitman's writings the word "debris" takes on rich and unusual meanings.[45] He looks beyond the idea of debris as leavings, trash, or refuse, to recognize the various ways in which debris, even in a context of loss, is valuable. Whitman explores the idea of death or destruction as both ruination and renewal, a process in which things are broken down to an elemental condition for whatever comes next.

The poet devoted an entire cluster to debris in both the 1860 and 1867 *Leaves of Grass*. Late in life, he even coined a term, "debrisity," to describe his living circumstances, a word underscoring "the confusion, the air of

---

[44] Sweet, *Traces of War*, 75.
[45] See Kenneth M. Price, "'Debris,' Creative Scatter, and the Challenges of Editing Whitman," in *Where the Future Becomes Present: Walt Whitman and Leaves of Grass*, ed. Michael Robertson and David Blake (Iowa City, IA: University of Iowa Press, 2008), pp. 59–80.

don't care, the unusual look and atmosphere."⁴⁶ Perhaps fittingly for poems called "Debris," the cluster was ultimately scattered, parts of it disappearing and other parts dispersed in subsequent publications. As we saw in the last chapter, in another Civil War-era poem, "Ashes of Roses," the debris of fallen northern and southern soldiers includes dust that creates a "solemn and strange cement" (he uses the cement metaphor in his late life lecture on Lincoln, too) that melds together a union once torn apart. Whitman's invocation of the dust and debris of death as the basis of the union offers no easy pastoral affirmation but only an agonizing one: this is not a restored nature again under patriarchal control, brimming with abundant crops and displaying harmony and tranquility, but instead an account of a desolate, scorched landscape. The cost had been enormous, but Whitman hoped that the trauma and bloodshed would at least yield a sloughing and a fresh beginning.

What we might call Whitman's aesthetic of "debrisity" resisted pastoral norms of coherence and hierarchical (social) order and highlighted the confluence of destruction and creation.⁴⁷ In *Drum-Taps*, *Memoranda During the War* (1875–76), and later *Specimen Days* (1882), Whitman abandons any narrative structure with an ordinary beginning, middle, and end. By virtue of the title *Memoranda During the War*, Whitman modestly offers informal notes or reports, as the word *memoranda* implies, not an overarching or controlling narrative. With *Specimen Days* his title promises individualized accounts of brief temporal units, avoiding explanations of causes. If a new and more thoroughgoing freedom was to emerge from the shredded remnants of the past, Whitman seems to say, it would be glimpsed in fragments. Much of what transpired and was sacrificed would go unsung, would remain invisible. Debris, specimens, limbs, shreds, patches: the world was shattered, young bodies and old dreams alike, just as the statue of freedom, discussed in an earlier chapter, lay in pieces on the capitol grounds, an image that caught Whitman's attention both as a detached observer and as a self-designated national poet. His own writing shifts from a pre-war romantic belief in wholeness and unified ideals to a new commitment to a realist mode: we get the partial, the disorderly, even the chaotic, and we get the raw and dusty as the elements of a new union as opposed to the ideal.

---

[46] *WWWC*, 9: 59.
[47] Cody Marrs, *Nineteenth-Century American Literature and the Long Civil War* (New York: Cambridge University Press, 2015), 150.

Whitman disrupts and exploits the pastoral even more dramatically in his prose than in his poetry. His complex handling of the pastoral—resisting and moving beyond its conventions—is evident in *Memoranda*, which was later incorporated into *Specimen Days*. Whitman's war-time prose and poetry are remarkably different: despite his fondness for lists and their specificity, he steers clear in his published poetry of naming political leaders, individual soldiers, and major battles. As Adam Bradford has argued of Whitman's Civil War poetry, *Drum-Taps*, "in the absence of markers of identity, the poetic soldiers become reflections of a reader's mind—constructions that were at the very least intimate projections from the reader's own consciousness."[48] In his prose, however, especially *Memoranda*, Whitman takes the opposite approach, piling detail upon detail, as he renders the characteristics and specificity of individual soldiers. These soldiers are neither generic types, like the mass-produced memorial statues that quickly dotted the country after the war, nor are they envisioned in nature, as part of a past or future republican Arcadia.

Whitman entertains no such illusions. When Whitman describes John Mahay, for example, who was "a mere boy in age, but old in misfortune," who had never known the love of parents, who had been placed in infancy in a New York charitable institution, and who was subsequently "bound out to a tyrannical master" (both the use of "master" and the scars visible on Mahay's back associate him with slaves), Whitman insists on the particularity of a specimen case—here a truly pitiable one. Mahay was shot at the battle of the First Bull Run with a bullet penetrating the lower part of his bladder and coming out the other side, leaving him—now in a Washington, DC, hospital—to "lay almost constantly in a sort of puddle," in extreme pain for weeks, enduring an endlessly weeping wound. Whitman is unblinking in the face of Mahay's painful puddle of blood and urine. Whatever solace there may be is not in nature, or land, or even in abstract Union, but only in fraternal physical sympathy.

Memoranda During the War is remarkable for how it disrupts pastoral conventions. In a chapter called "Cattle Droves About Washington," Whitman remarks:

> Among other sights are immense droves of cattle, with their drivers, passing through the streets of the city. Some of the men have a way of

---

[48] Adam Bradford, "Re-Collecting Soldiers: Walt Whitman and the Appreciation of Human Value," *Walt Whitman Quarterly Review* 27 (Winter 2010), 139.

leading the cattle on by a peculiar call, a wild, pensive hoot, quite musical, prolong'd, indescribable, sounding something between the coo of a pigeon and the hoot of an owl. I like to stand and look at the sight of one of these immense droves—a little way off—(as the dust is great.) There are always men on horseback, cracking their whips and shouting—the cattle low—some obstinate ox or steer attempts to escape—then a lively scene—the mounted men, always excellent riders and on good horses, dash after the recusant, and wheel and turn—A dozen mounted drovers, their great, slouch'd, broad-brim'd hats, very picturesque—another dozen on foot—everybody cover'd with dust—long goads in their hands—An immense drove of perhaps 2000 cattle—the shouting, hooting, movement, &c.[49]

These are cowboys of a modern era, reminiscent of shepherd-poets piping through a glade. Yet there are key differences: the drovers are a skilled team, in control within an urban landscape (except for the dust, a gritty annoyance associated with death), keeping intact an immense herd on its way to the slaughterhouse so an industrial-era citizen army could be fed. The sheer scale of this cattle industry precludes any intimacy of herdsmen and herd (in contrast, the "songs" of the herdsmen in Theocritus and Virgil offer details about individual animals and Theocritus gives names to various goats and sheep). Whitman's drovers express themselves in a way resembling a "barbaric yawp": their "wild, pensive hoot," is not that of prey, like pigeons, nor predators, like owls but of a human animal. They do not compose a poetry of artifice but embody and emit through their hoot something more elemental, something Whitman always sought, what he called in "Song of Myself" the "origin of all poems." Their hoot has depth and complexity, a sad thoughtfulness conveyed through its "pensive" note—the word *pensive* is explored in greater detail in the next chapter. This passage about cattle might seem like an insignificant passing observation if it weren't for Whitman's invocation of slaughterhouses and the key word "*strayed*" (Whitman's italics) in *Memoranda*'s climactic passage, "*The Million Dead, too, summ'd up—The Unknown.*" The unknown are strayed humans, and Whitman's juxtaposition of these passages underlines how men have been herded to slaughter, too. Disturbingly, the management of cattle in the city is depicted as successful while the management of people is not (see Figure 3.4). The chapter on "Cattle Droves About Washington" is immediately followed by

[49] *MDW*, 28.

Figure 3.4. Cattle on the mall, Washington, DC. Reproduced courtesy of the Library of Congress.

another titled "Hospital Perplexity" which describes the "confusion of this great army of the sick" and visitors facing the near-impossibility of finding sick or wounded loved ones.

In "The Wounded at Chancellorsville" Whitman describes a scene perhaps even more upsetting than the inability to locate a lost loved one. His description underscores his commitment to realism in war reporting rather than any type of evasive invocation of pastoral harmony:

> The night was very pleasant, at times the moon shining out full and clear, all Nature so calm in itself, the early summer grass so rich, and foliage of the trees—yet there the battle raging, and many good fellows lying helpless...the red life-blood oozing out from heads or trunks or limbs upon that green and dew-cool grass.[50]

This is not Andrew Marvell's world where the mind can make "Far other worlds, and other seas; / Annihilating all that's made / To a green thought in a green shade."[51] Whitman experiences not imaginary worlds but the actual

---

[50] *MDW*, 14.
[51] The quoted passage is from Marvell's "The Garden," *The Poems of Andrew Marvell* (2003; rptd. New York: Routledge, 2013), 152.

world remade in blood red. His dash in the passage above emphasizes both a break and a fundamental incongruity between the "calm" and "pleasant" night and the raging battle, an incongruity further highlighted by the rich foliage now colored by carnage.

In fact, as the description proceeds all hint of a reassuring pastoral scene is lost in fire that consumes the wounded who

> unable to move, are burn'd to death.........—O heavens, what scene is this?— is this indeed *humanity*—these butchers' shambles?... There they lie, in the largest, in an open space in the woods, from 500 to 600 poor fellows— the groans and screams—the odor of blood, mixed with the fresh scent of the night, the grass, the trees—that Slaughter-house!—[52]

Butchers' shambles are a long way from caring for the herd. When Whitman turns to the slaughterhouse to convey the essence of war, he invokes the antithesis of the pastoral. A shepherd tends his flock, and though he may cull it, a shepherd does not engage in mass killing, nor does he torture valuable animals through death by fire. Here people are the herd and have been brutally carved up.

As Cynthia Wachtell notes, by depicting war as a "slaughterhouse" and enumerating the "sickening" ways in which the soldiers are wounded, Whitman challenges the "romantic vision of warfare and the moral underpinning of battle."[53] He also challenges an outmoded social order:

> *A New Army Organization Fit for America Needed.*—It is plain to me out of the events of the War, North and South, and out of all considerations, that the current Military theory, practice, rules and organization, (adopted from Europe from the feudal institutes...) though tacitly follow'd, and believ'd in by the officers generally, are not at all consonant with the United States.[54]

The military order was "worse than deficient": it was "offensive, radically wrong." Whitman's pastoral, then, points blame at hierarchical long-established military and social orders.

---

[52] *MDW*, 14–15.
[53] Cynthia Wachtell, *War No More: The Antiwar Impulse in American Literature, 1861–1914* (Baton Rouge, LA: Louisiana State University Press, 2010), 94.
[54] *MDW*, 31.

An insistent emphasis on butchery occurs in both Whitman's public and private writings. In a letter to his mother, following the battle of Gettysburg, he noted how "one's heart grows sick of war... it seems to me like a great slaughter-house & the men butchering each other." And in another letter home he declared, "What an awful thing war is—Mother, it seems not men but a lot of devils & butchers butchering each other."[55]

The smells and sounds of butchering had been known to Whitman since his days in Brooklyn when he once lived not far from a slaughterhouse.[56] Until the mid-nineteenth century, the "nuisance trades," including butchers, tanners, soapmakers, bone boilers, and fat renderers, provided key domestic products even as their work yielded a terrible stench.[57] Modern readers have far less experience with the processes of slaughter since they occur in sequestered areas. For Whitman, in the antebellum city, the smell of rotting flesh was a common experience, and during the war the rank odor of both animal and human decay became even more common and could be overpowering in the streets of Washington, along the canal (a dank waterway often littered with rotting animal carcasses), and especially in the hospitals. When Whitman was free of stench in the capital it was noteworthy enough to mention in a letter ("Mother, I am sitting here by my window in the office—I dont have the smell of any streets or gutters—").[58]

In the climactic meditation on "The Million Dead" in *Memoranda* Whitman strives to come to terms with slaughter. Far from avoiding war's carnage, destruction, and loss of life, he catalogues a seemingly endless number of battles and amount of destruction. This loss of life is connected explicitly to herding and the pastoral. The fallen have gone astray:

> The Dead in this War—there they lie, strewing the fields and woods and valleys and battle-fields of the South—... the varieties of the *strayed* dead, (the estimate of the War Department is 25,000 National soldiers kill'd in battle and never buried at all, 5,000 drown'd—15,000 inhumed by strangers or on the march in haste, in hitherto unfound localities—2,000

---

[55] Walt Whitman to Louisa Van Velsor Whitman, July 7, 1863 and Walt Whitman to Louisa Van Velsor Whitman, March 22, 1864 (*WWA*).

[56] Judith Connors, "Biography of Walt Whitman" in Harold Bloom, ed., *Walt Whitman* (Philadelphia, PA: Chelsea House, 2003), 14.

[57] Jared N. Day, "Butchers, Tanners, and Tallow Chandlers: The Geography of Slaughtering in Early-Nineteenth-Century New York City," in Paula Young Lee, ed. *Meat, Modernity, and the Rise of the Slaughterhouse* (Durham, NH: University of New Hampshire Press; Lebanon, NH: published by University Press of New England, 2008), 179.

[58] Walt Whitman to Louisa Van Velsor Whitman, July 10–13, 1868 (*WWA*).

graves cover'd by sand and mud, by Mississippi freshets, 3,000 carried away by caving-in of banks, &c.)[59]

Whitman emphasizes the loss of fallen soldiers through the word "*strayed*" (his italics), depicting men as a wayward herd dying in massive numbers. These were the truly dispossessed—men who died together but without any connection to home or to the land. Whitman thus calls to mind the pastoral to emphasize how far this death-littered landscape is from a harmonious and productive rural setting.

The conditions described here point not to an orderly Arcadian scene but to a world scarred by loss of life, direction, and dignity. The scale of nineteenth-century warfare is again critical. Straying had been a frequent topic in classical pastoral—the herdsmen often interrupt one another to call a stray animal back—but the difference in Whitman is that the whole herd has gone wrong. Instead of a reassuring pastoral abundance, we have a natural world brimming with disconnected bodies, truly a harvest of death. What misguided shepherd or shepherds allowed this herd to lose its way? A rudderless democratic politics? Corrupt politicians? A higher power? If the "Lord is my shepherd" with God conceived as omnipotent and omniscient, then the war raises the type of theodicean concerns Lincoln grappled with in the lengthiest and most profound sentence of his Second Inaugural Address: "If we shall suppose that American Slavery is one of those offences which, in the providence of God, must needs come, but which, having continued through His appointed time, He now wills to remove, and that He gives to both North and South, this terrible war, as the woe due to those by whom the offence came, shall we discern therein any departure from those divine attributes, which the believers in a Living God always ascribe to Him?" One implication of such a concept of the divine is that the pastoral is unavailable precisely because of slavery.

Lincoln's "must needs come" expresses the cyclical nature of God's approval and disapproval, with harmony restored only after God's vengeance has been asserted. Whitman had available other models for thinking about the rise and decline of civilizations, including the course-of-empire idea, with its assumption of a civilization inevitably destroyed by its own luxuries and returned to a primitive state. If Whitman had embraced such a model, he could have argued that after the collapse of slavery, and the

[59] *MDW*, 56.

strayed herd, the United States would revert to a primitive state, and then gradually achieve the pastoral again.

But Whitman stands in a complicated relationship to the historical models of his time. He is progressivist in orientation, and the philosophical thinking supporting his outlook is a mix of Hegel, Humboldt, Darwin, Chambers, the Bible, Swedenborg, Emerson, and others. In his dismantling of the pastoral, Whitman offers readers a different view of America's position in the arc of history; his work strives to face the collapse straight on, with all its uncertainty for the US in particular and democracy generally, rather than imagining that the country was passing through a predetermined stage. The pastoral was attractive to Whitman as a foil to emphasize his commitment to the urgency of the present (rather than nostalgia for an imagined past) and the immense potential of everyday people. Messy and marked by debrisity, Whitman's world possessed immense possibility precisely because it was what he called in "A Song for Occupations" the "nearest, commonest, readiest." For Whitman, the pastoral—more staid, predictable, and hierarchical—was neither to be ignored nor eliminated, but wielded.

Cattle, Chattel, and the Anti-pastoral

In Chapter 1, I discussed two black girls Whitman encountered on 14th Street in Washington, near a contraband camp, at a muddy crossing. Whitman's interest was in the "prospect" before them. How would blacks—both those who had been free for generations and those only recently freed—fit into the landscape? Could African Americans be owners of the land they had long cultivated? What would be their new relation to the soil and the nation? Whitman struggled to come to clear resolutions on these issues, but his pictorial language invites consideration of the visual representations of African Americans in both the popular press and in the paintings of Civil War correspondents and artists Winslow Homer and Eastman Johnson. Like Whitman, they were attempting to picture freedom for millions who had been enslaved. Like Whitman, they resorted to the pastoral.

In nineteenth-century Anglo-American visual and literary texts there was a strong association between enslaved African Americans and cattle, whether in the influential McGuffey readers or speeches by abolitionist and educator Horace Mann:

> Sir, from the front of this Capitol, from the piazza that opens out from your congressional library, as you cast your eye along the horizon and over the

conspicuous objects of the landscape, —the President's Mansion, the Smithsonian Institution, and the site of the Washington Monument, you cannot fail to see the horrid and black receptacles where human beings are penned like cattle, and kept like cattle, that they may be sold like cattle, —as strictly and literally so as oxen and swine are kept and sold at Smithfield shambles in London, or at the cattle fair in Brighton.[60]

Whitman's commentary on cattle in Washington came when pro-slavery discourse equally if more approvingly depicted enslaved people as property and akin to livestock. As M. Jimmie Killingsworth notes, enslaved people were "legally defined as 'chattel,' a word etymologically equivalent to cattle and related to capital, the root meaning for which goes back to the word for head, as in heads of livestock, the countable items of property that can be reduced to a number and valued accordingly."[61] Illustrators from *Harper's Weekly* tried to turn the legal distinction or lack thereof into humor not long after the signing of the Emancipation Proclamation (see Figure 3.5). In this image, the chaotic lines of houses, like those in the "Man of Color's" clothes, suggest nature gone to seed. They contrast with the careful, neat depiction of the animals. The "Man of Color" is represented as ruinous of the pastoral in his preening self-regard, an attitude repeated in the much smaller figure in the front yard, whose chin also juts upward at a sharp angle, to highlight a false vanity. The future or potential property owner is characterized via vertical lines; his hopes and his relationship to the landscape are severely restricted by horizontal lines everywhere behind him, implicitly restricting his movement and confining him visually—as enslaved African Americans were often actually confined—and seeming to limit his destiny and that of his fellows. There is no arable land or prospect opening out in front of him.

As Michael Bennett argues, typically for early African American writers a "pastoral vision offer[ed] little solace for confronting the real travails of this world, which are obfuscated and kept in place by a mythic understanding of the relationship between humans and their environment."[62] We recall that in Frederick Douglass's famous narrative, he pines for Baltimore and wishes to escape not *from* but *to* the city. Like many African American writers from

---

[60] Horace Mann, *Slavery Letters and Speeches* (1851; repr. New York: Burt Franklin, 1969), 122 as quoted in John Davis, "Eastman Johnson's *Negro Life at the South* and Urban Slavery in Washington, D.C.," *The Art Bulletin*, 80, No. 1 (Mar., 1998), 75.

[61] Killingsworth, "'As if the beasts spoke': The Animal/Animist/Animated Walt Whitman," *Walt Whitman Quarterly Review* 28 (2010), 21.

[62] Michael Bennett, "Anti-Pastoralism, Frederick Douglass, and the Nature of Slavery" in *Beyond Nature Writing: Expanding the Boundaries of Ecocriticism*, ed. Karla Armbruster and Kathleen R. Wallace (Charlottesville, VA: University Press of Virginia, 2001), 199.

Figure 3.5. *Harper's Weekly*, January 17, 1863, p. 48.

Douglass forward, Whitman rarely displayed a view of the rural landscape as an ethically neutral or even beneficent space. African Americans questioned romanticized views of country life, not only because they were excluded from the pastoral's yeoman ideal, but because they too often encountered unpredictable violence and degradation on plantations. In fact, the Euro-American bias in pastoralism has prompted what Bennett calls a corresponding "tradition of anti-pastoralism in African American culture."[63]

Just prior to the war, Whitman made clear that he was alive to a diverse city, as "Give me the Splendid Silent Sun" shows, but he was also cognizant that the countryside was racialized. His "Longings for Home" (1860–61) is an anti-pastoral poem that he later retitled "O Magnet-South!" In a perceptive analysis of "Longings," Jacob Wilkenfeld notes that Whitman sets out "to deconstruct the idyllic vision of Southern pastoral, exposing an elision of the evils of slavery from Southern poetic representations" and thus "underscores Southern hypocrisy"; he does this by adopting "a discourse similar to

---

[63] Bennett, "Anti-Pastoralism, Frederick Douglass, and the Nature of Slavery," 205. Sarah Wagner-McCoy has demonstrated that the case of Charles Chesnutt is exceptional in that he invokes the pastoral not to counter it but instead to claim a place for African American culture within the pastoral. See her "Virgilian Chesnutt,"199–220.

that of the Southern pastoral republican mode," even speaking in the voice of a Southerner. Yet after offering a "catalogue of the natural splendors of the South" and the productive fields of crops of cotton, rice, sugar, hemp and corn, Whitman shifts tone and undermines the "idealized Southern pastoral mood" when he describes the "Southern swampland" with the "fugitive slave" in "his concealed hut."[64] Southern depictions of pastoralism in the visual arts ordinarily erased slave labor. Whitman demonstrates a sophisticated awareness that the meanings of nature, especially in nature's nation, are dependent upon one's subject position as a white or as a free or enslaved black.

In a key parenthetical line, Whitman brings to light what the "pastoral"— or in this case the South—has repressed: "The piney odor and the gloom— the awful natural stillness, (Here in these dense swamps the free-booter carries his gun, and the fugitive slave has his concealed hut.)" As in Virgil, the dispossessed—here the speaker as pseudo Southerner—longs for the idyllic countryside, where human life follows natural rhythms. But Whitman exposes this as a false harmony, based on coercion and racial ideology, not nature. The fugitive slave hut in the Southern landscape disrupts the pastoral and its legitimacy. Moreover, the *free-booter* (a word applied to plunderers, robbers and armed trackers of slaves) underscores the dangers so often hidden in accounts of Southern pastoral. Whitman's poem is an early refutation of the Southern pastoral myth that would most fully develop during Reconstruction and the post-Reconstruction years—a myth rooted in white supremacy and misleading about the role of slavery.[65]

As has been already suggested, and as David Miller notes, for many nineteenth-century Euro-American readers the swamp was seen as "weird and noxious ... fixing it as a repulsive if intriguing emblem of evil, a natural hell."[66] This generalization is far less true for Native Americans, African Americans, and those sympathetic to them. The swamp signified differently for those in asymmetrical conflicts. To besieged African Americans and Native Americans, a swamp could change the power balance, offering sanctuary, camouflage, and a defensible position. Whitman describes the

[64] Jacob Wilkenfeld, "Re-Scripting Southern Poetic Discourse in Whitman's 'Longings for Home,'" *Walt Whitman Quarterly Review* 29 (Fall 2011/Winter 2012), 53–54.
[65] This myth was advanced with lamentable success in the work of such writers as William Gilmore Simms, John Pendleton Kennedy, Caroline Lee Hentz, William Alexander Caruthers, and Joel Chandler Harris. See Wagner-McCoy, "Virgilian Chesnutt," 203.
[66] David Miller, *Dark Eden: The Swamp in Nineteenth-Century American Culture* (Cambridge: Cambridge University Press, 1989), 92.

swamp in "Longings for Home" as "half-impassable...infested by reptiles, resounding with the bellow of the alligator, the sad noises of the night-owl and the wild-cat, and the whirr of the rattlesnake."[67] If any place functions as an anti-pastoral setting it is the swamp sought out by fugitives. A locale paradoxically dangerous and safe, functioning differently across racial lines, the swamp-as-haven highlights that the ordinary settings fugitives had fled from could be even more terrifying. If the swamp was a "natural hell," it often seemed better than the humanly produced hell of everyday life. In the swamp at least there was a chance for seclusion and escape.

An 1856 *Harper's Monthly* account of "The Dismal Swamp," where Nat Turner's "banditti" fled after his rebellion, included an illustration of an African American man, Osman (see Figure 3.6). The name associates him with the founder of the Ottoman dynasty, a larger-than-life leader. It is reasonable to assume Whitman saw this illustration since he was a reader of *Harper's Monthly* and *Harper's Weekly* in these years. Osman, in this engraving by David Hunter Strother, appears to have melded with the swamp: the lines in his shirt are nearly indistinguishable from the snaky thicket from which he half-emerges. This image clarifies how the swamp can be both a refuge and place of bondage of a different sort—Osman has broken the chains of slavery by immersing himself in a thicket of natural entanglements. The only straight lines in the picture show his gun, held in a powerful bare arm. Independent, moving forward, and capable of self-defense, Osman is nonetheless not threatening—his rifle points away from the viewer and is not ready to be fired. He has white hair associated with age, wisdom, and a lack of aggression. His glance, turned slightly aside but nonetheless riveted on the viewer, expresses a gentleness and sensitivity all the more remarkable in light of the foregrounded over-sized hands. The key difference between "Longings for Home" and Strother's engraving is that Whitman's fugitive slave is not seen with a rifle—only the freebooter in Whitman's poem "carries his gun," emphasizing their imbalance of power.

Whitman's Civil War landscapes are ambiguous—recurrently marked by destruction and debris, swamps and scorched earth—and they highlight moral uncertainties and quandaries. The messiness, misunderstandings, and challenges facing any effort to recuperate the past with its history of exploitation characterize his "Ethiopia Saluting the Colors," a poem composed in 1867 though not published until 1871. On a variety of grounds, this

---

[67] *LG* (1860–61), 390.

Figure 3.6. David Hunter Strother, *Osman, Harper's New Monthly Magazine*, 13, no. 76 (September 1856), 452.

poem has made many Euro-American critics since then cringe. But it was praised by Langston Hughes as "one of the most beautiful poems in our language concerning a Negro subject," and other black artists, including the poet Melvin Tolson and the composers Samuel Coleridge-Taylor, Margaret Bonds, and Harry T. Burleigh have revered it as well.[68] Ed Folsom has argued that it has "always seemed that African American writers and critics

---

[68] The Anglo-African Samuel Coleridge-Taylor composed a march on "Ethiopia Saluting the Colours" in 1902. Harry Burleigh also set "Ethiopia Saluting the Colors" to music in about 1915. Hughes lavished great praise on Whitman himself in "Langston Hughes Calls Whitman Negroes' First Great Poetic Friend, Lincoln of Letters," *Chicago Defender*, July 4, 1953, 11, col. 6. In addition, Melvin Tolson praises "Ethiopia Saluting the Colors" in his review of *Selected Poems of Claude McKay*, in *Poetry* 83, no. 5 (February 1954), 287. For discussion of Harry T. Burleigh, Margaret Bonds, and "Ethiopia Saluting the Colors," see Jean E. Snyder, *Harry T. Burleigh: From the Spiritual to the Harlem Renaissance* (Urbana, IL: University of Illinois Press, 2016), 181. Bonds remarked: "I myself had never suffered any feelings of inferiority because I am a Negro, and I had always felt a strong identification with Africa, but now here was a poem which said so many different things I had known and was not able to verbally express" (181).

see and hear something in the poem that most white readers do not."⁶⁹ If in fact the poem is seen and heard differently along racial lines, it may be because of the differing ways two key terms—"Ethiopia" and "Sherman"—can be understood. The soldier in the poem baldly states what many Europeans and Euro-Americans believed: people from Africa, like the elderly woman he observes, were "hardly human." Whitman's various comments on Ethiopia in both private drafts and published writings are far more complex. He described Ethiopia as the bedrock foundation of civilization, a key precursor, if nonetheless primitive in outlook.⁷⁰ In an 1860–61 poem eventually titled "Song of the Broad-Axe," Whitman mentions the "venerable and harmless men of Ethiopia." Even this limited praise of Ethiopia led to parodic treatment of his views in pro-slavery publications and in *Vanity Fair*.⁷¹ In the United States, views of Ethiopia in the 1860s and 1870s could fall anywhere on the spectrum from those who mocked Whitman's comments about that land's "venerable and harmless" men to those who held that "Ethiopia" (or "Aethopia" as it was sometimes spelled) was a land "favored by the gods" and that Ethiopians were "closest to the gods."⁷² This latter line of thinking, available in classical dictionaries and possibly through oral tradition, too, would resonate for African Americans. Also important for African Americans were General William Tecumseh Sherman and his ill-fated effort to set aside land for African Americans. Sherman in fact provides an opportunity to see through the pastoral to the issues at stake in this poem.

As a postwar reflection on the conflict and its implications, this poem is controversial because of its (belated) treatment of race. Whitman did not address slavery and emancipation in any meaningful way in the initial publication of *Drum-Taps*, though he added this poem to the "Drum-Taps" cluster of *Leaves of Grass* in 1881. However, Whitman's dramatization of an encounter between an elderly black woman and a soldier joined many other verbal and visual treatments in the northern press of African American women and children encountering federal troops.⁷³ As early as

---

⁶⁹ See Ed Folsom's online MOOC, available at https://iwp.uiowa.edu/whitmanweb/en/writings/civil-war/week-35/ethiopia-saluting-the-colors
⁷⁰ See the notebook, "In his presence" (*WWA*).
⁷¹ Eric Conrad, "Whitman and the Proslavery Press: Newly Recovered 1860 Reviews," *Walt Whitman Quarterly Review* 27 (Spring 2010), esp. 229–30.
⁷² See Charles Anthon, *A Classical Dictionary*, entry under "Aetheopia," (New York: Harper, 1872), 64.
⁷³ Peter H. Wood and Karen C. C. Dalton, *Winslow Homer's Images of Blacks* (Austin, TX: University of Texas Press, 1988), 54.

1862, for example, *Harper's Weekly* depicted an African American woman and her children greeting Union soldiers, in which it offered a mocking rendering of black dialect (see Figure 3.7). Although the caricatured woman ostensibly seeks freedom, her position behind three thick horizontal bars of a fence makes her appear just as far from emancipation as Osman in his swampy entanglement. The image offers no sign of blacks and whites sharing the same space nor does it give the woman access to an open pastoral landscape. The woman's smiling face, open arms, and widely spread legs distance her from ideals of white bourgeois womanhood, of course, and the fencing suggests that firm barriers are in place to block any efforts to escape, something her dialect signals, too. Yet the one child pushing through the fence and another wriggling under it suggest that separation or segregation is doomed to fail, at least for this future generation.

Whitman's own imagining of the interaction between an African American woman and Sherman's army was almost certainly shaped by such depictions in the popular press. To take another example of this theme, an unknown artist in *Harper's Weekly* caricatured an open-mouthed slave along with the purported comment, "Is All Dem Yankees Dat's Passing?" (see Figure 3.8). The African American woman appears stunned

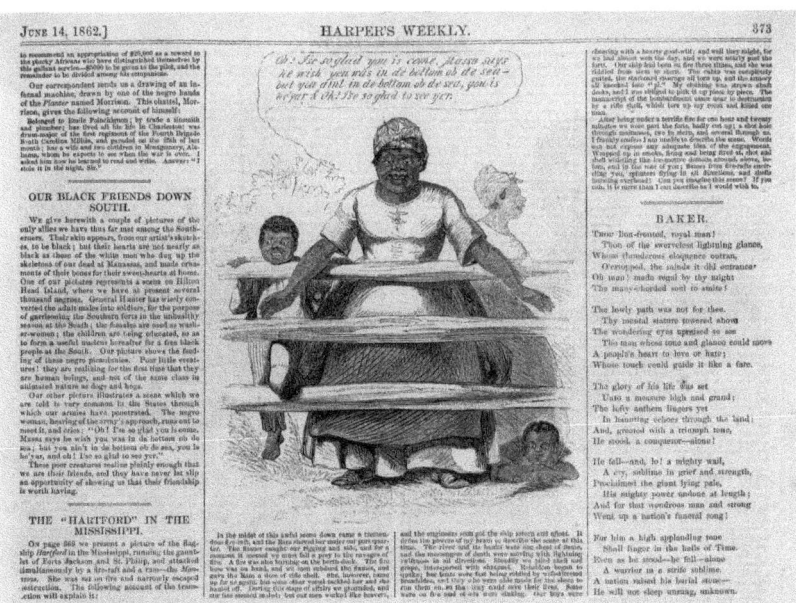

Figure 3.7. Unknown artist, in *Harper's Weekly* (June 14, 1862), 373.

Figure 3.8. Unknown artist, "Is All Dem Yankees Dat's Passing?" in *Harper's Weekly* (January 7, 1865), 16.

and possibly alarmed. There is a discrepancy between the text and image here that was fairly typical, as *Harper's* writers were often more sympathetic than illustrators who came from a tradition of caricature and satire. In the picture, a porch railing leaves the woman fenced in, and limited black mobility is also emphasized in the caption describing her as "one of the 'colored population'" who watched from the plantation "from which, probably, she was never ten miles in her life." However, the plantation setting in which she theatrically addresses an off-stage mistress or master suggests some agency, though it is tied to the movements of "all dem" marching soldiers. Indeed, the viewer, following her gaze, is in on the joke—the endless number of Yankees is precisely what the slave's seeming astonishment underscores: the prospect is of her master's defeat.

In contrast, Whitman's elderly woman, Ethiopia, though she may seem a caricature, too, differs importantly from popular depictions of enslaved women. She has both self-awareness and agency, and her evident understanding not only of the significance of the northern invasion and its implications for her freedom is matched by her refusal to disavow her African roots. She is neither shocked nor overwhelmed by the prospect of freedom, and she is not caught between staying put and crossing over to the Union army. In the poem as a whole, she epitomizes much of African American history up until the moment of encounter with a soldier from Sherman's army: African childhood and capture, Middle Passage crossing of the Atlantic, long decades as an enslaved person, and ultimate seizing of the opportunity of emancipation.

Whitman's poem, like the popular illustrations, employs black dialect. Widely understood as a comic mode at this time, Whitman uses it to satirize white Southern pastoral.

> *Me, master, years a hundred, since from my parents sunder'd,*
> *A little child, they caught me as the savage beast is caught;*
> *Then hither me, across the sea, the cruel slaver brought.*[74]

Whitman's language rings false because our minds have been shaped by later achievements of Dunbar, Chesnutt, Hughes, Faulkner, Morrison and a host of other artists who have highlighted the range and eloquence of black dialect. The problem in "Ethiopia Saluting the Colors" is not that Whitman has presented African American speech as a barbarous deviation from a norm (unlike *Harper's*, he does not strive for comic effect and he avoids eye dialect) but that he failed to recognize the extraordinary expressive capacity of black dialect when rendered realistically. In treating black dialect, Whitman and the popular press exhibit different types of failures of authenticity. The diction Whitman attributes to the elderly woman is overly poeticized with its inversions, two instances of internal rhyme, and a chiasmic heroic simile (caught me as the "savage beast" is an inversion

[74] *LG* (1871–72), 357.

that speaks back to and disputes the northern soldier's claim that she is "hardly human"). The language of Ethiopia is akin to eighteenth-century antislavery poetry and is in some ways reminiscent of Phyllis Wheatley and a poem published in 1773:

> I, young in life, by seeming cruel fate
> Was snatched from Afric's fancied happy seat:
> What pangs excruciating must molest,
> What sorrows labor in my parent's breast?

Antique diction is not altogether inappropriate if Ethiopia is indeed 100 years old.[75]

We only need to separate author from narrator to see that Whitman's depiction of white racism is not the same as his endorsing it. The elderly woman resists dehumanizing interpretations, indignities, and deprivations that one of Sherman's soldiers shows little eagerness to correct:

> ('Tis while our army lines Carolina's sand and pines,
> Forth from thy hovel door, thou, Ethiopia, com'st to me,
> As, under doughty Sherman, I march toward the sea.)

The poverty of the hovel—again a biased view of the racist soldier, not necessarily a truthful perception like the wild lines in "Cutting his old Associates" in *Harper's*)—is not consistent with the pastoral. Instead, what comes to mind through the naming of Sherman, and what would resonate particularly for African American readers, is the possibility of an improved life precisely through the promise of land possession, land promised via Sherman's Field Order 15. In this famous order of January 16, 1865, Sherman gave African Americans "possessory rights" to a strip of coastland stretching from Charleston, South Carolina to northern Florida, along with nearby sea islands, after consulting with a group of black ministers. These orders—serving to redistribute roughly 400,000 acres of land in forty-acre segments to newly freed black families—are commonly understood as the origin of the "40 acres and a mule" promise. The Union army confiscated land abandoned by fleeing whites (Sherman's motivation was in part to rid himself of the estimated 19,000 African Americans who attached themselves

---

[75] My thanks to Matt Cohen for informative discussions about this poem.

to his army. It is also worth noting that the forty-acre plot accords with the pastoral view of Thomas Jefferson, except for the racial dimension, of a nation built on small forty-acre single farms).[76] Whitman no doubt read about this order in a variety of places, including in his government work and in the daily papers—for example in the February 5, 1866 *Washington Daily National Republican*. Regrettably, this order was rescinded by the government not long after.

The double dealing of the government may explain some of the oddities of the poem, including Ethiopia's initial greeting of the American flag as a sign of liberation. In the first stanza, Sherman's soldier is more confused by her liberation than the elderly woman, so he asks: "Why, rising by the roadside here, do you the colors greet?" By the end of the poem, though the woman remains respectful—she "curtseys to the regiments"—she also goes silent, wagging her head "with turban bound—yellow red and green." She wears the colors of the Ethiopian flag, displaying pride in her African roots even as she honors an American flag "strange and marvelous" that could both conceive of land redistribution and betray its promise.

Ed Folsom has speculated that Elihu Vedder's painting of *Jane Jackson, Formerly a Slave* (1865) may have influenced "Ethiopia."[77] Jane Jackson was an elderly black woman who sold peanuts near the artist's studio on Broadway in New York City. Whitman knew Vedder from his bohemian days in New York at Pfaff's beer hall. But "Ethiopia" may also be profitably read in conjunction with Winslow Homer's *Near Andersonville* (1865–66), a painting known previously as *At the Cabin Door* and *Captured Liberators* before Homer's own title for the painting was discovered (see Figure 3.9).[78] Whitman almost certainly did not know of this painting (it was not exhibited and seems to have only been seen briefly at auction in New York City on April 19, 1866 when Whitman was in Washington), so rather than arguing for its influence on him, we can recognize a commonality of concern and subject matter. Homer covered the Civil War for *Harper's*, which as we've seen, regularly published images and stories of former female slaves encountering Union soldiers. As noted, Whitman read *Harper's*, and his poem is

---

[76] Megan Rowley Williams, *Through the Negative: The Photographic Image and the Written Word in Nineteenth-Century American Literature* (New York: Routledge, 2003), 44.
[77] Ed Folsom, "Lucifer and Ethiopia: Whitman, Race, and Poetics before the Civil War and After," in *A Historical Guide to Walt Whitman*, ed. David S. Reynolds (Oxford: Oxford University Press, 2000), 66–67.
[78] For the history of this painting and the discovery of the title Homer gave it, see Peter H. Wood, *Near Andersonville: Winslow Homer's Civil War* (Cambridge, MA: Harvard University Press, 2010), 9–29.

Figure 3.9. Winslow Homer, *Near Andersonville* (1865–1866; previously known by other titles). Newark Museum.

unusual in comparison in envisioning the black woman and white soldier on the same road, with no barriers separating them, sharing the same national space. Homer's painting clarifies how difficult this was to do (see Figure 3.9).

Both Whitman and Homer depict an African American woman emerging alone from a modest building, wearing a turban.[79] In Whitman's poem it is the African American woman who acts as an individual whereas the soldier, part of a marching unit, is part of a herd, though he does have agency and his thoughts and words shape the poem. So, too, in Homer's painting soldiers are in the background, prisoners of war being marched to Andersonville, the Civil War prison camp infamous for its high death rate. A young adult

---

[79] Peter H. Wood sees the building in Homer as more ambiguous: "The largest portion of the painting is not the military scene or the foreground figure; it is the building that surrounds her. This element is also the most ambiguous.... Are we looking at the front of the woman's small home, or at a plantation outbuilding, or at the back corner of a white-owned mansion?" (*Near Andersonville*, 61). It is impossible to exclude any one of these possibilities, though if this building is part of a mansion, Homer did nothing to indicate that.

woman in an individualized pose is framed in the doorway, in the foreground, absorbed in thought, seeming to muse stoically on the Union prisoners—now captured and under the Confederate flag—no doubt justifiably concerned about not only them but a future her gaze cannot discern. Any hope for landowning or pastoral harmony is remote from this scene. Generally speaking, Homer saw promise in the younger generation of blacks and painted them with sensitivity and insight; like *Harper's*, his depiction of the older generation of blacks was more caricatured—they were less literate and thus, he seems to imply, less capable of citizenship. This woman, in her dignity and self-awareness, is akin to the woman in "Ethiopia Saluting the Colors."

Eastman Johnson's *Union Soldiers Accepting a Drink* (circa 1865), a striking work in its own right through its handling of spatial dynamics, also sheds light on "Ethiopia Saluting the Colors" (see Figure 3.10). The painting overturns conventions of nineteenth-century American art about the decorum for representing African Americans and whites together. Albert Boime has "demonstrated that the convention of deploying figures in a composition to mirror social hierarchies in real life applies especially to

Figure 3.10. Eastman Johnson, *Union Soldiers Accepting a Drink* (ca. 1865). Carnegie Museum of Art, Pittsburgh.

pictures of racial types."[80] In this painting, the African American woman is in the highest position, at the apex of the triangle of adult figures. Unlike Homer's *Near Andersonville* (but like Whitman's poem), Johnson's painting offers a view of Union soldiers interacting directly with an African American woman. In their paintings both Johnson and Homer position the African American woman as framed by the threshold. Of the images considered here, this is the only one with any direct claims to the pastoral. Strikingly, the figure with an intriguing opening to the land, to the promise of the pastoral, is a child-sized African American woman in the shadows, near the exact center of the painting, watching the older woman's hospitality. She is, perhaps, not the initial focus of interest in a painting ostensibly about the warm welcome white Union soldiers received from people of color in the south, highlighting a sentimental dimension to the painting. Yet the girl and her sunlit path toward an open field and future, small but promising, in the distance behind her, rivals the *seemingly* more important reinscription of a service role for African Americans (the adult woman provides beer and cake for the soldiers, as the sign above her indicates). There are rocks in front of the younger woman as she looks on at this moment of service, but there is only light and smooth ground ahead of her, if she turns toward the light, the opening, and the land. And, painted later than Homer, its sunny vistas suggest Reconstruction along the lines of pastoral social harmony—no threat is posed to a white patriarchy.

In this painting, the visual field is divided into thirds, and a further dimension is added by the mysterious red swath in the leftmost third of the painting that appears to be a young white woman in a red dress, standing in a pose very similar to the young black woman in the shadows. She is more distant and more embodied in the pastoral, sunny world. This red splotch, despite its lack of clarity, is a significant element in the painting, since it is what the eye is drawn to in that segment of the painting. That all but indecipherable hot spot captures the uncertainty of race relations as the war ended and new possibilities for fundamental social reshuffling were contemplated.[81]

---

[80] The quoted phrase is Patricia Hills's summary of Boime's argument. See Hills, "Painting Race: Eastman Johnson's Pictures of Slaves, Ex-Slaves, and Freedmen" in Teresa A. Carbone, Patricia Hills, et al., *Eastman Johnson Painting America* (New York: Rizzoli International Publications, 1999), 138.

[81] My thanks to Ed Folsom for suggestive remarks about this painting. Email to the author, June 20, 2019.

Whitman's poem, in contrast, has Ethiopia venturing out to the roadside, moving beyond service and domesticity: she is at a significant remove from her "hovel." She travels further and interacts in more complex ways with the soldier than the women depicted by Homer and Johnson. In fact, in Whitman's poem there is an interesting quality of movement, different from that of a fugitive or a soldier. By crossing to the Union lines, she acts more independently than is possible for either. The mere fact of travel is significant since slave codes had restricted black mobility. Nor in "Ethiopia" does the woman serve white soldiers—she serves herself.

Whitman's "Ethiopia Saluting the Colors" does not place the elderly woman in a domestic context: her positioning highlights the more open-ended future for those newly emancipated. In Homer we feel for soldiers through the woman's empathy; that is not her function in Johnson and Whitman. The poet depicts an anti-pastoral scene in the Carolina "sand" and brings an aged and resilient black woman to the center of attention. She has labored a hundred years only to have land promised and denied.

The Pastoral Hut, the Urban Shanty, and the Grand Mausoleum

Virgil's slave shepherds, like enslaved people in the United States, were not land owners—they were the dispossessed. In considering Whitman, slavery, and pastoralism, we need also to consider his writing on land ownership and the relationship between nature and the "home." In 1856 a reviewer writing in the Washington *Daily Intelligencer*, one of the nation's leading Whig newspapers, argued that Whitman himself belonged with hooved creatures:

> Mr. Whitman thinks, however, he would like to turn and live awhile with the animals.... Every one to his liking, as remarked the venerable dame in the proverb when she kissed her cow.... It behooves him also to bear in mind that according to all accounts the condition of the Irish peasantry is not greatly elevated over "the rest of mankind" by their hereditary custom of assigning to the "placid" porker and domestic cow a cozy corner in the cabin along with its other inmates. If much good was to be expected from turning and living with the animals, Ireland would have convinced the world of it long before Mr. Whitman's day, and if he had properly studied her history we question whether he would have considered it a matter

worth boasting of that he feels himself—"Stucco'd with quadrupeds and birds all over."[82]

This caustic reviewer recognizes that Whitman at times questioned the animal-human hierarchy that others took to be self-evident, as when he wrote both that he "could turn and live awhile with the animals" and that "I am enamoured of growing outdoors, / Of men that live among cattle or taste of the ocean or woods."[83] Again, Whitman calls hierarchy into question, specifically the dominion humans have claimed over non-human domesticated animals.

The hovel or hut (associated frequently with enslaved people or formerly enslaved people), the cottage of the rural poor and the rustic cabin (associated with both blacks and whites), the urban shanty (associated with the Irish, but not exclusively so[84]),—these real and imagined dwellings did not always sharply separate humans and non-human animals. The shanty, defined as a "mean dwelling" in the nineteenth century, was especially important to Whitman. (The OED indicates that shanty probably comes from the French, in the French Canadian context, and from lumberjacking camps. It is not surprising that Whitman was taken by a foreign word that had been reshaped in a North American work setting.)[85] As early as 1842 Whitman wrote about a "shanty" as a source of "cheerfulness and content," available to blacks and whites alike.[86] For both Louisa Van Velsor Whitman and her son Walt, a "shanty" referred to the most modest level of self-respecting free-standing housing. Both Whitman and his mother yearned to own a shanty, to possess a stable home, a modest dwelling. The poet suggested that the war itself had taught him to keep aspirations in check for any type of excess luxury. He wrote to his mother: "Do you then think of getting new apartments, after the 1st of May? . . . —the kind of house to build is quite a consideration, (if any house,) I should build a regular Irish shanty myself, two rooms, and an end shed—I think that's luxury enough, since

---

[82] [Review of *Leaves of Grass* (1855)], *The Washington Daily National Intelligencer*, February 18, 1856: 2 (*WWA*).
[83] *LG* (1855), 21.
[84] Whitman's brother Thomas Jefferson Whitman ("Jeff") referred to the "shanties" where dead bodies, many of them Irish immigrants, were removed after the police regained control of the city after the New York City draft riots. Thomas Jefferson Whitman to Walt Whitman, July 19, 1863 (*WWA*).
[85] John Russell Bartlett, *Dictionary of Americanisms* (1848).
[86] Whitman, "'Black and White Slaves,'" *New York Aurora*, April 2, 1842: [2] (*WWA*).

I have been down in the army."[87] Louisa Van Velsor Whitman wrote to her friend Helen Price on October 9, 1872, shortly after moving to Camden: "i would rather have my own shanty and my good friends come to see me." She indicated in a letter to the same friend that a shanty could be desirable but only if she owned or controlled it: "i wouldent mind living here if i had a place of my own but this...not being boss of your own shanty aint the cheese."[88] For Walt, a fantasy of dwelling in Arcadia could be contemplated—we recall the manuscript discussed above in which he wished to own nothing but to own all in imagination—but for the poet and his mother the more urgent wish was to find a reasonable place to rent or, better, to own a small actual home, an unassuming dwelling, a non-luxurious space of one's own.

Both Whitman and his mother writing separately value the shanty for its assurance of (modest) independence. Both sought stability after tumultuous lives that had each of them moving from one rented lodging to another often yearly, when not more frequently.[89] Whitman sometimes imagined sharing a harmonious life in a shanty with soldiers he had grown fond of during the Civil War—Thomas Sawyer and Lewy Brown, for example.[90] Perhaps Whitman thought of this yearning as a nineteenth-century remaking of Virgil's Alexis and Corydon and their simple life charged with an amorous aura: in one letter he wrote, "wherever I am in this world, while I have a meal, or a dollar, or if I should have some shanty of my own, no living man will ever be more welcome there than Tom Sawyer."[91] Whitman, however, never seemed to imagine a pastoral or wilderness setting for such a life—he was drawn instead to urban life. His musings about economic independence had a basis in reality: the shanty he imagined was within practical reach,

---

[87] Walt Whitman to Louisa Van Velsor Whitman, February 6, 1863 (*WWA*). A letter from Louisa to her son just after the war is typical: "well Walt here we all are without so much as a shanty to cover us and all the houses or the most of them for sale the most of people say that rents will come down but i gess they will be high enoughf for the most of us" (Louisa Van Velsor Whitman to Walt Whitman, [March 26 (?),1866]) (*WWA*).

[88] Louisa Van Velsor Whitman to Helen Price, October 9, 1872 and April 18 (?), 1873 (Pierpont Morgan Library).

[89] John Burroughs, always attentive to Whitman's preferences, invited the poet for a visit in October 1882, invoking language geared to be appealing: "You need a change. I dearly wish that as soon as you are well enough you would come up here & spend a few weeks with us. We could have a good time here in my bark-covered shanty & in knocking about the country." See John Burroughs to Walt Whitman, October 29, 1882 (*WWA*).

[90] During the war, Whitman became tremendously attached to Maryland native Lewy Brown, and the poet spent two nights on a cot near Brown's bed after the soldier suffered the amputation of his lower leg.

[91] Walt Whitman to Thomas P. Sawyer, November 20 (?), 1863 (*WWA*).

within his relatively modest means. He made plans to purchase a home in Washington, though that did not come to fruition.[92] He was at home in cities, and when he imagined possessing a shanty, it was in an urban environment. Whitman's imagined dwelling place was in keeping with a country that was growing increasingly urban. The shanty also implied a different labor model at odds with the yeoman farmer and the family-based labor. The shanty offered some of the independence of the farmer's homestead even as it was adaptable to increasingly urban and industrial conditions and to the lives of immigrant communities.

Interestingly, near the end of his life, and after he had departed Washington for Camden, New Jersey, Whitman chose to build a grand mausoleum for himself and his family (see Figure 3.11). He spent nearly

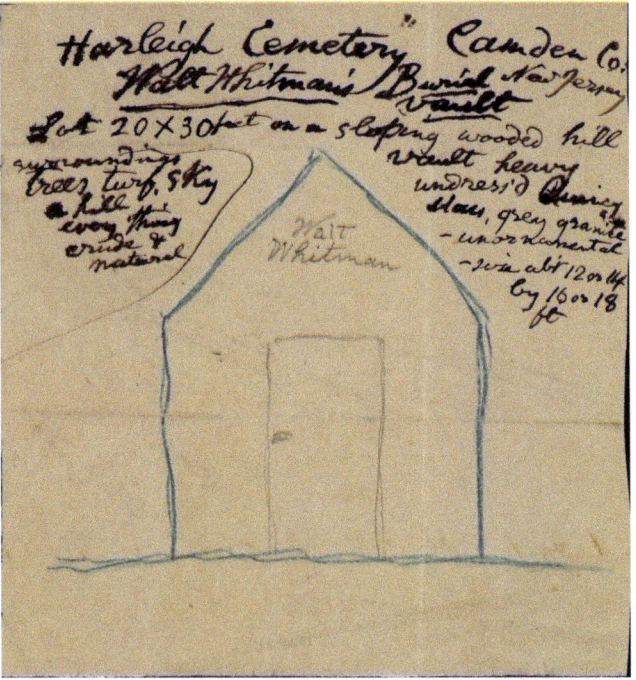

Figure 3.11. Courtesy Walt Whitman Papers in the Charles E. Feinberg Collection, 1763–1985, Library of Congress.

---

[92] Walt Whitman referenced the possibility of purchasing a house in Washington in his March 1, 1873 letter to Mannahatta Whitman and in his February 23 and March 28, 1873 letters to Louisa Van Velsor Whitman (*WWA*).

twice as much on his tomb as on his Camden home: he lived in humble quarters while alive and then indulged in splendor for death.[93] He manifested an anxiety felt by many Romantic artists: what was to happen to a dead poet, to dead leaves, to dead pages. These questions resonated with special force for a poet whose main book title evoked leaves. His tomb, built into a hillside, is in a pastoral setting in Harleigh cemetery in Camden. Yet its pastoralism is, like so much in Whitman, paradoxical. It is also on the edge of the cemetery, near marshy, swampy ground.[94]

Curiously, the poet who urged us to look for him under his bootsoles and who lived in modest places throughout his life, became ostentatious in the face of death, raising anew questions about nature, pastoralism, and home. Amanda Gailey has argued that the "larger purpose behind Whitman's interest in the tomb...was an end-of-life attempt to shore up his legacy."[95] Like his publication of the *Complete Poems and Prose*, his tomb offered a second means of ensuring Whitman's legacy, a prominent tangible monument supplementing *Leaves of Grass*. Whitman worried about an issue that had become more acute in an age of mass reproduction of versions, of copies, of paper: did it all amount to scattered ephemeral leaves? The tomb—*et in Arcadia ego*—attempted to mitigate that threat.

Typical statements about pastoral fit Whitman poorly. The view that he invoked the pastoral in wholly unironic or wholly ironic ways is too simple to accord with the evidence. Like most writers of his generation, he associated the Republic with nature, and he tried to fathom all of the Civil War deaths within that context. He recognized that if he wished to be the national poet, he had to reckon with extraordinary carnage. But there is an escapist tendency in pastoralism, and evading the war or the city was not Whitman's approach in either his life or his writing. He strove to own rather than evade this cataclysm and build a more democratic society worthy of the sacrifice, not to restore the old order. Whitman's poetry and prose of the war years and Reconstruction rarely invoke the pastoral to wax nostalgic about the past. He focused instead on the crises of the present and the vistas of the future.

---

[93] Loving, 479.

[94] Amanda Gailey notes Whitman's friend William Sloane Kennedy was "careful to point out that the tomb was Whitman's idea, not the imposition of friends who failed to grasp his philosophy, and that 'rural Harleigh' is 'in the woods and nowhere else,' his tomb specifically 'in the out skirts of an almost empty cemetery in a grove, and abutting on vast fields which will always remain so.'" See *Proofs of Genius: Collected Editions from the American Revolution to the Digital Age* (Ann Arbor: University of Michigan Press, 2015), 68.

[95] Gailey, 66.

4
Social Calamity, Personal Perturbations, and Office Decorum
How *Leaves of Grass* Grew Pensive

If Whitman at times romanticized a snug home in a shanty, an existence of self-reliant independence, he in fact lodged in a series of never entirely satisfactory quarters in Washington DC. He lived in at least seven different residences during his decade in the capital as a clerk, dependent on partisan patronage for his job.[1] His lodgings included a room in the same house where his fellow bureaucrat William Douglas O'Connor and wife Ellen O'Connor also rented rooms just above him, and in various other boarding houses (in 1870, one quarter of federal workers in Washington lived in boarding houses with non-relatives, so Whitman's experience was common but not the statistical norm).[2] At the end of his decade in the capital, Whitman lived in a solitary unheated garret. Fortunately, he found a remarkable degree of comfort unexpectedly in another location, his perch in the Treasury Building where he worked in his longest-running government job. Earlier, in Brooklyn, Whitman could write at his various lodgings, usually shared with other family members, or in an editorial office, or wherever his jaunts took him. All of these had been places of relative independence, and like an artisan or a bohemian he could control much of his labor and his ways. In Washington, in contrast, he became part of the creation of the first white-collar bureaucracy in the United States through the federal government's employment of primarily white native-born professionals—male in most cases but increasingly including women, too. Federal workers were well educated, with the great majority having received

---

[1] Kim Roberts, "A Map of Whitman's Washington Boarding Houses and Work Places," *Walt Whitman Quarterly Review* 22 (Summer 2004), 23–28 and Kim Roberts, "A Corrected Map of Whitman's Washington Boarding Houses and Work Places," *Walt Whitman Quarterly Review* 22 (Fall 2004/Winter 2005), 136–37.

[2] Cindy Sondik Aron, *Ladies and Gentlemen of the Civil Service: Middle-Class Workers in Victorian America* (Oxford: Oxford University Press, 1987), 20.

at least a secondary education while many had attended college or professional schools. Whitman entered a system filled with intelligent, well-trained individuals who held far-reaching authority but little autonomy.[3]

Whitman's various roles as a government clerk shaped his life and writing from 1863 to 1873. Whitman's years in the attorney general's office coincided with his revising of *Leaves of Grass*, especially the creation of an annotated volume known as the "Blue Book," considered in detail below, and the writing of *Democratic Vistas*, considered in the next chapter. I argue that there is a relation between the decorum required of an employee—a clerk in a government office—and the evolution of Whitman's creative life in these years, particularly his treatment of sex and the body. Compared to his editorial labor on newspapers, Whitman's government stint has received less attention, though it is illuminating to view him through this lens, as he tried on new identities during the war and in the immediate postwar years. His government work provided him with a network of contacts different from the bohemian world of New York or New Orleans journalists, but his new milieu nonetheless offered him friendship, collaboration, and intellectual stimulation. The identification of nearly 3,000 documents in Whitman's handwriting from his clerking years leaves us now better able to study this portion of his life in its full complexity and to reevaluate his literary accomplishments. His scribal documents let us see how his roles as poet of democracy and clerk in bureaucracy were more entangled than we've ever known or imagined. He was joining a long history of writers who sought patronage from governments or landed aristocrats and that way entered a conventional stream. Government work may have checked some of his bolder poetic claims, as patronage relationships so often did, but it also broadened and nuanced his cultural analysis.

Whitman as poet and care-giver has been of such great interest that his government work, which seemingly possesses little originality, has been overlooked. Yet the Washington city directory listed him not as "author," nor as "journalist," nor again as "missionary to the wounded" but instead as "Whitman, Walt, clerk." As a clerk, he spent much of his time as a scribe or copyist of documents and letters; writing in a clear, fair hand was

---

[3] For a helpful study of federal employees, see Aron, *Ladies and Gentlemen of the Civil Service*, 18. For a broad consideration of middle-class life in the period, see Timothy R. Mahoney, "Middle Class Experience in the Gilded Age, 1865–1900," *Journal of Urban History*, 31 (2005): 356–66. For the role of women in the federal workplace, see Jessica Ziparo, *This Grand Experiment: When Women Entered the Federal Workforce in Civil War-Era Washington, D.C.* (Chapel Hill, NC: University of North Carolina Press, 2017).

required for official documents and to preserve records of letters sent. In fact, Whitman's handwriting seems to have been key to his employment.[4] His initial salary of $1200 per year—once he was appointed as a clerk in the Department of the Interior in January, 1865—gave him a new financial stability. The word clerk has a religious origin related to cleric, though in modern usage, as the OED notes, the term is applied to one "employed in a subordinate position in a public or private office, shop, warehouse, etc., to make written entries, keep accounts, make fair copies of documents, do the mechanical work of correspondence and similar 'clerkly' work."[5] Particularly in the United States, the term clerk was used for a shop assistant. Unlike city clerks involved in sales and exchange, a clerk for the federal government held a desk job. Beginning in 1863, Whitman worked in the Army Paymaster's office, then for the Bureau of Indian Affairs in the Department of the Interior, and lastly in the Attorney General's office (in 1872 he was transferred to the Office of the Solicitor of the Treasury, though this was still within the Attorney General's office). The extant records of his government work are almost entirely from the Attorney General's office and date from 1865–73.[6] In becoming a clerk, Whitman was part of the vast expansion of the federal government in the latter half of the nineteenth century. As Cindy Sondik Aron notes, "in 1859, only 1,268 employees worked in the federal government offices in Washington, D.C.; at the turn of the century that number had mushroomed to more than 25,000 federal workers, nearly 9,000 of whom were clerks."[7]

Most of the surviving 3,000 scribal documents are letters with all words, including the signature of another person, in Whitman's handwriting. These were internal office copies of letters typically going out over the name of the attorney general or the assistant attorney general, though in one case we have a letter in Whitman's hand inscribed for President Andrew Johnson. There are at least 350 letters inscribed by others that include Whitman's

---

[4] William D. O'Connor instructed Whitman: "The object of your writing the letter is to get a specimen of your hand. Pick out, then, a good pen and write as fairly as you can a letter formally applying for a clerkship. Then enclose a copy of this letter to Ashton, so that he can follow it in to the Secretary" (O'Connor to Walt Whitman, December 30, 1864, *WWA*). William T. Otto, Assistant Secretary in the Department of Interior, told Whitman: "Upon reporting at this Department and passing a satisfactory examination you will be appointed to a First Class Clerkship" (Otto to Walt Whitman, January 12, 1865, *WWA*).

[5] *The Oxford English Dictionary* online.

[6] These records in the National Archives are now filed with the papers of the Department of Justice, though that department did not exist until 1870.

[7] Aron, 3.

annotations—often these annotations are in the margin and are of a summarizing nature and serve an indexing function. A few additional documents are notes or summaries or index pages in Whitman's handwriting.

Dixon Wecter published a valuable article in 1943 on "Walt Whitman as Civil Servant," noting these records, but until recently no one built on Wecter's work perhaps because he made no estimates about the number of available documents in Whitman's handwriting.[8] Wecter discusses about a dozen items but never implies that there are thousands of other documents to be explored. When other scholars have described Whitman's government work, they suggest he took things casually, sauntered into work when he wanted to, put in a few hours, and left when it suited him, a picture that corresponds to a romantic concept of a poet whose day job was largely meaningless to him. The evidence I have collected paints a very different picture. He worked steadily and produced a prodigious amount of material. Or as Whitman himself told Horace Traubel when reminiscing about his time as a clerk: "'It is a great mistake to suppose the positions all or mostly sinecures—some of the clerks work like beavers.'"[9]

Whitman ultimately embraced his employment as a clerk, a result that could not have been foreseen in light of his earlier comments emphasizing how clerks were "peculiar" or "ridiculous." In 1849, in his series "Letters From a Travelling Bachelor," he mocked clerks for their impatience as they waited for New York's Fulton Ferry: "It is perfect agony for them to be just half a second too late for the boat.... The time until the arrival of the next boat, (which extends from a second to three quarters of a minute,) these excited youths pass in a state of mind which must be felt before it can be realized. Then...the sharp glance around, to see whether there are any fashionable coats aboard.... Ah, these city clerks are a peculiar race."[10] "Paumanok," his pseudonym for the "Travelling Bachelor" series appearing in a cheap Sunday paper, reinforces the contrast with his own identity (and perhaps that of the reader), free of the demands and punishments of the time clock and genteel expectations of the business world that govern these clerks. His novel *Jack Engle* (1852) features a clerk, Wigglesworth, described as a "ridiculous old codger," indicating that from an early date Whitman perceived incompatibility between the roles of conservative clerk and radical modern poet—the name

---

[8] *PMLA* 58, no. 4 (Dec. 1943), 1094–09.   [9] *WWWC*, 6: 33.
[10] Paumanok [Walt Whitman], "From a Travelling Bachelor," *New York Sunday Dispatch*, December 23, 1849: [1].

Wigglesworth calls to mind Michael Wigglesworth, the Puritan minister and poet famous for *The Day of Doom*.[11]

A few years later, after the appearance of *Leaves of Grass*, Whitman again spoke disparagingly about clerks, holding in contempt foppish clerks on Broadway (the city's main, fashionable shopping street, with new department stores catering to women) befouled in perfume and hair oils: they were "a slender and round-shouldered generation...trig and prim...[with] hair all soaked and 'slickery' with sickening oils. Creatures of smart appearance, when dressed up;...how ridiculously would their natty demeanor appear if suddenly they could all be stript naked!"[12] As Ruth Bohan notes, in an age that "placed a premium on manliness and masculinity, these clerks occupied a conflicted and sexually ambiguous position within the city's rapidly growing subculture of urban males."[13] In Whitman's view, the problem is that these clerks care about a genteel decorum that excludes working class men and women who can't afford expensive oils. Bohan points out that Whitman may have the counter jumper in mind, a new urban type who was of interest to the poet and his bohemian friends at Pfaff's beer hall. The counter jumper—a dry goods clerk catering to women, ready to jump over a counter to serve buyers in the feminized environment of dry goods stores—was laughable to Whitman and other Pfaffians, and yet to a remarkable degree Whitman was vulnerable to satiric treatment via the counter jumper, as parodies in *Vanity Fair* and *The Saturday Press* make clear[14] (see Figure 4.1).

At the time of the third edition of *Leaves of Grass* (1860–61), Whitman remained dismissive of clerks, associating one of their tasks, copying, with a lack of independence and originality. In the first of the "Chants Democratic" he asked: "Who are you indeed who would talk or sing in America?" In a test of authenticity, he asks: "Have real employments contributed to it? original makers—not amanuenses?"[15] In number 13 of "Chants Democratic" he goes further, calling the copyist's courage into question: "There shall be no subject but it shall be treated with reference to the ensemble of the world, and the compact truth of the world—And no coward or copyist shall be

---

[11] Whitman, *Life and Adventures of Jack Engle: An Auto-Biography* (1852; rpt. Iowa City, IA: University of Iowa Press, 2017), 6.
[12] [Walt Whitman,] "Broadway," *Life Illustrated*, August 9, 1856: 116 (*WWA*).
[13] Ruth L. Bohan, "Vanity Fair, Whitman, and the Counter Jumper," *Word & Image* 33 no. 1 (2017), 57.
[14] Bohan, "Vanity Fair, Whitman, and the Counter Jumper," esp. 63–67.
[15] *LG* (1860–61), 119.

Figure 4.1. Public domain image from *Vanity Fair*, March 17, 1860, 183.

allowed."[16] Like the clerks described above who were effeminate because they copied a fashionable mold, rather than preserving individuality, copyists were timid and imitative rather than offering anything authentic. Whitman's association of copying with cowardliness is related to his idealized masculine role—the copyist risks being effeminate. Whitman was critical of copying because it was a threat to originality and self-reliance. Of course, the irony is that Whitman emerged out of a journalistic background in which he regularly copied from sources high and low, typically without giving credit. Like Shakespeare and many other writers, Whitman appropriated the writings of others, including his own previous writings, as fodder for new creations.

When Whitman first arrived in Washington, his need for income led him to consider supplementing his freelance journalism with office work, though he foresaw no happiness in that milieu. In April 1863 he wrote to Thomas

[16] *LG* (1860–61), 185. This poem was ultimately titled "Laws for Creations."

P. Sawyer, a young soldier he had fallen in love with in the hospitals, and explained:

> When I stopped here, last January... I thought I would... see if I could not get some berth, clerkship or something—but I have not pushed strong enough... and I don't know as I could be satisfied with the life of a clerk in the departments anyhow.... I enjoy a kind of vagabond life... I go around some, nights, when the spirit moves me,... just to see the sights. Tom, I wish you was here. Somehow I don't find the comrade that suits me to a dot—and I won't have any other, not for good.
>
> Tom, you tell the boys of your company there is an old pirate up in Washington, with the white wool growing all down his neck—an old comrade who thinks about you & them every day, for all he don't know them, and will probably never see them, but thinks about them as comrades & younger brothers of his, just the same.

The last thing Whitman wanted was for Sawyer to see him as a clerk bound to rules and regulations, and to party—far better to be an aging but dashing rogue or rough—a vagabond, pirate, or some other scofflaw.[17] Whitman wanted Sawyer to see his aversion to the ways of Washington, his reluctance to push "strong enough" by calling on powerful recommenders or political contacts for his own advancement. In fact, though, a February 13, 1863 letter to his brother Thomas Jefferson ("Jeff") Whitman indicated that Whitman had already talked with Charles Sumner, Senator from Massachusetts, and Preston King, Senator from New York, and had plans to contact Secretary of State William Seward as well. Whitman also enlisted Ralph Waldo Emerson to advocate for his worthiness as a potential federal employee.[18] These efforts were part of what Whitman called "getting better and better acquainted with office-hunting wisdom, and Washington peculiarities

---

[17] This letter also has many more references to God and an afterlife than is typical in Whitman, suggesting that Sawyer was religious and that Whitman wanted to speak to that. Although "vagabond" is used in a postive way in the letter to Sawyer, it is worth noting that when Whitman took on the Washington newspaper dailies to defend Peter Doyle's brother, a policeman who was widely criticized for arresting a young boy on charges of theft, he was sharply critical of the "increasing swarms of juvenile thieves & vagabonds who infest the streets of Washington." Martin G. Murray, "Whitman Takes on D.C.'s Dailies," *Yale University Library Gazette* 70 (October 1995), 50. Since "vagabond" was a pseudonym of one of the writers at Pfaff's, his remark about "vagabonds who infest the streets of Washington" may signal his shift away from the New York City Pfaffians.

[18] Ralph Waldo Emerson to Salmon P. Chase, January 10, 1863 (*WWA*).

generally."[19] Despite seeking eminent allies, Whitman found it harder than many others to land a salaried job in Washington (John Burroughs was able to secure one in two weeks while it took Whitman two years to find a suitable position). John Trowbridge, a friend trying to assist Whitman, gleaned the problem from Salmon P. Chase, Secretary of the Treasury: the poet's "writings have given him a bad repute," Chase explained, "and I should not know what sort of place to give to such a man."[20] It may be relevant that Chase was raised by his uncle, Ohio's Episcopal Bishop, and remained deeply religious, like many anti-slavery leaders.

In seeking a clerk's job in Washington during the war years, Whitman was joining the many other mostly white men predominantly from eastern states who sought the posts vacated by those who joined the Union army and the new posts being created by a rapidly expanding bureaucracy and increasingly centralized government. When Whitman joined the federal workforce it was both growing in size and changing in nature. In 1859 there were only eighteen female names in the *Register of All Officers and Agents, Civil, Military, and Naval, in the Service of the United States*, all of them employed at the Government Hospital for the Insane. By 1871 that figure had risen to over 900 women, an increase of over 5,000 percent.[21] The number of African American men and women employed is harder to judge because of gaps in the evidentiary record for many of the lower level jobs African Americans were typically limited to—scrub women, sweepers, office messengers and the like. Cindy Sondik Aron notes that the "very small number of blacks who achieved federal jobs was testimony to the racism endemic in Washington," though when African Americans did receive federal jobs they worked alongside white federal workers (it was only in the administration of Woodrow Wilson that federal officials openly suggested racially segregated offices for various Washington agencies).[22] Whitman joined the federal workforce when people from a variety of states (after the war, including from the former Confederate states) flocked in large numbers to Washington where jobs of intellectual interest and attractive remuneration were often hotly contested for.

Once experienced rather than imagined, clerking agreed with Whitman as letters sent to his mother and to his English ally, poet, editor, and full-time

---

[19] Walt Whitman to Thomas Jefferson Whitman, February 13, 1863 (WWA).
[20] Quoted in Gay Wilson Allen, *The Solitary Singer: A Critical Biography of Walt Whitman* (1955; New York: New York University Press, 1967), 311.
[21] Ziparo, *This Grand Experiment*, 1.   [22] Aron, 30.

civil servant, William Michael Rossetti indicate. Whitman was certainly more contented with his clerking positions than many of his acquaintances, including his close friend William Douglas O'Connor, who worked as a clerk of the Lighthouse Board in the Treasury Department and Charles Eldridge, his former publisher, who worked for the Internal Revenue Bureau, also in the Treasury Department. Even as O'Connor and Eldridge complained bitterly about their positions (fitting the melancholic model of the clerk described by Thomas Augst), Whitman in contrast enjoyed his work, particularly in the Attorney General's office, for a host of practical reasons.[23] Although briefly stationed in the Freedman's Savings Bank Building, Whitman for the most part was situated in the Treasury Building. There he labored within a seven-room suite with the attorney general, assistant attorney general, and nine clerks. These quarters became a retreat suitable for after-hours study, too, with warmth and an overhead reading lamp (a "splendid astral-lamp, to burn gas by a tube"), and a library of law books and more than 500 miscellaneous volumes. He told his mother: "I am getting many books for the...office Library...that I have long wanted to read at my leisure— & can get any book I want, in reason."[24] For a writer who was chronically short of paper and known to compose drafts on discarded tax forms, repurposed incoming letters, and even pieces of wallpaper, it is notable that he was writing on Department of Justice stationery, blank except for the letterhead, as late as 1890, nearly two decades after he had left employment there.[25] He also drafted poems and essays on the flip side of documents that were for various reasons rejected material from the office. In such cases the blending of his roles as bureaucrat and poet inheres in individual artifacts.[26] The attorney general's office also served as his literary postal address.[27]

[23] Thomas Augst, *The Clerk's Tale: Young Men and Moral Life in Nineteenth-Century America* (Chicago, IL: University of Chicago Press, 2003), 207–54.
[24] Walt Whitman to Louisa Van Velsor Whitman, March 12, 1867 (*WWA*).
[25] Walt Whitman to William Sloane Kennedy, November 12, 1890 (Charles E. Feinberg Collection, the Library of Congress, Washington, DC).
[26] See, for example, the poetry manuscript "Crusades." On the verso is a cancelled list of references to letters in the *House Executive Documents, 38th Cong.* which correspond to several individual documents transcribed on the cancelled versos of other crusade manuscripts also in the Harned collection. Another example is an item held at the University of Texas: on one side we have a draft letter in an unknown hand written for the US Attorney General to the Little & Brown publishing company. On the flip side of the leaf, we find a title, note, and verse fragment, approximately twenty-five words, probably related to the poem "Warble for Lilac-Time," which was first published in *The Galaxy* in May 1870. See Whitman Archive ID: tex.00045 in the "Catalog of the Walt Whitman Literary Manuscripts in the Walt Whitman Collection, Harry Ransom Humanities Research Center at the University of Texas at Austin" (*WWA*).
[27] When Whitman requested thirty copies of *Broadway*, a magazine that printed his poem "Whispers of Heavenly Death," he asked for the shipment to go to "my address, Attorney Gen's office, here." Walt Whitman to Edmund Routledge, March 22, 1868 (*WWA*). On another

As a clerk, Whitman found himself acting as an *amanuensis*, a role he also played when he wrote letters for Civil War soldiers who could not write for themselves because of illness, injury, or illiteracy. The word has its roots in two different structures of authority, one embodied, one textual: slavery and signatures. In ancient Rome, the word *amanuensis* applied to "a slave at hand" performing any command; it was also applied to a trusted servant acting as a personal secretary.[28] The word can also refer to someone who signs a document on behalf of an authority. In his poetry, Whitman's protean sense of self famously inhabits (or appropriates) a slave's identity in "Song of Myself" and does the same more effectively in the draft manuscripts of "The Sleepers."[29]

In his role as an amanuensis, Whitman inhabited a space that in its structural subordination had more of a rhetorical than an actual similarity to the life of an enslaved person. Nonetheless, the language of closing with "your obedient servant," widely used in the scribal documents, was sometimes visualized before the war in terms of slavery. For example, in 1843 when the amateur artist, adventurer, and architectural designer J. Goldsborough Bruff composed a letter to the National Institute for the Promotion of Science, he employed a visual shorthand, substituting small drawings for words. When he wrote "Your very obedient" he followed it with a pictograph of a black man, hat removed, bending low and at a steep incline in a gravity-defying show of humility and deference to an unseen master (see Figure 4.2). It is not clear that Whitman knew Bruff, though he, too, worked in the Treasury Building and was responsible for the ornamentation on the south and west wings of the building itself near the location of Whitman's office.

As a salaried clerk, did Whitman—the poet who had asked "How dare ... an obedient man write poems for These States?"—in some sense become "owned" by the Republican government, with the self-described poet of democracy now

occasion, he gave instructions to "Please unlock the case where my books & pamphlets are in Mr. French's room & send me by bearer 6 copies 'Democratic Vistas.'" Walt Whitman to Mr. French, [April 14, 1873] (*WWA*).

[28] "In Latin, the phrase servus a manu translates loosely as 'slave with secretarial duties.' (The noun manu, meaning 'hand,' gave us words such as manuscript, originally meaning a document written or typed by hand.) In the seventeenth century the second part of this phrase was borrowed into English to create amanuensis, a word for a person who is employed (willingly) to do the important but sometimes menial work of transcribing the words of another." See https://www.merriam-webster.com/dictionary/amanuensis

[29] See Folsom, "Lucifer and Ethiopia: Whitman, Race, and Poetics before the Civil War and After," in David S. Reynolds, ed., *A Historical Guide to Walt Whitman* (New York: Oxford University Press, 2000), 45–53 and my *To Walt Whitman, America* (Chapel Hill, NC: University of North Carolina Press, 2004), 9–36.

Figure 4.2. Detail of letter from J. Goldsborough Bruff to Francis Markoe, August 14, 1843. This public domain image was obtained from the Smithsonian Institution.

subordinate within a hierarchical order outside the marketplace?[30] Nearly 250 documents Whitman inscribed as a clerk close with a formulaic declaration of subservience: "your obedient servant." In contrast, there is not a single instance of Whitman signing this way as a private citizen. Of course, the upper-class language of self-deprecating servitude had been a conventional sign-off since the emergence of commodified gentility in the late seventeenth century. In the eighteenth century, the Anglo-American male gentry were known to greet or depart from each other with mutual declarations of being one another's "obedient servant." With the emergence of the civil servant, many from class backgrounds unfamiliar with niceties of deference, Anglo-American letter writing manuals proliferated and conventions of letter writing were explicitly tied to forms of general polite behavior.[31]

---

[30] *LG* (1860–61), 109.
[31] See Deirdre M. Mahoney, "Bibliography of Nineteenth-Century Letter Writing Manuals" in *Letter-Writing Manuals and Instruction*, ed. Carol Poster and Linda C. Mitchell (Columbia, SC: University of South Carolina Press, 2007), 319–26.

The act of repeatedly inscribing a closing such as "your obedient servant" no doubt had some effect on Whitman. Even if he told himself he wasn't speaking in his own voice, the compartmentalization of a mind is rarely so complete as to prevent seepage. For Whitman literal writing (the material marks he made) and literary writing (his development of verbal content) were never entirely separate processes. What was crucial was that if he believed mercantile clerks lost their individuality in conforming to the genteel dictates of fashion and profitably pleasing others, government clerks could claim that they lost their individuality in serving the broader public good.

A revealing language of decorum certainly appears in Whitman's letter to John Binckley, Assistant Attorney General, when the poet initially declined to seek the position of pardon clerk. Here as his own person, as an employee, rather than as a ventriloquist or copyist, he wrote on March 24, 1868:

> In reference to the brief conversation between us a few days since, allow me in candor to say, that I should decidedly prefer to retain my present post as Record Clerk, the duties of which I feel that I can fulfil properly—& that I would therefore, as far as my personal choice is concerned, wish to be not thought of in view of the pardon clerkship.
>
> Only in case of urgent wish on your or [the attorney general's] part, would I deem it my duty to waive the preference mentioned, & obey your commands.[32]

At one level, this is routine employee-employer correspondence. Yet it is also fascinating as written by a poet who once claimed "I cock my hat as I please indoors or out" and asked (with the obvious answer being "no"): "Shall I venerate and be ceremonious?" Of course, the contextual situation of these varying utterances is entirely different. Did a poet, especially an unconventional one like Whitman, risk being constrained when he asked for allowances from a stultifying bureaucracy? His role as a clerk threatened to restrict his individuality, not least by forcing upon him some of the genteel tics he lampooned in *Democratic Vistas*: "Do you call those genteel little creatures American poets? Do you term that perpetual, pistareen, paste-pot work, American art, American drama, taste, verse?"[33] But his ceremonious official language in this case was not only for politeness's

---

[32] Walt Whitman to John M. Binckley, March 24, 1868 (*WWA*).
[33] Whitman, *Democratic Vistas* in *Complete Prose Works* (Philadelphia, PA: David McKay, 1892), 225 (*WWA*).

sake; it was designed to conceal real political differences. The position of pardon clerk dealt with sensitive matters, and Whitman certainly noticed in December 1867 when "one of the clerks, the youngest, was dismissed, (or suspended,) lately for selling some information about pardons to the Herald—the Attorney Gen'l [Henry Stanbery] was very mad about it, & gave him a sharp talking to."[34] The pardon clerks were responsible for processing appeals by ex-Confederates who wanted to regain the ability to vote, hold public office, acquire property, sue in court, and exercise other powers they had lost. Andrew Johnson's policy was to approve nearly all pardon applications he received, and the attorney general, through whom applications were funneled, did not want troublesome attention.[35] Whitman, after initially declining to seek the position of pardon clerk during the Johnson administration, then later applied for the position, in January 1871, during the Grant administration, though the position was left vacant. Ed Folsom has argued that "this is where Whitman wanted to be, helping reintegrate Confederates into the Union," but the picture was more complicated than this implies, with Whitman's attitude altering with the different presidential administrations.[36] His hesitancy to take the position earlier, and his application only when he served under Attorney General Akerman, a fierce opponent of the Ku Klux Klan, is notable.

This is not to minimize Whitman's belief in a public policy of leniency, whether toward Confederates or anyone else. Early in life as a journalist, he opposed the death penalty, and in a late-life discussion with Traubel over the Haymarket Affair massacre, he again indicated he "did not want to see [the defendants] executed—I wanted to see them reprieved." When Traubel asked him to explain, he said: "'Well—much for reasons I would have urged for Jefferson Davis and those associated with him: for our own sakes, all our sakes—America's, humanity's. But the men were hung.... I never wished the severe penalty enforced: to me, too, it was grievous.'"[37] In fact, his awareness of his personal tendencies may have given him pause in the process of applying for position of pardon clerk in both administrations.

---

[34] Walt Whitman to Louisa Van Velsor Whitman, January 15, 1867 (*WWA*).

[35] Initially, Johnson was purposefully slow to approve pardons. Whitman noted that "there are between 4 & 5000 pardons issued from this Office, but only about 200 have been signed by the President—The rest he is letting wait, till he gets good & ready—." Walt Whitman to Alfred Pratt, August 26, 1865 (*WWA*).

[36] Ed Folsom, "'A Yet More Terrible and More Deeply Complicated Problem': Walt Whitman, Race, Reconstruction, and American Democracy," *American Literary History*, 30 (2018), 548.

[37] *WWWC*, 2: 486.

An unpublished pair of poetic lines, probably drafted around 1860 when Whitman experimented with aphoristic poems called "Thoughts," illustrate again that even before he began his government work he was concerned with the interplay of public and private roles:

> What would it bring you to be elected and take your place in the capitol?
> I elect you to understand yourself; that is what all the offices in the republic could not do.[38]

Here "offices" do not advance and may actually undermine self-understanding. How then did Whitman navigate the demands of these years? How did it change him not just to speak within the government, but to speak as the government, to embody the government, to enact policy and law through his fingertips?

One answer comes from the way he found some of the comradeship that he told Tom Sawyer he worried about losing, outside the hospitals. On the whole, Whitman admired his fellow federal employees. He asserted that "honesty" was the "prevailing atmosphere" in government offices. When a friend laughed skeptically, Whitman retorted:

> Let me explain that. I do not refer to swell officials—the men who wear the decorations, get the fat salaries (they are mostly dubious enough, though not all): I refer to the average clerks, the obscure crowd, who after all run the government: they are on the square. I have not known hundreds—I have known thousands—of them. I went to Washington as everybody goes there prepared to see everything done with some furtive intention, but I was disappointed—pleasantly disappointed. I found the clerks mainly earnest, mainly honest, anxious to do the right thing—very hard working, very attentive. Why, the clerk jobs are often the worst slavery: the clerks are not overpaid, they are underpaid. Washington is corrupt—has its own peculiar mixture of evil with its own peculiar mixture of good—but the evil is mostly with the upper crust—the people who have reputations—who are better than other people.[39]

---

[38] "What would it bring you," The Henry W. and Albert A. Berg Collection of English and American Literature, The New York Public Library.
[39] *WWWC*, 1: 148.

Whitman felt enough kinship with his fellow clerks to support in November 1867 a "memorial," as it was called, appealing to Congress to increase their wages. Pay had stagnated since the beginning of the war, even as the cost of living rose dramatically. Whitman signed for the Attorney General's office, joining with other departments in the bid for an increase. He signed in solidarity and in sympathy with the claim that the "amount of money imperatively demanded for the subsistence of ourselves and our families is rather increased than diminished, and we still find it impossible, with the most rigid economy, to meet the demands made upon us."[40] The debate over the pay increase of 1867 initially snagged, though it was ultimately approved, on the question of why women were paid less than men for the same work, marking an important early instance of the debate over equal pay for equal work.

In other circumstances, Whitman noted to Rossetti that his salary left him with "quite a free margin."[41] He also explained that he could live on one-third of his salary and that he gave two-thirds to others (this claim seems plausible for the war years but unlikely afterward). In a draft journalistic puff piece on the "Wealth of Poets," apparently never published, Whitman indicated that the salary he received was more than adequate for his own modest needs. His complaint in "Wealth of Poets" is not about his government pay but about the lack of the "first shilling of return from his poetic volumes." In contrast, he noted that "Tennyson and Victor Hugo are wealthy, and Browning and Swinburne receive handsome and regular incomes." Moreover, American writers "Emerson and Whittier are well off, and Longfellow and Bryant are rich." Walt Whitman alone, this piece insists, "keep[s] up the tradition of narrow means and wide afflatus."[42] Whitman often overstated his neglect and sometimes his financial straits. In fact, it would be accurate to see his government work as achieving what his friend and champion O'Connor originally sought for him: "a regular income, &c, leaving you time to attend to the soldiers, to your poems, &c,— in a word, what Archimedes wanted, a place on which to rest the lever."[43] Nathaniel Hawthorne may have seen labor in the Customs house, a reasonably common job for writers with political friends, as extinguishing his ability to write, but Whitman was more prone to see government work as

---

[40] "Memorial to Congress of the Clerks and Other Civil Employees," National Archives, Record Group 233, HR 40A, F2.10- HR 40A, F 2.11. Email from Jessica Ziparo to the author, April 19, 2019.
[41] Walt Whitman to William Michael Rossetti, January 30, 1872.   [42] *NUPM*, 3: 961.
[43] William D. O'Connor to Walt Whitman, December 30, 1864 (*WWA*).

enabling. In 1872, he went so far as to comment on the advantages of Washington as a winter residence and to list the authors living there. His list emphasized not the poet in the garret but those who, like himself, were employed in the federal government (postings "not incongenial with literary pursuits") and the surrounding apparatus of newspapers, magazines, and major cultural institutions, including the Library of Congress and the Smithsonian.[44]

In viewing Whitman's efforts to constitute a new circle of comrades, one can look both to his lodgings and to his office. In both locales, most of his interactions were with white men. There were no women in the attorney general's relatively small office (the Department of Interior, where Whitman worked in the Bureau of Indian Affairs, was much larger, and did employ women copyists until Harlan fired most of the female clerks when he became secretary of the interior in 1865.[45] Whitman commented that Harlan was a "sincere, often deadly sincere, though a fiercely impossible bigot."[46]) The poet boarded with two women clerks in 1870: Mrs. Newton Benedict, his landlady, worked in the Treasury Department; another white woman with the last name of Asenath, a thirty-seven-year old clerk, also boarded there. Like Whitman, these two women were originally from New York. Also living with the Benedicts were nineteen-year-old Hattie Gross and twenty-three-year-old Winnie Robinson, each listed as "black female domestic." Black women (and men) were increasingly employed in the federal government too, but in jobs that had less political fluctuation and drew primarily from local populations. Whitman interacted, then, with white women and with African Americans who embodied the US government through their actions and employment status, even as their access to suffrage and other basic rights was roundly denied. As discussed in the next chapter, such issues are key as Whitman hopes to see, even as he sometimes muddies, the vistas ahead.

A considerable amount of information about the Attorney General's office and those employed there can be gleaned from a long letter Whitman inscribed for John M. Binckley, Assistant Attorney General, on January 24, 1868, in response to a thirty-seven question circular from Representative T. A. Jenckes of Rhode Island, a conservative Republican and a member of

---

[44] Martin G. Murray, "Two Pieces of Uncollected Whitman Journalism: 'Washington as a Central Winter Residence' and 'The Authors of Washington,'" *Walt Whitman Quarterly Review* 20 (Winter/Spring 2003), 151–76.
[45] Mary Elizabeth Massey, *Bonnet Brigades* (New York: Knopf, 1966), 133.
[46] *WWWC*, 3: 470.

the Joint Select Committee of Congress on Retrenchment, who sought information from all department heads (Jenckes became known as the "Father of Civil Service Reform").[47] Binckley replied that "all the subordinates of this office are under my control. Their grades and classes are as follows: One Law Clerk, one Chief Clerk, two fourth-class clerks, three third-class clerks, two first-class clerks, and two laborers—being eleven in all, of whom one third-class clerk, and one first-class clerk are temporary."[48] The pay scale of the government distinguished between first-, second-, third-, and fourth-class clerks. First class clerks earned $1200 annually, a figure first established in 1853 and that remained in place when Whitman began work in the Department of the Interior in 1865. A promotion entailed an increase of $200 in each of the next categories. Binckley's further answers to Jenckes are also intriguing:

> 19. The Law Clerk was a clerk in one of the Bureaus of the Treasury Department. The Chief Clerk was a merchant. One fourth-class clerk was a printer, the other a stenographer and lawyer; one third-class clerk, a clerk—one, an author, and another a teacher and stenographer. Of the first-class clerks, one was a soldier, and the other for many years a messenger. The Law Clerk and opinion clerk have both pursued a regular course of study in the law,—and the latter also of the art of stenographic writing.
>
> 20. No appointment has been made since I entered this office for political considerations.[49]
>
> 23. One was a soldier for three years in the union armies. One was prominently identified with the Sanitary organizations in the field. One was a printer. One was an author.—The allotted labor of each clerk being in great degree different, no standard of comparison of efficiency in the same class would be satisfactory.
>
> 25. One of our subordinates is under twenty-five years of age; between that age and thirty, one; between thirty and forty, four, (or, including myself,

---

[47] Ari Hoogenboom, "Thomas A. Jenckes and Civil Service Reform," *The Mississippi Valley Historical Review*, 47, no. 4 (1961), 636 and 647.

[48] John M. Binckley to T. A. Jenckes, January 24, 1868 (*WWA*).

[49] The Jenckes bill of 1866–67 sought to curtail government spending and to abandon the practice of patronage appointees in favor of nonpartisan employees retained because of their knowledge or talents. President Ulysses Grant was reputed to be in favor of the Jenckes bill, though his administration was only partially able to institute civil service reform.

five;)—between forty and fifty, two; between fifty and sixty, one. Of the messengers, (colored,) one is of middle age, and the other younger.

Assuming Binckley was accurate in his account, Whitman was the second oldest person in a mostly middle-aged and white-collar office. And like so much else in the US at this time, the work in the Attorney General's office was segregated and stratified by race and gender. Jenckes's inquiries served his aim of civil service reform—an effort both to curtail the rising cost of government and to abandon the patronage system for one dependent on qualifications such as efficiency and aptitude for the work.[50] Jenckes is also known for introducing a bill that created the Department of Justice in 1870. Although many discussions of the emergence of the Department of Justice connect it with efforts to safeguard the rights of newly emancipated African Americans, the creation of this new department resulted more directly from efforts to offset the ineffectiveness of a dispersed legal force and to reduce expenditures. The creation of the Department of Justice ultimately led to the elimination of approximately one-third of the legal staff used by the federal government (because the hiring of outside counsel—earlier much relied upon—was disallowed). These losses were hardly offset by the creation of the Office of the Solicitor General, despite the qualifications and strong commitment to civil rights of its first occupant, Benjamin Helm Bristow. The net loss of legal personnel came precisely when cases of abuses of civil rights were rising sharply in numbers.[51] As Jed Handelsman Shugerman has noted, Jenckes's committee "lacked any members who cared deeply about black civil rights" and that "if you came to Washington to shrink the federal government and to roll back Reconstruction, you probably were interested in getting on the Joint Select Committee on Retrenchment."[52]

Whitman regularly relied on other government workers for reports, information, and even topics for poems. William Conant Church, one of the editors of the New York monthly literary magazine *The Galaxy*, enlisted O'Connor in persuading Whitman to write "Carol of Harvest," a poem celebrating the 1867 harvest reaped by soldiers now returned from the war. This was hardly the only time O'Connor fed material to Whitman: "Glad you got the Report on Armored Vessels," O'Connor said on another

---

[50] For a succinct summary of some of the issues surrounding civil service reform, see Ron Chernow, *Grant* (New York: Penguin Press, 2017), 730–33.
[51] Jed Handelsman Shugerman, "The Creation of the Department of Justice: Professionalization without Civil Rights or Civil Service," *Stanford Law Review*, 121 (2014), 123.
[52] Shugerman, 143–44.

occasion. "I thought it might yield hints for poems. At all events, it gives one a good idea of what the Monitors are and can do."⁵³ Whitman also corresponded with F. A. Walker, Acting Superintendent of the Census Office in the Department of the Interior, to get demographic statistics. The poet wished to know "the number of persons, male and female, in the United States, between the ages of 5 and 20."⁵⁴ (His interest here is consistent with his life-long fascination with factual information—the same impulse that led to his compilation of a massive homemade Geography notebook—as he sought to ground his poetry and cultural criticism on the most solid footing possible.) At still another time, Whitman sent a copy of his "Proud Music of the Sea-Storm," published in the *Atlantic Monthly* in February 1869, to Julius Bing, a clerk of the Joint Select Committee on Retrenchment in 1867 and 1868 and an energetic advocate for civil service reform.⁵⁵ In response, Bing wrote a lengthy letter outlining in remarkable detail how Whitman should write a poem about the Child Crusades. The poem was attempted by Whitman but never realized.⁵⁶

In the Attorney General's office, and to a surprising degree in his poetry as well, writing was accomplished through the bustle of *collective* effort. As the work of many hands, the scribal documents help adjust our view of nineteenth-century textual production. These documents remind us to be wary of our intellectual habits, editorial history, and conventions of scholarship to the extent that they obscure the collaborative nature of literary production generally. The myth of Whitman as a solitary singer or individual authorial genius may retain some appeal, but it is more accurate to see him as a networked creator, not only in New York City, but in

---

⁵³ William D. O'Connor to Walt Whitman, August 13, 1864 (*WWA*). The item O'Connor had sent to Whitman was *Report of the Secretary of the Navy in Relation to Armored Vessels* (Washington: Government Printing Office, 1864).

⁵⁴ Francis A. Walker to Walt Whitman, 1871 (*WWA*).

⁵⁵ Julius Bing to Walt Whitman, January 21, 1869 (Thomas Harned Collection, The Library of Congress, Washington, DC). Bing (dates unknown) served as the clerk of the Joint Select Committee on Retrenchment in 1867 and 1868 and ghostwrote the 1868 report "Civil Service of the United States" before being appointed diplomatic agent for Crete later that year. A major advocate for reform of the Civil Service, Bing wrote a series of articles on the civil service for the *North American Review* and *Putnam's Magazine* in 1867-68. For more on Bing, about whom little is known, see Ari Hoogenboom, *Outlawing the Spoils: A History of the Civil Service Reform Movement 1865-1883* (Urbana, IL: University of Illinois Press, 1968), especially 40-49. Although Whitman must have sent at least one letter to Bing, since Bing thanked Whitman for sending a copy of the *Atlantic Monthly* that included Whitman's "Proud Music of the Sea-Storm" (the poem was published in the February 1869 issue of the magazine), no additional correspondence between Bing and Whitman has been identified to date.

⁵⁶ Whitman's notes on the topic and trial lines are in the Thomas B. Harned Collection of the Library of Congress.

Washington.⁵⁷ However, the marks of that network are oddly erased by the very nature of his job. For example, a July 14, 1868, letter in Whitman's hand, having to do with pensions, has a marginal note, also in Whitman's hand, saying: "This letter has been withdrawn and cancelled—is to be considered as never having been written. W.W."⁵⁸ (see Figure 4.3). The practice of cancelling a document is straightforward. However, the phrasing here is curious, perhaps even nonsensical. How can one look at writing, one's own especially, and regard it as never having been written? But the

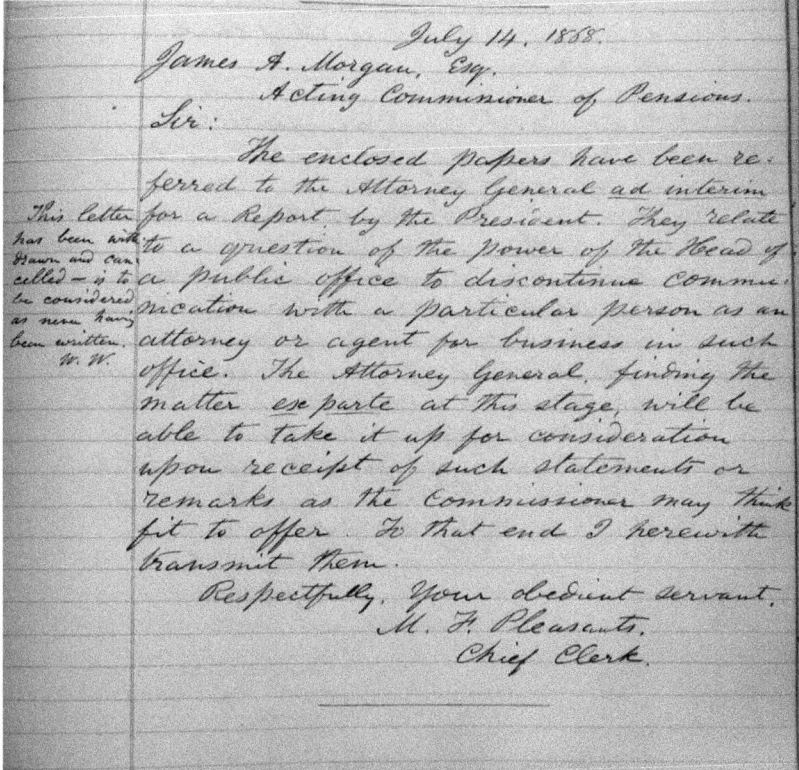

Figure 4.3. Letter from M. T. Pleasants to James A. Morgan, July 14, 1868, inscribed by Walt Whitman. Courtesy National Archives and Records Administration, Washington, DC.

---

⁵⁷ Ed Whitley, "Networked Literary History and the Bohemians of Antebellum New York," *American Literary History*, 29 (2017), 287–306.

⁵⁸ Matthew F. Pleasants to Benjamin Helm Smith, July 14, 1868 (*WWA*).

comment serves as an apt description of how Whitman's most collaborative work as a scribe has been treated—as cancelled, non-consequential, writing that somehow left no mark either on the writer or the world.

Late in life, when Whitman was asked about his government work, he told Traubel that he had been "put in charge of the Attorney General's letters." Whitman did not specify which one of the several attorneys general he served, perhaps implying that it was a common practice for them all. Whitman continued by saying "cases were put into my hands—small cases: the Attorney General could not attend to them all so passed some of them over to me to examine, report upon, sum up." At other times, Whitman is more specific in his remarks to Traubel, as in these comments about Henry Stanbery, the attorney general under Andrew Johnson, both of whom were opponents of Reconstruction, before Stanbery stepped down in order to defend Johnson during his impeachment. Given their opposition to Reconstruction, it is disconcerting to hear Whitman tell Traubel: "I was the Attorney General's clerk there," he said, "and did a good deal of writing. [Stanbery] seemed to like my opinions, judgment. So a good part of my work was to spare *him* work—to go over the correspondence,—give him the juice, substance of affairs—avoiding all else."[59] Of course, it is possible that Stanbery liked Whitman's judgement on matters distinct from Reconstruction policy, but it is also true that no one in the chain of command from Johnson to Stanbery to Whitman forcefully advocated for black civil rights or black suffrage at this time.

Whitman was more than just a passive functionary in his government work, more than a mindless copyist or neutral channel unaware of the import of the documents at hand. On October 28, 1866, he wrote a letter to Attorney General Stanbery successfully petitioning for a pardon for Erastus Otis Parker on the grounds that "the whole theory on which he was convicted was but an inference from an inference" and that Parker had "already served four years in prison."[60] Whitman became interested in the case—Parker had been charged with seven counts of theft—and worked on it for months, upon the urging of his Brooklyn friend Abby H. Price and her family.

Without doubt, the scribal documents were once present in Whitman's mind and passed through his fingertips. Beyond that, we have uncertainty. For the scribal letters, Whitman probably acted sometimes as mere copyist

---

[59] *WWWC*, 3: 156 and 6: 147.
[60] Walt Whitman to Henry Stanbery, October 26, 1866 (*WWA*).

and other times as co-author or even author. Whitman's involvement in formulating documents (not just inscribing them) seems likely because we know his intellect and writing ability were valued by those in the office. There is evidence that some attorney generals called on Whitman to complete partially drafted material of consequence. In 1866, for example, Attorney General James Speed (much more of a radical than Stanbery) wrote to J. Hubley Ashton, his Assistant Attorney General, letting him know of plans to dedicate a bust of Abraham Lincoln in Speed's home town of Louisville, Kentucky. Too busy with other obligations to complete his speech, Speed asked Ashton to "see our friend Walt Whitman and ask him whether he will take my rough draft of an address and revise and finish it.... I have a notion that if he has the time and is in the mood he can do it better than any man I know."[61] Collaboration was vital to Whitman's authorship in and beyond the office.[62]

Whitman at times posed as if he were lackadaisical about his government work (an extension of his poetic pose as an observer inclined to "lean and loafe" at his ease). He told Abby Price while he was working for the Attorney General: "I am still in the same Office— find my work mild & agreeable, & the place one remarkably well suited to a lazy, elderly, literary gentleman."[63] Yet this version of himself was as limited and misleading as his earlier claim to be a "rough." It was often observed, for example, that he left the office by mid afternoon, but in fact the regular hours for clerks were 9–3.00 p.m., as John Binckley noted in his letter to Jenckes describing his office staff. Certainly when Whitman found a temporary replacement for himself in 1870 so he could oversee the publication of several books, his substitute did not find the work easy, as Whitman noted to Peter Doyle: "I have rec'd a letter from John Rowland who is working for me in the office, complaining that he has to work too hard."[64] Whitman told his mother that he personally preferred intense work over slack days: "We are all quite busy to-day in the

---

[61] M. Lynda Ely, "Memorializing Lincoln: Whitman's 'Revision' of James Speed's Oration Upon the Inauguration of the Bust of Abraham Lincoln," *Walt Whitman Quarterly Review* 14 (Spring 1997), 176.

[62] For an extended consideration of Whitman and collaboration, see my "'Many long dumb voices... clarified and transfigured': The Walt Whitman Archive and the Scholarly Edition in the Digital Age" in *Nuovi annali della Scuola speciale per archivisti e bibliotecari* 28 (December 2014), 241–56. Also relevant is Kenneth M. Price and Janel Cayer, "'It might be us speaking instead of him!'": Individuality, Collaboration, and the Networked Forces Contributing to 'Whitman,'" *Walt Whitman Quarterly Review* 33 (2015), 114–24.

[63] Walt Whitman to Abby H. Price, March 13, 1867 (*WWA*).

[64] Walt Whitman to Peter Doyle, September 9, 1870 (*WWA*).

office... we have to fly around— Well I enjoy it just as well when I am busy during office hours, or rather I like it better."⁶⁵

His closest friends and family asked frequently for assistance based on his government position. These people included his brother George, who hoped he might get him a job inspecting pipes for the city of Washington; and William H. Mills, Jr., a soldier boy who hoped to be remembered by Whitman (addressed as "Uncle") and to land a position in the Interior department. In an exchange that points to Whitman's engagement in political lobbying, or at least bureaucratic influence, as well as his continuing hostility to gentility, he turned down a sizable paycheck. On March 25, 1867, Abby Price wrote "to ask your assistance in behalf of Our Ruffle Manufacture and if you succeed in doing what we ask, or in getting it done I am authorised to offer you a 1000 dollar check as soon as it is done! think of that. It is only a simple act of justice." In response, he told her there was "little or no chance of getting Congress to pass... a special resolution or law putting the ruffles on the list of exempts—There is no Committee of Ways & Means yet appointed in the H[ouse] of R[epresentatives]—True, any member could offer such a Bill... but there are too many, both in House & Senate, who would almost certainly object—one objection would be that ruffles are matters of extra ornament &c. &c. and ought to pay a tax, if any thing does." Though Whitman did not pursue the offer of money, he said he would "try what I can do— I will see a few of the members, forthwith—I have one in my mind, I think may be the best one I can get to offer a Bill, & if he is willing." He added, "Had I known it when the Committee & House were cooking the Bill, I have no doubt I could have got it put in with the... shirt-bosoms, &c.—But that's poor consolation."⁶⁶

Whitman felt as if he was treated with "'distinguished consideration' by all the Attorney Gen's—Mr. Speed, Mr. Stanbery, & the present one Mr. Browning—I couldn't wish to have better bosses."⁶⁷ However, there was tension with a fellow worker, Matthew F. Pleasants, who served initially as pardon clerk—a new position created to help address the appeals to reinstate the power of those who had sworn allegiance to the Confederacy—and then became chief clerk in the attorney general's office. On October 9, 1868, O'Connor wrote cryptically to Whitman: "I had a long and free

---

⁶⁵ Walt Whitman to Louisa Van Velsor Whitman, August 13, 1868 (*WWA*).
⁶⁶ Abby H. Price to Walt Whitman, [March 25, 1867] and Walt Whitman to Abby H. Price, March 27, 1867 (*WWA*).
⁶⁷ Walt Whitman to Abby H. Price, April 10, 1868 (*WWA*).

talk... about Mat Pleasants... in connexion with you." The conversation was with Attorney General William M. Evarts and J. Hubley Ashton, Assistant Attorney General, and the situation made O'Connor "feel quite anxious, but I guess all's right, while Ashton is there. Pleasants is a miserable devil. I wish I had power in that office for a little while. I'd put a spoke in the wheel of his vendetta, which would carry it and him to a safe distance."[68] Ashton and O'Connor, both with anti-slavery roots and both strong supporters of Reconstruction, were more radical than Pleasants, an Andrew Johnson appointee. At this time, as O'Connor noted, "there have been many dismissals of clerks in the Departments," perhaps an indication that Pleasants was angling to have Whitman forced out. It is not clear if the nature of the problem between Whitman and Pleasants was personal or political, but the retrenchment underway at this time heightened tensions for federal workers generally.

Whitman and his friends had reason to be concerned about any threat to his livelihood. He had lost his job with the Bureau of Indian Affairs in 1865 when James Harlan, head of the Department of the Interior and a former Methodist minister, discovered a copy of the 1860-61 edition of *Leaves of Grass*, the famous Blue Book, at Whitman's desk. What Harlan, a Lincoln appointee, saw as unsavory is now regarded as the single most valuable and informative copy of the 1860-61 *Leaves of Grass* in existence: this was Whitman's personal copy, heavily annotated in anticipation of a never-realized future edition. Harlan was offended by what he took to be the immorality of *Leaves*.[69] Whitman's firing and Harlan's refusal to reinstate him upon appeal led to O'Connor's spirited and influential pamphlet "The Good Gray Poet." This defense of the poet shaped Whitman's reputation and to some extent his own subsequent self-depictions.

The juxtaposition of Whitman's scribal documents and the Blue Book can be illuminating for literary studies generally because of the way they have been read (or more accurately not read). In the case of the scribal documents, this neglect results from their apparent non-literary and non-authorial status, and in the case of the Blue Book, the neglect results from its existence outside of the temporalities and material forms (final

---

[68] William O'Connor to Walt Whitman, October 9, 1868 (The Charles E. Feinberg Collection of Walt Whitman, The Library of Congress).
[69] This is the usual interpretation of these events, though Harlan later defended himself by saying he was merely downsizing the office. For a view of the events more favorable to Harlan, see Johnson Brigham, *James Harlan* (Iowa City, IA: State Historical Society of Iowa, 1913), 208–10.

intentions, clear, traceable contribution to a published text) within which the work of authors has typically been understood. In some ways, they are opposites—the scribal documents are formally and materially clean yet not authorial in any clear or traditional sense; the Blue Book is formally and materially messy yet is intensely authorial with its innumerable revisions inscribed onto Whitman's own previously authored text (see Figure 4.4). Together they speak to the nature of Whitman's time in Washington, disjointed from his creative and New York-based lives in some ways, but inseparable from them in others. These documents make possible new insights about the connections among Whitman's professional, poetic, and personal lives. They also reveal the ways in which Whitman's life and actions can be mapped onto the life and actions of the country beyond his efforts to consciously make that connection. Finally they provide a spur to reflection on literary practice and priority, what kinds of things have been invisible to critics and how that blindness has affected the stories that have been told

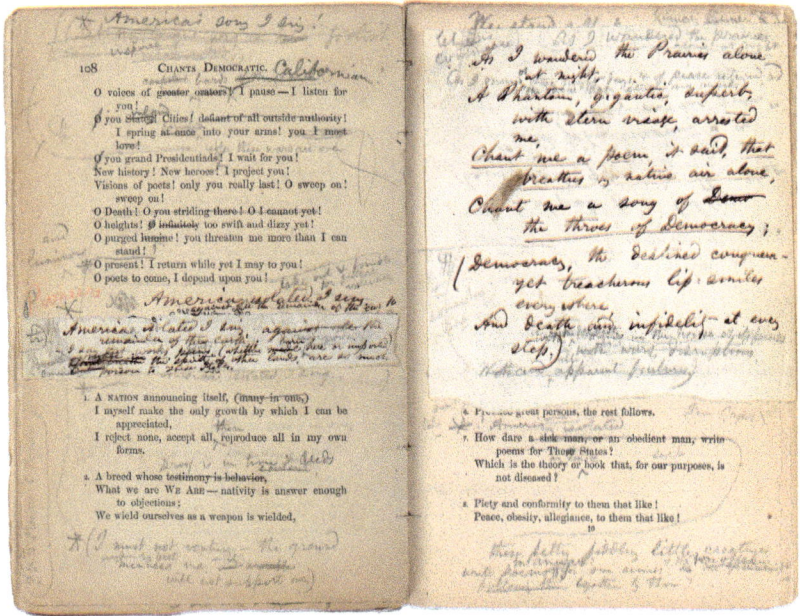

Figure 4.4. This fairly typical page from the Blue Book gives a sense of the intensity of Whitman's efforts at revision. Photo courtesy of the New York Public Library, Oscar Lion collection.

about Whitman and the stories that have been told about the processes and products of creative work in general.[70]

As noted, the Blue Book has been understudied in Whitman criticism. As a work partly composed in the US Department of the Interior, and as a work that led to his dismissal from a government post, it can be useful to evaluate the volume through the lens of Whitman's government employment specifically and of his Washington experience generally. We cannot be certain when Whitman began work on the Blue Book.[71] What is known is that the Blue Book was one of several advance copies prepared for reviewers—and probably also for Whitman's final proofreading—in May 1860, just before the third edition was published. (At least two other pre-publication copies of this edition still exist, bound in brown paper, and one of these was clearly meant to be a review copy.[72] Since the Blue Book has a frontispiece, one of the last parts of the book to be prepared, this advance copy probably did not reach Whitman until the month of publication, May 1860.[73] Arguably, then, Whitman could have begun his annotations on the Blue Book even before the publication of the 1860 edition, though it seems more likely that he began annotating the book in the latter part of 1860 or early 1861.

We do know that Whitman, still at a high creative pitch in July 1860, proposed to Thayer and Eldridge a new, cheaper edition of *Leaves of Grass*. Soon, however, Whitman's writing and publishing plans evolved into the idea for *The Banner at Day-Break*, a volume of poetry which was advertised in October 1860 but, because Thayer and Eldridge failed in December, never came to fruition. Reorienting his creative efforts after the collapse of his publisher, Whitman made considerable progress toward a new edition of *Leaves of Grass*. He drafted an introduction the following year that begins: "I commenced Leaves of Grass my thirty-sixth year, by publishing their first issue.—Twice I have issued them since, with increased matter—the present one making the fourth issue, with the latest increase. I am to-day, (May 31, 1861,) just forty-two years old—for I write this introduction on my birthday—after having looked over what I have accomplished."[74]

---

[70] For points made in this paragraph, I am indebted to email exchanges and other communications with Nicole Gray.

[71] Interestingly, in the volume of textual commentary accompanying the facsimile edition of the Blue Book published in 1968, Arthur Golden says nothing about when he thought Whitman began work on the Blue Book; *Walt Whitman's Blue Book*, ed. Arthur Golden, 2 vols. (New York: The New York Public Library, 1968), vol. 2.

[72] Scrawled on one copy at the University of Virginia are the words "Sunday Currier."

[73] I base this statement on an email from Ted Genoways, July 17, 2010.

[74] "I commenced Leaves of Grass" in *NUPM*, 4:1484.

Certainly by December 1862, before Whitman left Brooklyn to go to the Virginia front in search of his wounded brother George, he had made significant annotations on *Leaves of Grass* as he worked toward the publication of the next edition. In March 1863, having recognized that he might remain in Washington to care for wounded soldiers, he wrote to his mother expressing concern "*especially* [about] the copy of Leaves of Grass covered in blue paper, and the little MS book 'Drum Taps.'...I want them all carefully kept."[75] Interestingly, he pairs these concurrent literary efforts. By this time, then, Whitman had inscribed enough changes in the Blue Book for him to value it highly. Many more changes would be added through the remaining years of the war—and some after the war, as dated passages indicate.[76]

For Whitman, to write a text was to want to rewrite it; to compose a poem was merely to begin an ongoing process. His changes are recurrent, seemingly compulsive. Some critics are distinctly negative about Whitman's approach, arguing that it conflicts with his stated Romantic ethos. For example, Mark Bauerlein argues: "In his attempt to improve and update [*Leaves of Grass*], Whitman violates the supposedly universal, irrefutable, and immutable language of his heart, and commits the pure emotive idiom to calculated editorial emendation. By performing this self-revision, Whitman positions his creations squarely within the semiotic sequence of translations, quotations, displacements, and reinterpretations that he intended his language to halt."[77] Bauerlein seems unwilling to have artists—or at least Romantic artists—modify their writings as their views and circumstances evolve. The chain of ideas underlying Bauerlein's criticism—authoring is vital; revising is not authoring but editing; editing is sterile—flies in the face of what is known about Whitman's habitual compositional practices, and such ideas have contributed to the marginal place of the Blue Book in Whitman studies.

The Blue Book is one of the most dramatic manifestations of Whitman editing himself—recasting, rejecting, rearranging, repurposing *Leaves of Grass* on the basis of one of its earlier incarnations, the 1860–61 edition. When Whitman gave the book to Horace Traubel on May 23, 1890, he remarked: "This will help you to see how the book grew....The book is a

---

[75] Walt Whitman to Louisa Van Velsor Whitman, March 31, 1863 (*WWA*).
[76] The only explicitly dated revisions in the Blue Book are between December 1864 and July 1865. However, it seems to me highly likely—in part because of Whitman's letter to his mother of March 1863—that many of the annotations are from a much earlier date.
[77] Mark Bauerlein, *Walt Whitman and the American Idiom* (Baton Rouge, LA: Louisiana State University Press, 1991), 15.

milepost....This gives you a glimpse into the workshop."⁷⁸ The book vividly displays Whitman's compositional practices and evolving thinking. Recognizing its value, Traubel tried to make available a facsimile copy of Whitman's extensively annotated text as long ago as 1902. Those initial efforts foundered, but his goal was finally achieved in 1968 when textual editor Arthur Golden, working with financial support from Oscar Lion and the cooperation of the New York Public Library, reproduced the volume in facsimile, accompanied with a volume of commentary.⁷⁹ For more than fifty years, however, Golden's two-volume study has been insufficiently integrated into the ongoing critical discussion, in part because it was always expensive and is now out of print. *The Walt Whitman Archive*, with cooperation from the New York Public Library, now provides free Internet access to high-quality facsimile page images of the Blue Book. The *Archive* regards revisions as essential to Whitman's creativity and does not view them as mistakes or insignificant alterations reducible to a record of variants. The wider availability of this document should lead to renewed interest in Whitman's revisions and enable a reconsideration of the manifold ways the Civil War and Whitman's Washington life shaped his writing.

The Blue Book illuminates Whitman's artistic response to the war. Differing significantly from the 1867 edition of *Leaves of Grass* because many of its revisions were never implemented, the Blue Book is a unique document, a shadow edition. It is neither the 1860–61 nor the 1867 *Leaves* but something else, related to yet independent of both, and very much a product of its own time and circumstances. Just as we think of *Drum-Taps* as a volume of war poetry, we should consider the Blue Book as a volume of war-inflected poetry. The former treats war directly; the latter is everywhere shaped by the war.

We need more comprehensive studies of textuality that appreciate all features of a text, including pencil and pen markings in more than one hand, typography, ornamentation, word choice—in short, the entire range of features that contribute to textual meaning. In this case, we need to read the Blue Book as it stands as an artifact, and that of course includes the spermatoid typeface and design features inherited from the underlying 1860–61 edition. As Ed Folsom notes regarding the 1860–61 *Leaves*, "the

---

[78] This comment, in Horace Traubel's handwriting, is part of the front matter of the Blue Book. Images of the pages in question are available at the *Whitman Archive*: http://www.whitmanarchive.org/manuscripts/figures/nyp.00015.005.jpg and http://www.whitmanarchive.org/manuscripts/figures/nyp.00015.006.jpg

[79] Oscar Lion contributed $30,000 to help offset the publication costs.

letters of the... title page work figuratively to evoke sperm," and this highly suggestive typography is reinforced by the ornamentation of the book, particularly in the "Calamus" cluster of poems. Readers attentive to both the linguistic and the bibliographic codes of the Blue Book will experience an artifact that is arguably at odds with itself: the typography highlights sexuality, even as the later manuscript annotations—including Whitman's decision to mark eleven of the Calamus poems for deletion—serve to curtail that sexuality. An interesting fact about the Blue Book is the absence of any response by Whitman to the spermatoid design features of his own book (he annotated seemingly everything else, marking all but thirty-four of 456 pages), perhaps suggesting that design decisions for him were separate from content decisions. He makes no comment about typography in the Blue Book, so it is unclear if he means to reinforce, maintain, or abandon his sexually suggestive typeface and ornamentation.

Wary of biographical interpretations, Golden says little about Whitman's writing circumstances. But it is useful to think of the Blue Book as developing primarily out of the writing and emotional conditions of two distinct environments: the work-a-day world of a Washington, DC, copyist (and later clerk) and the world of the hospitals. David Haven Blake has observed: "It is hard to imagine a less auspicious time to emphasize oneself as a hyperbolic, self-involved poet than in the years after the Civil War."[80] The same of course could be said about the war years themselves. It is on just these grounds that I argue that his government work was a much more significant part of his writing life—and his emotional-mental-psychic life—than we have realized.

In fact, the government context, more than any misgivings about same sex love itself, may help explain Whitman's crises, including over the "Calamus" poems, his breakthrough account of passionate love between men, and the "perturbations" he experienced (his word to describe his mental and emotional state) over his love affair with the Washington horse-car conductor, Peter Doyle.[81] He had lost a job at the Department of the Interior over the candor of *Leaves of Grass*, and in the early post-war years he was acutely aware of continuing threats to his position through retrenchment or through the possible return of heavy-handed moralism.

---

[80] David Haven Blake, "Whitman's Ecclesiastes: The 1860 'Leaves of Grass' Cluster," *Huntington Library Quarterly* 73, no. 4 (2010), 627.

[81] It is worth noting that Whitman told O'Connor that "Drum-Taps has none of the perturbations of Leaves of Grass." See Walt Whitman to William D. O'Connor, January 6, 1865 (*WWA*).

At the time of Whitman's firing, Harlan had issued an official directive asking for the names of employees who disregarded "in their conduct, habits, and associations the rules of decorum & propriety prescribed by a Christian Civilization."[82] Whitman was well aware of this self-righteousness, and he occasionally punctured it with irony, as in the postscript to a letter of August 25, 1866, to his much younger fellow clerk, Andrew Kerr: "I must not neglect to impress upon your youthful mind—also upon that of Mr. F. Stitt [another clerk]—the original & solemn advice, 'Be *virtuous*—& you will be happy.'—from your Christian friend—*Walter*."[83] Whitman could joke about this, but he also recognized the power of prejudices and repressive forces. He would later explain to Abby Price in April 1868 that changing political circumstances were not likely to alter "the pleasantness & permanency of my situation here...unless [Benjamin Franklin] Wade, coming in power, should appoint Harlan, or some pious & modest Radical of similar stripe, to the Attorney Generalship—in which case, doubtless, I should have to tumble out."[84] Wade, a senator from Ohio, and a leading radical Republican, was a bitter opponent of Andrew Johnson and at odds with the decidedly unRadical tendencies of the Johnson administration.

It is possible, then, that Whitman's interest in and ongoing battles with sanctimonious officials explain why he preserved in his personal records an unusual letter sent to the attorney general's office that emphasizes "*Sodomy*" (see Figure 4.5). The letter was crafted to defend the notorious Confederate army Captain Henry Wirz. Born in Switzerland, Wirz ultimately became commandant of Camp Sumpter (commonly known as "Andersonville" from the nearby town of that name in Georgia) and the only man executed following the Civil War for war crimes. Fairly or not, Wirz was held responsible for the disease, starvation, and high death rate at the camp. The issue of sodomy, invoked by the letter writer, or the "crime against nature," was a weighty legal matter; it had been a capital offense in some states in the eighteenth century, and many states regulated it as a serious felony after independence. Ironically, as William Eskridge observes, "for centuries no English-language statute defined precisely what conduct constituted the crime against nature. Case law specified sodomy to include anal intercourse by a man with a woman or girl, another man or boy, or a beast;

---

[82] Jerome Loving, *Walt Whitman's Champion: William Douglas O'Connor* (College Station, TX: Texas A&M University Press, 1978), 57.
[83] Walt Whitman to Andrew Kerr, August 25, 1866 (*WWA*).
[84] Walt Whitman to Abby H. Price, April 10, 1868 (*WWA*).

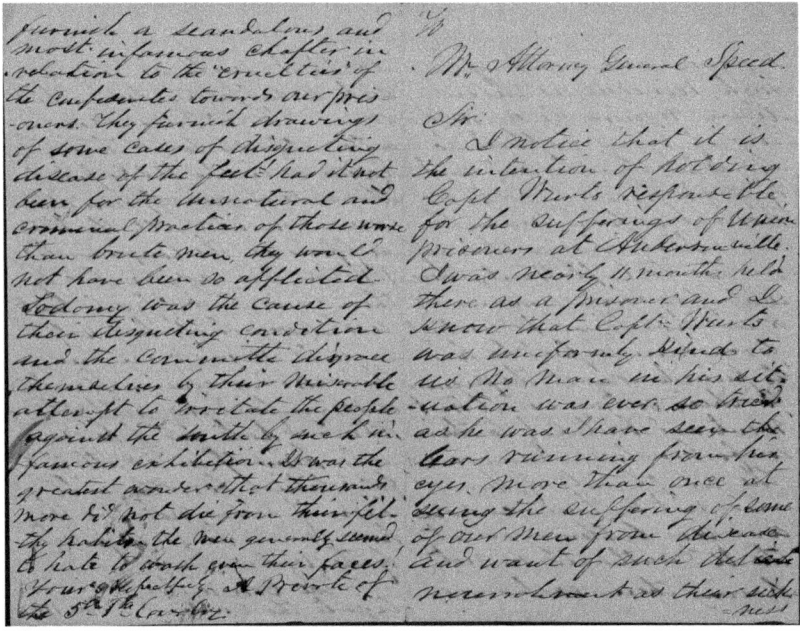

Figure 4.5. Letter to Attorney General James Speed, August 1865, with the word *Sodomy* emphasized through underscoring. Courtesy Walt Whitman Papers in the Charles E. Feinberg Collection, 1763–1985, Library of Congress, Washington, DC.

women could only commit sodomy by lying with a beast."[85] Whitman was clearly interested when (I assume) an anonymous southerner or southern sympathizer posing as a Pennsylvania soldier attempted to secure the government's mercy on Wirz's behalf. The letter speaks well of Wirz and argues that the hardships and disease suffered by captured Union soldiers at Andersonville were not a result of mistreatment but instead followed from the "unnatural and criminal practices of those worse than brute men.... *Sodomy* was the cause of their disgusting condition."[86]

The letter survives not in Department of Justice records, as might be expected, but in Whitman's papers. With the letter is an envelope with a single afterthought comment on it in Whitman's handwriting: "bogus?"

---

[85] William N. Eskridge, Jr., *Dishonorable Passions: Sodomy Laws in America, 1861–2003* (New York: Viking, 2008), 2.

[86] A Private of the 5th Pa. Cavalry to Attorney General James Speed, August, 1865 in the Charles Feinberg collection, the Library of Congress, Washington, DC.

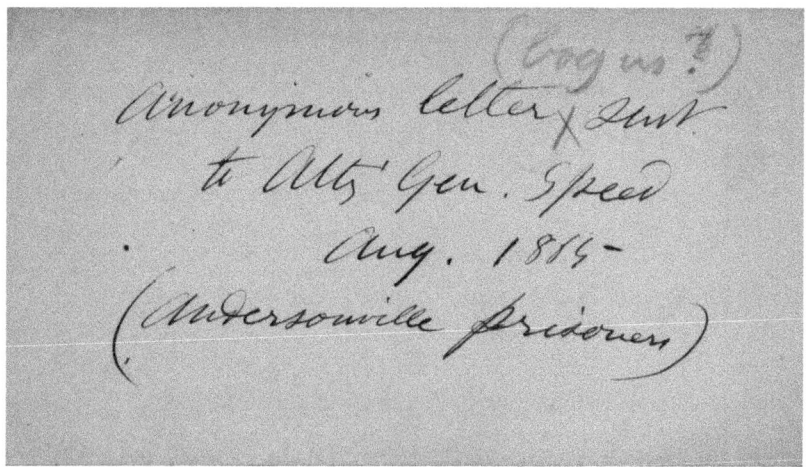

Figure 4.6. Envelope with Whitman's annotations. Courtesy Walt Whitman Papers in the Charles E. Feinberg Collection, 1763–1985, Library of Congress, Washington, DC.

(see Figure 4.6). Was the document taken (with or without permission) by Whitman for its historical interest, or had it been judged by the Attorney to be fraudulent and not worth keeping? We don't know—all that is certain is that it was still in Whitman's personal custody late in life and was briefly discussed with Horace Traubel. Reading such letters must have underscored how sexual morality could be weaponized by the courts and government, and that written documents in a government setting acquired authority even when their author was unknown.

Whitman of course knew and was often reminded that he was seen as bold and norm-breaking in his treatment of sex and the body. In 1872 Senator Matt Carpenter of Wisconsin sent him a letter inscribed with purple ink and marked "confidential." Whitman thought of the letter as a "curio" and remained unclear about Carpenter's intent. The letter opens as follows: "Examining some old papers, the other day, I found an extract from an argument of the late Hon. A. D. Smith, a Judge of the Sup. Ct. of Wisconsin, delivered by him when practising before that Court about twenty years ago, in a case about alleged rape, followed by conception; maintaining that the fact of conception was conclusive evidence of consent on the part of the prosecutrix."[87] (This belief continues to be held in some quarters and as

---

[87] Matt H. Carpenter to Walt Whitman, January 31, 1872 in *WWWC*, 4: 120.

recently as 2012 derailed Todd Akin's Missouri senate campaign when he infamously claimed "If it's a legitimate rape, the female body has ways to try to shut that whole thing down."[88]) Whitman remarked to Traubel: "It has always been a puzzle to me why people think that because I wrote Children of Adam, Leaves of Grass, I must perforce be interested in all the literature of rape, all the pornograph of vile minds. I have not only been made a target by those who despised me but a victim of violent interpretation by those who condoned me." Whitman thought Matt Carpenter was "a brilliant of the first water," but he also "had a reputation more or less *outré*."[89]

The general governmental stress on probity may explain the oddity of the planned "Calamus" deletions and also the "perturbations" that bothered Whitman as he contemplated his relationship with Peter Doyle in a notebook he inscribed within the physical space of the attorney general's office. I can find no evidence of Whitman expressing comparable qualms about same-sex love in the 1850s in New York. However, in Washington, Whitman coded a notebook, "After an Extract from Heine's Diary," using the numbers 16 and 4 for the letters P and D, and he twice erased the pronoun "him," altering it to "her." Just below noting that Congress is adjourning with excitement at the outbreak of the Franco-Prussian War, Whitman exhorted himself to give up the "undignified pursuit" of Doyle. He did not specify what made the pursuit undignified—asymmetries in their levels of interest and their ages (Doyle was twenty-four years younger than Whitman) are possibilities. But the most likely possibility is the same-sex nature of the attachment, given the effort to avoid using Doyle's name and the "him" to "her" alterations. The dramatic coloring and unusual inscription and reinscription, as he writes over his own words to chisel them into the firmest of resolutions, is then reinforced further with two red manicules—here the body, via the hand, and inscription, are one. The entire document is aligned with the violent end to the French Empire—a convulsion not so different from the US Civil War.

Whitman also expresses concern about "disproportionate adhesiveness." The overall context of this notebook shows his interest in what makes for a balanced and healthy life that will lead to longevity. He is drawing on interests earlier articulated in *Manly Health and Training*, and showing his ongoing fascination with phrenology as a way to perfect one's mental health (the literature of phrenology used the term "perturbation" itself).

---

[88] John Eligon and Michael Schwirtz, "In Rapes, Candidate Says, Body Can Block Pregnancy," *The New York Times*, August 20, 2012, A13.
[89] *WWWC*, 4: 119–21.

Intriguingly, in this context, Whitman implores himself to remember Fred Vaughan, a man he had lived with in New York and who probably inspired the "Live-Oak, with Moss" manuscript sequence, a sequence that was never published as such but led to the "Calamus" poems first appearing in the 1860–61 edition. Whitman and this particular loving comrade ultimately became estranged, with Vaughan later marrying in 1862 and fathering four children. On the "perturbation" document we now find a government seal, affixed at a later date by staff at the Library of Congress in a misguided attempt to protect against theft, thereby damaging the very object they wished to protect (see Figure 4.7). By chance or design, the seal is situated between the two manicules, with each drawn hand pointing to "perturbation" but also now to governmental authority. Despite twice committing to "remove" himself from Doyle in June and July 1870, and despite societal and governmental pressure against this type of romantic bond, Whitman ultimately reaffirmed male-male attachments by retaining nearly all of the "Calamus" poems in subsequent editions of Leaves of Grass and continuing in his love for Peter Doyle for years beyond this notebook.[90]

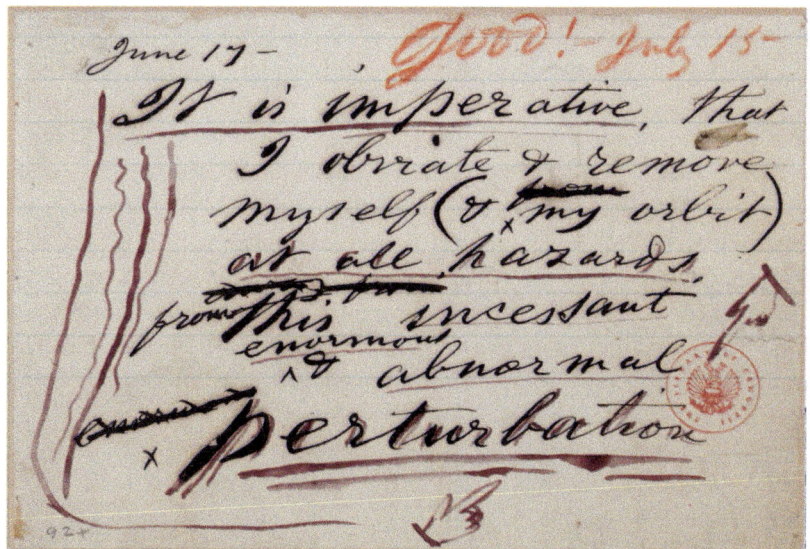

Figure 4.7. Inscribed and reinscribed page from a notebook "After an Extract from Heine's Diary." Courtesy Thomas Biggs Harned Collection of Walt Whitman Papers, 1842–1937, Library of Congress, Washington, DC.

---

[90] For discussion of the perturbations that preoccupied Whitman, see Jonathan Ned Katz, *Love Stories: Sex Between Men Before Homosexuality* (Chicago, IL: University of Chicago Press,

In an intriguing essay, Nicole Gray proposes four ways of thinking about the value of Whitman's scribal documents, and one of these is their "political value as evidence of the embodied presence of a queer poet in the government office primarily responsible for enforcing hegemony, in the form of legal and punitive action in the nineteenth-century US."[91] Despite the force of Gray's essay, with its attentiveness to self-surveillance, it seems to me that a personal document, like the one concerned with "perturbation," albeit written in the Attorney General's office, is more indicative of queer embodiment than official letters in Whitman's hand. The latter suppress indications of queer embodiment, even though Whitman's identity could never be altogether severed from his job status—he both gained and lost jobs as the author of *Leaves of Grass*. If we can see the official documents of Whitman in the Attorney General's office as at all *outré* (to borrow his term about Matt Carpenter), it is indirectly at best in the documents he retained (such as the one treating sodomy) or the ones sent to him (such as Matt Carpenter's letter about rape and pregnancy). Whitman's idea of the "abnormal"—too convulsive passions and movements, like those that led to war and disturbed planetary orbits—remained consistent. In these years he sometimes wished instead to be "imperturbable," a trait he claimed to detect in the native delegations who visited Washington. In "An Indian Bureau Reminiscence," appearing in *November Boughs* (1888), he describes "chiefs [possessing] heroic massiveness, *imperturbability*, muscle, and that last and highest beauty consisting of strength—the full exploitation and fruitage of a human identity, not from the culmination-points of 'culture' and artificial civilization, but tallying our race, as it were, with giant, vital, gnarl'd, enduring trees, or monoliths of separate hardiest rocks, and humanity holding its own with the best of the said trees or rocks, and outdoing them" (emphasis added).[92] This passage, confusing, fanciful, and blinkered all at once, is nonetheless illuminating in one respect: it speaks to Whitman's own desire for steadiness, calm, and resolve in the face of societal and governmental attempts to police and confine him. In fact, there is a complex struggle going on here between internal policing and external policing: the Indians here are viewed as naturally manly, whereas Whitman works at

2001), 170–73 and Gary Schmidgall, *Walt Whitman: A Gay Life* (New York: William Abrahams; Dutton, 1997), 138–43.

[91] Nicole Gray, "Toward an Embodied Poetics of Appraisal: Walt Whitman in the National Archives," *Archivaria* 89 (Spring 2020), 121.

[92] *Complete Prose Works*, 409.

manly health and training, as one of his tracts called it. The source of perturbation is both from within and without.

Whitman interlaced his various roles—professional, poetic, and private—in these years. His service as a scribe links, if it does not fully unite, his roles during this time: he served as a scribe, drafting letters home for soldiers, drafting routine reports and correspondence in governmental offices, drafting poetry that speaks in a "multitude" of voices, and redrafting his own work in the Blue Book. He gained life experience as a ventriloquist of sorts—throwing his voice to become soldiers as he wrote as and through them to their friends and loved ones, just as he regularly assumed the identity of others as he conducted his work as a government scribe. These Washington experiences of inhabiting another's view—always part of Whitman's poetry, of course, but now acted out quite literally in life—accelerated his developing tendency to write from the perspective of various personae. These personae, especially notable in the latter part of his career, are more thoroughgoing and more sustained alterations of identity than the rapid but typically brief shape-changing of the speaker in the 1855 poem eventually titled "Song of Myself." We see such sustained personae in a variety of late poems, including "Ethiopia Saluting the Colors," "Prayer of Columbus," and "Osceola."

The annotations in the Blue Book, produced primarily in, and shaped by, the Civil War hospitals and the clerk's office, can be regarded as the hinge on which Whitman turns toward his late style. We can see this in many ways, including such a seemingly small matter as a change in his use of parentheses.[93] In 1855, the poem now known as "Song of Myself" included only a single set of parentheses:

> The prostitute draggles her shawl, her bonnet bobs on her
> tipsy and pimpled neck,
> The crowd laugh at her blackguard oaths, the men jeer and
> wink to each other,
> (Miserable! I do not laugh at your oaths nor jeer you,).[94]

The 1856 edition replicates the first edition in using a single set of parentheses in this poem, and the 1860 edition increases that number slightly to five. In

---

[93] For a discussion of Whitman's use of parentheses, see C. Caroll Hollis, *Language and Style in Leaves of Grass* (Baton Rouge, LA: Louisiana State University Press, 1983), 57.
[94] *LG* (1855), 22.

contrast, in the Blue Book Whitman adds at least thirty-nine new sets of parentheses. If parentheses are ordinarily used to indicate that the enclosed material is of marginal importance, something that could be excluded and is not fundamental to meaning or grammar, for Whitman the parenthetical remark often conveys the essence of what is at stake in a poem, a re-articulation of its issues in another register, tone, or voice. Rather than conveying the least important information, the parentheses often convey the most important meaning. Whitman may have relied heavily on parentheses at this time because he regarded the Civil War itself as a parenthetical moment—a break from normalcy in the national history—and a clarifying realization of American purpose and ideals. He also seems to have anticipated Virginia Woolf in recognizing the power of parentheses to allow for the expression of what has been called "multipersonal consciousness."[95]

The impact of the war on the Blue Book has been effectively analyzed by Golden, but the impact of Whitman's government work on his poetry has been ignored. One result of his steady work as a government employee was his absorption of a governmental propriety, a gradually internalized sense of what suited official documents. More than prudishness, the sheer orderliness of the documents he created for the government—so different from the fairly chaotic nature of his private manuscripts—helps explain some of the taming of Whitman's language in the Blue Book. A new restraint linked to this orderliness and propriety is likely behind his cutting of "suck and a sell" and "cock" from one page, and "Thruster holding me tight" a few pages later.[96] In the 1860-61 edition of *Leaves* Whitman retained a bold idea first articulated in 1855: "Outbidding at the start the old cautious hucksters, / The most they offer for mankind and eternity less than a spirt of my own seminal wet."[97] In the Blue Book, he dropped the second line but retained the earlier "hucksters," so that the passage retained something of its original meaning. Whitman does not abandon sexual expression in the Blue Book and in the postwar *Leaves*, but he does recalibrate it.

Both Gay Wilson Allen and Arthur Golden argue that Whitman's revisions in the Blue Book were for stylistic improvements and were not a form of self-censorship. More recently, Jimmie Killingsworth has effectively

---

[95] In a discussion of *Mrs. Dalloway*, Yaxiao Cui notes how the "syntactic independence of a parenthetical gives it a degree of freedom to digress from its host, which makes the construction a convenient device to bring in new sources of consciousness and thus shift the...viewpoint from one character to another." See Ciu, "Parentheticals and the Presentation of Multipersonal Consciousness: A Stylistic Analysis of *Mrs. Dalloway*," *Language and Literature* 23 (2014), 175.

[96] *Walt Whitman's Blue Book*, ed. Arthur Golden, 48 and 51.   [97] *LG* (1860-61), 86.

challenged their interpretation.[98] I would like to build on Killingsworth's study through close attention to a single word in Whitman's lexicon: *pensive*. The poet's use of the word can be a barometer of his outlook. The word gained frequency as Whitman's career progressed in the years before the Civil War. He used the word not at all in the 1855 *Leaves*, only once in 1856, and ten times in 1860. (The overall word count for the 1860 edition did not even double that of 1856, so the tenfold increase in the use of the word is striking.) Even as he was relying on this word heavily in 1860, he expressed misgivings about what it might suggest about his overall meaning: "I must change the strain—these are not to be pensive leaves, but leaves of joy."[99] A similar attraction and repulsion is, if anything, even more apparent in the Blue Book, where the word *pensive* was added once as an annotation only to be deleted. Moreover, another three uses of *pensive* in the underlying 1860–61 edition were marked for deletion in the Blue Book. *Pensive* thus stands out as a word that fascinated *and* troubled Whitman, especially in the 1860–65 years. The word resonates broadly in Whitman's work and has importance both within and beyond the realm of sexuality.

The word *pensive* was defined in the 1848 Webster's dictionary as "*Literally*, thoughtful; employed in serious study or reflection; but it often implies some degree of sorrow, anxiety, depression, or gloom of mind; thoughtful and sad, or sorrowful." The word did not match the buoyant tone Whitman often achieved in his poetry, but it came to be increasingly relevant as his anxiety increased about the future, both for himself and the nation.

The word *pensive* registers a sad thoughtfulness when Whitman feels separated from something he needs and expresses a lack of bonding or unity. This feeling of being separated operates in both sexual and political contexts. During the war he watched the nation suffer from separation and strove to redress it, and he saw innumerable limbs separated from soldiers' bodies via amputations. Whitman, increasingly pensive himself, strove to overcome the separation between soldier and family, comrade and fellow comrade, North and South. It is hardly surprising that he felt strongly yet ambivalently toward *pensive* in his Blue Book revisions. For Whitman, the war years highlighted separation and the hope for unity.

---

[98] See Golden, *Blue Book*, 2:lvi–lvii; Gay Wilson Allen, *The Solitary Singer* (1955; rev. ed. New York: New York University Press, 1967), 349; Jimmie Killingsworth, *Whitman's Poetry of the Body* (Chapel Hill, NC: University of North Carolina Press, 1989), 144–49.

[99] *LG* (1860–61), 359.

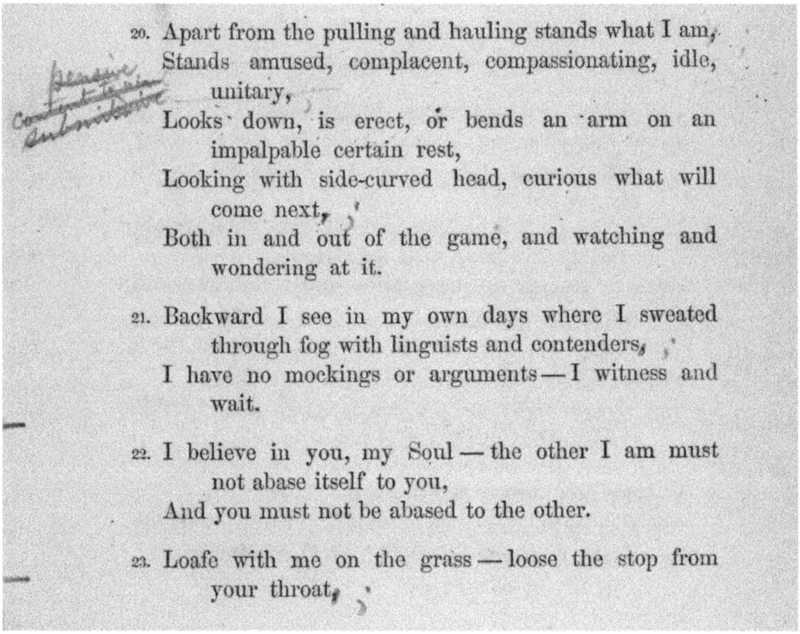

> 20. Apart from the pulling and hauling stands what I am,
> Stands amused, complacent, compassionating, idle, unitary,
> Looks down, is erect, or bends an arm on an impalpable certain rest,
> Looking with side-curved head, curious what will come next,
> Both in and out of the game, and watching and wondering at it.
>
> 21. Backward I see in my own days where I sweated through fog with linguists and contenders,
> I have no mockings or arguments — I witness and wait.
>
> 22. I believe in you, my Soul — the other I am must not abase itself to you,
> And you must not be abased to the other.
>
> 23. Loafe with me on the grass — loose the stop from your throat,

Figure 4.8. Detail of page 27 of the Blue Book. Reproduced with the permission of the New York Public Library.

In the Blue Book, Whitman contemplated revising a key moment of self-definition in "Walt Whitman," the poem later called "Song of Myself" (see Figure 4.8). As the very faint pencil strikethrough indicates, Whitman considered deleting the line "Stands amused, complacent, compassionating, idle, unitary." In many ways it is not surprising that he considered cutting "unitary." He had made "Walt Whitman" and "America" interchangeable terms, and the poet now faced the profound and painful self-division of Civil War. This famous passage immediately follows a section that stresses the difference between the "me" and the "Me myself." For the poet as an individual in the prewar years, a "unitary" identity was a hope and a potential only occasionally realized, as in the magical moment of lovemaking joining the "I" and the "Soul." Whitman's contemplated pencil revision, "Pensive, content to wait submissive," invites a sexual reading even as it relates to a broad philosophical outlook. Whitman's contemplated revision deserves careful attention because the passage is so patently autobiographical and because it sheds light on how the war influenced his thinking and poetry. After revising this passage, he then thought better of it, presumably because the revised passage did not adequately fit his persona. Sad thoughtfulness was also risky for a poet who had embarked on an effort, fully articulated in the 1860–61 *Leaves*, to give voice to same-sex love: it is one thing to suggest that love in general often leads to unhappiness, but it is another thing to register this about a type of love that has been criticized as morbid or depraved.

The poet regularly invokes pensiveness at moments of conflict or opposition. Contradiction and discord can at times be neutralized by extended thought that leads to a more encompassing outlook. Yet to seek for a mystical, metaphysical reconciliation can seem indecisive, uncertain. In the midst of the Civil War, does Whitman want to strive for the now-seemingly-hopeless "unity" of the original passage or to position himself as pensive, contemplative, and submissive? Which is more convincing and ultimately powerful—to suggest he is fundamentally unaffected by events, or to say he is considering them, allowing them to affect him?

Pensive became a much more prominent word for Whitman, especially in contexts treating love and sexuality. More important than the frequency of its use is its association with love and its psychological accompaniments. Whitman's breakthrough work in treating same-sex love did not appear without psychological stress. In the 1860 edition, the word *pensive* is invoked in the opening poem, "Proto-Leaf":

> What do you seek, so pensive and silent?
> What do you need, comrade?
> Mon cher! do you think it is love?

Even as he used *pensive* in the 1860–61 edition and in the Blue Book, Whitman sometimes felt uneasy about it, resisted it, and at times tried to shun the word. Whitman is not characterizing same-sex love itself as a cause of pensiveness, but indicating that the lack or loss of such love causes melancholic musing. To the extent that pensiveness requires a remedy, it is to be found in comradeship.

As is well known, Whitman held that adhesiveness was a unifying power capable of saving the union, but there was a sad wistfulness about it too for him, just as there was about the union. Even as late as "Poetry To-Day in America—Shakspere—the Future," first published in 1881, Whitman would say: "Lately, I have wonder'd whether the last meaning of this cluster of thirty-eight States is not only practical fraternity among themselves—the only real *union*... but for fraternity over the whole globe—that dazzling,

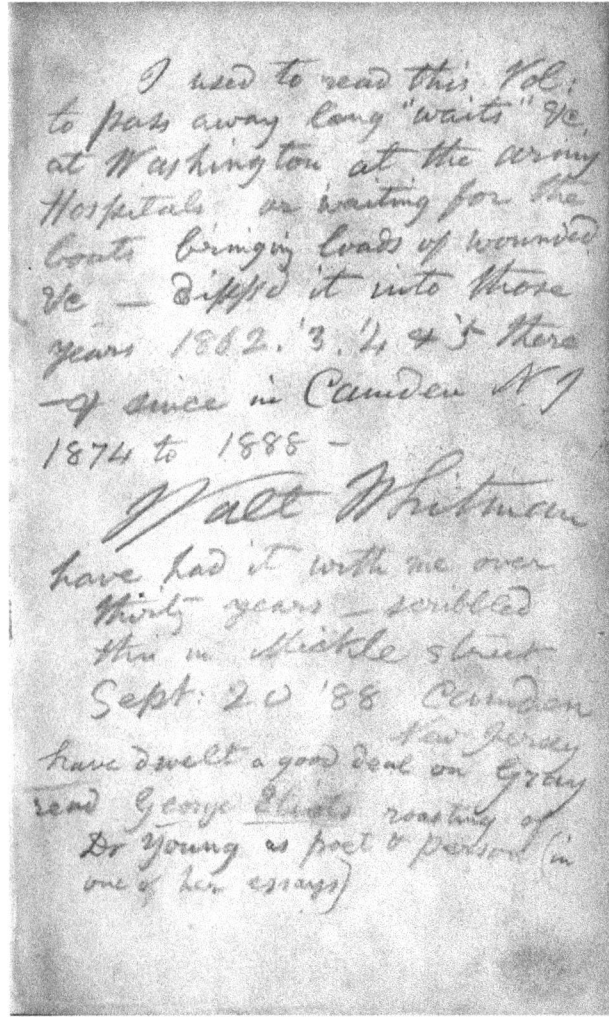

Figure 4.9. Whitman's comment on the flyleaf of his copy of *Milton, Young, Gray, Beattie, and Collins* (Philadelphia, 1841). This particular volume is now held in the Bryn Mawr College Special Collections Library. The image of the flyleaf is reproduced with permission.

pensive dream of ages!"[100] Ultimately, Whitman comes to accept, even embrace, *pensive*. In his late prose the word is regularly linked to one of two poles of existence that he describes in (nuanced and fascinating) dualisms: poetry and prose, day and night, or joy and melancholy.[101] Whitman's dualistic descriptions may have been shaped by his reading during the war of John Milton's "L'Allegro" and "Il Penseroso," poems that balance and harmonize joyousness and melancholic thoughtfulness. (The 1844 Webster's dictionary includes the Italian *pensieroso* when tracing the etymology of *pensive*.) Both "L'Allegro" and "Il Penseroso" were included in a volume he consulted regularly during the war titled *Milton, Young, Gray, Beattie, and Collins*. His comment on the flyleaf is illuminating: "I used to read this Vol: to pass away long 'waits' &c, at Washington at the army Hospitals, or waiting for the boats bringing loads of wounded &c—dipped it into those years 1862, '3, '4, and '5" (see Figure 4.9). Intriguingly, where we expect to read that Whitman "dipp'd into it" during the War years, he says instead that he "dipp'd it into" the war years, as if he tried the poetry in the fire of the times, just as he tested and altered his own poetry in the crucible of Civil War.

If we give attention to all features of the Blue Book—from the front matter, to typography, to contemplated and then rejected revisions, to individual word choices—we can better understand a writer with a living work in hand, always ready to revise, ever responsive to historical crisis and local circumstances. And we can hear, in the growing pensiveness that comes to pervade this book, a dialing down of faith in the future, a hesitancy that works its way into his poetry through the decorum encouraged by his government work and through the hundreds of rethinkings he records in the Blue Book, where the slowing down of thought itself is registered in the increasing number of parenthetical statements, pauses in his lines as he gazes more and more pensively on his life, his nation, and the nation's dead.

---

[100] Walt Whitman, *Complete Prose Works* (Philadelphia, PA: David McKay, 1892), 296.
[101] Whitman, *Complete Prose*, 282, 101, and 158.

5
Multi-racial Democracy and Black Democratic Vistas

> In his interests, in his associations, in his habits of thought, and in his prejudices, he was a white man. He was preeminently the white man's President, entirely devoted to the welfare of white men.
>
> Frederick Douglass, oration dedicating a statue to Abraham Lincoln (1876)

Democratic Vistas and Whitman's later poetry and prose writings were shaped by his experiences in Washington, DC, a key site of experimentation with multi-racial democracy, and a city where local experiments had national implications. Washington was the nation's first emancipated city and after the Civil War the combined forces of newly gained suffrage and effective political organizing led to a brief but remarkable surge in African American political power. Yet after promising initial gains, multi-racial democracy foundered, and ultimately democratic government itself was lost in the city when in 1874 it became governed by a presidentially appointed board of three commissioners. Whitman's mid-career achievements and failures can be illuminated against the backdrop of these local developments and the national scope of his work within the attorney general's office. Was Washington to become what Charles Sumner called "an example for all the land," enabling the United States increasingly to embody the ideals of liberty and equality, or would the city, and the nation, remain mired in state-supported white supremacy?[1] As Whitman watched these questions play out from a clerk's perch, he allowed an increasing chasm to develop between the ideals most central to *Leaves of Grass* and the misgivings he had about Radical Reconstruction.

---

[1] Speech by Charles Sumner, April 1, 1870 in *Charles Sumner: His Complete Works* (Boston, MA: Lee and Shepard, 1900), 18: 21.

Whitman in Washington: Becoming the National Poet in the Federal City. Kenneth M. Price,
Oxford University Press (2020). © Kenneth M. Price.
DOI: 10.1093/oso/9780198840930.001.0001

Congress exercised authority over Washington, without needing to engage with state or local authorities, allowing Radical Republicans to implement their policies with few impediments.² During the Civil War, Radicals understandably resented the widespread pro-South sentiment in the District, and in the postwar period they continued to be suspicious of the local white population. Whitman too was well aware of the southern-leaning inclination of the white residents, as he explained in later years to Traubel: "You are just on the edge of the South there—you begin there to penetrate Dixie."³ During Reconstruction, Radical Republicans regarded Washington as a testing ground for policies that could later be pursued throughout the South. However, even among Republicans, black suffrage was controversial. The moderate Republican newspaper in Washington, *The Evening Star*, became more conservative as the decade wore on, and it criticized Congress for enfranchising black men (a long legislative process beginning in 1865 and extending to 1867), declaring it a "war on the rights of the white laboring men of the whole Union." The editors went further, arguing that to give the franchise to the "most ignorant and incapable contraband negroes" would "africanize the city" and turn it into a "negro Utopia." The Republican *Chronicle*, in contrast, advocated for a restricted suffrage, with former slaves and men without property excluded. Only the Radicals supported "universal" manhood suffrage. For those doubting the wisdom of giving black men the vote, Indiana representative George Julian had a ready answer: in contrast with "white rebels, who deserve to be hung," black men were "eminently fit."⁴

In 1868 African American voters proved decisive in the mayoral election of Sayles J. Bowen, a Radical Republican, over Democrat John T. Given. What Bowen lacked in political charm, he made up for, especially in the African American community, with his backing of black public schools and fervent support of black men's suffrage. The determination of African Americans to participate in the political process was striking: one study of voters in Washington city observes that "despite being only 30 percent of the population, by election time black men were nearly 50 percent of registered voters." After he was elected, Mayor Bowen appointed African Americans to nearly one-third of the positions in his administration.⁵ A new day seemed

---

² Chris Myers Asch and George Derek Musgrove, *Chocolate City: A History of Race and Democracy in the Nation's Capital* (Chapel Hill, NC: University of North Carolina Press, 2017), 122.
³ *WWWC*, 4: 266.   ⁴ Asch and Musgrove, *Chocolate City*, 143–46.
⁵ Asch and Musgrove, *Chocolate City*, 147, 150.

to be at hand when political clout would no longer be restricted to white men. Whitman found this unsettling, as he noted to his mother in June 1868:

> We had the strangest procession here last Tuesday night, about 3000 darkeys, old & young, men & women—I saw them all—they turned out in honor of *their* victory in electing the Mayor, Mr. Bowen—the men were all armed with clubs or pistols—besides the procession in the street, there was a string went along the sidewalk in single file with bludgeons & sticks, yelling & gesticulating like madmen—it was quite comical, yet very disgusting & alarming in some respects—They were very insolent, & altogether it was a strange sight—they looked like so many wild brutes let loose—thousands of slaves from the Southern plantations have crowded up here—many are supported by the Gov't.[6]

Whitman's comment is disturbing on various grounds from its slur on "darkeys" to its resentment of government aid directed toward needy migrants, to the mention of "insolent" behavior, as if African Americans didn't know their deferential, respect-showing place. Whitman expressed dismay about an armed procession (despite his attempt to dismiss the possible threat as "comical"), but African Americans, in a city where they had long been treated unlawfully, needed self-protection, wished to assert a second amendment right exercised by others, and sought to mark their independence from white authority.[7] Despite Whitman's moving paeans to freedom and democracy in *Leaves*, the pressures of lived experience in a city where most people in the federal bureaucracy—as Frederick Douglass observed—felt their first loyalty was to white men at times routed the poet's loftier hopes and claims.

Like many Washingtonians, Whitman was disconcerted by the "torrent of black migration to the city" that followed the Compensated Emancipation Act

---

[6] Walt Whitman to Louisa Van Velsor Whitman, June 6–8, 1868 (*WWA*).

[7] For a discussion of the unlawful treatment of African Americans in the nation's capital, see Kate Masur, "Washington's Black Codes," *The New York Times*, December 7, 2011, online. She notes that "Senator John Hale of New Hampshire offered a broad indictment of the District's justice system: 'No matter how long a man has lived here, no matter how correct a life he has led, no matter how exemplary he may be in all the walks of life,' if his 'complexion' was dark, he was 'liable to be at once arrested and carried to jail, and kept in confinement.' Congress had a duty, Hale declared, 'to look into the administration of justice in this District, and to see to it that those who have been ground to the earth heretofore may not be ground still more under your auspices.'"

of 1862 and continued thereafter. Washington's black population tripled by 1870, jumping from 19 percent of the city's total population to 33 percent. Most of the migrants were unskilled, poor, and, with rare exceptions, illiterate, in contrast with a 70 percent literacy rate for the free black people in the District. The migrants arrived in the capital, White House tailor Elizabeth Keckly recalled, "with all their worldly goods on their backs."[8]

The local white population responded with a concern that bordered on hysteria. Following passage of the Fifteenth Amendment (prohibiting the federal government and each state from denying a citizen the right to vote based on that citizen's "race, color, or previous condition of servitude"), an outraged Washington Board of Aldermen nevertheless passed a resolution demanding that the mayor conduct a special election "to ascertain the opinion of the people of Washington on the question of negro suffrage." On December 21, 1865, the polling occurred, with 6,591 against black suffrage and only thirty-five in favor (Georgetown voted 712 against and one in favor).[9] Chris Myers Asch and George Derek Musgrove note that the referendum, "restricted to white voters and boycotted by white Republicans [,] ... yielded predictable results."[10] The totals from the referendum notwithstanding, the Republican Congress was eager to give the franchise to African Americans, perhaps rightly fearing opposition would only become more entrenched if they waited. They also recognized that black votes could potentially give control of city government to the Republicans.[11] What many whites saw as the oddity of black people voting and monitoring the election was depicted in a *Harper's Weekly* illustration from 1867 in which two white men stare intently and incredulously at their fellow black election monitor, even as a black voter hovers over the ballot box without supervision, implying that an obsession with black suffrage leads to neglect of more practical issues at hand—for example, checking to verify that a voter doesn't stuff the ballot box (see Figure 5.1).

In this time of cultural transition, Whitman indisputably held prejudicial attitudes widely shared among whites, even white Republicans. T. J. Stiles notes that "in 1860, four free states had constitutional prohibitions on the immigration of black people across their borders; in 1865, only five of 20 Union states allowed black men to vote. A race-neutral definition of

---

[8] For both quotations, see Asch and Musgrove, *Chocolate City*, 123.
[9] Ed Folsom, "The Vistas of *Democratic Vistas*," in *Democratic Vistas: The Original Edition in Facsimile* (Iowa City, IA: University of Iowa Press, 2010), xxvii.
[10] Asch and Musgrove, *Chocolate City*, 144.
[11] For discussion, see Folsom, "The Vistas of *Democratic Vistas*," xxvi–xxvii.

SIGNIFICANT ELECTION SCENE AT WASHINGTON, June 3, 1867.—[Sketched by A. W. M'Callum.]

Figure 5.1. *Harper's Weekly*, June 22, 1867, p. 397.

citizenship and individual rights, let alone black enfranchisement, seemed absurd to most white men."[12] Yet Whitman's intellectual circle in Washington included numerous people advocating such an agenda,

---

[12] "The Constitutional Amendment that Reinvented Freedom" *The New York Times*, July 26, 2018.

including William and Ellen O'Connor, Charles Eldridge, and John Trowbridge (strong supporters of abolition, women's rights, and black suffrage). In short, he had allies available to him had he chosen to translate the egalitarian drive of the pre-war *Leaves of Grass* into practical progressive politics (or poetry) in Reconstruction-era Washington, DC. Instead, he generally left these questions out of his poetry or kept them at a mostly abstract level. In his prose he often limited them to footnotes printed once and not later reprinted, a practice that manifests a hesitant, half-embarrassed strand of thought, a strand that is surprising given the perceptions and commitments of the early Whitman.[13] In his early years, Whitman had himself been critical of the growing conservatism he thought he detected in his major English language competitors: "Of the leading British poets many who began with the rights of man, abj[i?]ured their beginning and came out for kingraft priestcraft, obedience, and so forth.—Southey, Coleridge, and Wordsworth, did so.—"[14] There are ironies here, of course. If Whitman's British counterparts retreat from a growing democratic fervor to the traditions of hierarchy inherent in monarchy and Anglican religion, the later Whitman retreats from a widening democratic embrace of African Americans to reaffirm the traditional hierarchy of white nationalism. Whitman becomes an advocate for the hierarchy of race (just as he criticized the British writers for becoming advocates for other forms of hierarchy) at precisely the time his own associates were pushing for a widening and less hierarchical definition of democracy.

Whitman's early manuscript drafts and the first edition of *Leaves of Grass* are remarkably compelling, if uneven, in their treatment of race, and one of the most bracing aspects of his pre-war poetic achievement is its unprecedented inclusiveness—of master and slave, of immigrant and yankee, of butcher and drayman. He rarely wrote of the wealthy and the elite, and rightly so: they had never lacked for representation and celebration. Over time, however, Whitman's adherence to the cause of African Americans declined. Notably, he never manifested as much interest in Native Americans as African Americans, though a gradual decline in his regard for native peoples can also be traced. Why Whitman lost interest in or

---

[13] For perceptive analysis of this problem, see especially two essays by Ed Folsom, "Erasing Race: The Lost Black Presence in Whitman's Manuscripts" in Ivy G. Wilson, ed., *Whitman Noir: Black America and the Good Gray Poet* (Iowa City, IA: University of Iowa Press, 2014), 3–31 and "'A yet more terrible and more deeply complicated problem': Walt Whitman, Race, Reconstruction, and American Democracy" *American Literary History* 30 (Fall 2018), 531–58.

[14] "What are inextricable from the British poets" in *WWA* marginalia.

lessened his commitment to people of color is perplexing, even if it was typical of his generation, because it deviated from one of his own defining values about the necessity of brotherhood across "hues" for a successful democratic republic. Of course, Whitman as always is complex, and even in his later years, he could be outspoken in support of people of color—for example, in his support for Chinese immigration and in "The Spanish Element in Our Nationality," by which of course he meant what would now be called Hispanic or Latinx Americans.[15] Certainly, Whitman's life-long sense of special kinship with working-class whites led him to fear that emancipated African Americans, as job seekers, would threaten the standing and livelihood of white men, but additional factors also contributed to his declining sympathy for African Americans.

Ed Folsom has rightly lamented how American writers, including Whitman, failed to offer accounts of what a vibrant multi-racial democracy might look like.[16] To discuss what is not present can be perilous, and some may question whether it is fair to critique writers for what they don't write. Whitman once said: "If you want to know what I mean watch what I do."[17] But to fully understand what he did requires us to consider what was left undone, too. In Whitman's postwar years in particular, with the rare exception of "Ethiopia Saluting the Colors," we find a pattern of avoidance of African American concerns and civil rights that is too consistent to be accidental.

In 1888, Whitman himself commented on gaps and lacunae—and the regret over what is left not achieved—in connection with his terminally ill friend O'Connor:

> It is almost tragic to see a man endowed as he is so largely silent—so much of him just fired up and never expressed. A nobler genius never walked the earth. William has a world all his own—a potential world: I used to think he would some day give it birth: but the days pass, the years pass, by and

---

[15] In remarks to Horace Traubel, Whitman said: "Restrict nothing—keep everything open: to Italy, to China, to anybody. I love America, I believe in America, because her belly can hold and digest all" (*WWWC*, 1:113). For Whitman's discussion of "The Spanish Element in Our Nationality," see *Complete Prose Works* (Philadelphia, PA: David McKay, 1892), 386–87. The poet also came to the defense of Jews as a persecuted minority. On August 9, 1890, he discussed with Traubel his former employer, the publisher Mordecai Manuel Noah: "I remember Col. Noah, in New York—it was long ago—I knew him well, intimately, even. He was a Jew—oh!—a Jew of the Israelites! possessing the grand virtues we read of in Old Testament characters—fraternal feeling, kindness, generosity, love of domestic life" (*WWWC*, 7:46).
[16] Folsom, "'A yet terrible and more deeply complicated problem,'" 541.
[17] *WWWC*, 3:577.

bye William will pass, I am afraid, with the work undone. That damned job in Washington ties him down to a few feet of grass: I ought not to growl at it: it is splendid work: but somehow I resent it—just a little, anyway.[18]

As a government official, O'Connor worked in the Treasury department for the lighthouse board, and while this engaged him in documenting lifesaving efforts (his book *Heroes of the Storm* was published posthumously in 1904), Whitman suggested that his real strength was unrealized and in a different arena altogether. Given O'Connor's commitment to progressive causes, that "potential world" might very well have been his never-realized writing about the rich, diverse, and inclusive democracy so needing to be born. Since Whitman and O'Connor had a decade-long falling out over black suffrage, with O'Connor supportive and Whitman unsympathetic, it is hardly far-fetched to believe Whitman may have been thinking of civil rights. O'Connor, given his eloquence, literary talent, and passion for justice, was capable of offering a ringing endorsement of equality across the races (see Figure 5.2). Whitman indicates that O'Connor's government work, regardless of its practical value, sapped his energies and constrained his literary scope and vision.

The reference to a "few feet of grass" also suggests that in describing O'Connor, Whitman was thinking of his own diminished outlook. Though the poet commented positively about clerking in Washington, he may later have wondered if it had compromised or curtailed his own imaginative productions; *Democratic Vistas*, a major postwar prose work, lacked the visionary character of his pre-war poetry. Whitman's figurative language here is striking, calling to mind not only the title *Leaves of Grass* but more particularly his celebration of grass as a "uniform hieroglyphic," and its wonderful lack of discrimination as it sprouts, nourishes, receives, and teaches "alike in broad zones and narrow zones, / Growing among black folks as among whites."[19]

Whitman's Silences

Whitman prided himself on breaking silence. He famously asserted in the 1855 *Leaves* that it was the defining characteristic of "Walt Whitman, an

---

[18] *WWWC*, 1, 181.   [19] *LG* (1855), 16.

Figure 5.2. William Douglas O'Connor carte de visite. Courtesy Walt Whitman Papers in the Charles E. Feinberg Collection, 1763–1985, Library of Congress, Washington, DC.

American, one of the roughs, a kosmos." He was the poet who believed that "Whoever degrades another degrades me," and he further asserted:

> I speak the password primeval....I give the sign of democracy;
> By God! I will accept nothing which all cannot have their counterpart of on the same terms.
>
> Through me many long dumb voices,
> Voices of the interminable generations of slaves,
> Voices of prostitutes and of deformed persons,
> Voices of the diseased and despairing, and of thieves and dwarfs,
> Voices of cycles of preparation and accretion,

And of the threads that connect the stars—and of wombs,
   and of the fatherstuff,
And of the rights of them the others are down upon,
Of the trivial and flat and foolish and despised,
Of fog in the air and beetles rolling balls of dung.

Through me forbidden voices,
Voices of sexes and lusts.... voices veiled, and I remove the veil,
Voices indecent by me clarified and transfigured.[20]

The early Whitman thus movingly gave voice to a diverse US, celebrating the teeming and varied "nation of nations." Yet, he later manifested indifference—at times even ill will—toward African Americans. While he generally kept such comments out of his enduring writings, some nevertheless made it into print, and much is conveyed through these conscious and unconscious evasions.

Silence does not necessarily mean indifference. Whitman collected newspaper clippings on the crucial contributions of African Americans to the Union war effort, but never celebrated their achievements. Nor did he do anything to celebrate emancipation, what Charlotte Forten called "the most glorious day this nation has yet seen."[21] (In a manuscript note, perhaps a draft of newspaper article, he observes that the Emancipation Proclamation is in all the papers but has been met with a "phlegmatic coolness all through Washington." He also commented more positively on the effects of black emancipation when he recalled the effects of the New York emancipation acts, noting how those acts "diversified" the crowd that gathered in Brooklyn when he was a boy to see Lafayette.[22]) Whitman was silent about the Fifteenth amendment, too, that right articulated in the negative—prohibiting the exclusion of voting rights on the basis of race or previous condition of servitude. Moreover, he rarely used the term Reconstruction, with its implications of radical social change. Such silences led one Washington contemporary, Charles Eldridge, to conclude that Whitman

---

[20] *LG* (1855), 29.
[21] *The Journals of Charlotte Forten Grimké*, ed. Brenda Stevenson (Oxford: Oxford University Press, 1988), 428. In fact, one of Whitman's additional comments on emancipation to his mother sounds anything but supportive: "We had the greatest black procession here last Thursday—I didn't think there was so many darkeys, (especially wenches,) in the world—it was the anniversary of emancipation in this District." Walt Whitman to Louisa Van Velsor Whitman, April 23, 1866 (*WWA*).
[22] *NUPM*, 2: 545 and 1: 33–34.

was "one of the most conservative of men. He believed in the old ways... and thought no change could be made in the condition of mankind except by the most gradual evolution." He noted that the poet "had no sympathy" for the abolitionists: "While opposed to slavery always, he thought the radicals considered the subject too all important and were incendiary in their methods." Eldridge further remarked that "Of the negro as a race he had a poor opinion.... I never knew him to have a friend among the negroes while he was in Washington."[23]

Eldridge's comments are consistent with a contribution Whitman made to his late collection of poetry and prose, *November Boughs* (1888). Titled "Small Memoranda" and subtitled "Thousands lost—here one or two preserv'd," it is comprised of three items: one headlined "Attorney General's Office" and dated August 22, 1865, treating pardons; another headlined Washington and dated "*Sept. 8, 9, &c.,* 1865," further treating pardons and, in comments on black suffrage, suggesting that suffrage complicates efforts at north-south reconciliation; and a final item, "A Glint inside of Abraham Lincoln's Cabinet appointments," discussing Lincoln's decision-making as he considered James Harlan and Colonel Jesse K. Dubois of Illinois for Secretary of the Interior. Together these three pieces in "Small Memoranda" make up only four pages in *The Collected Writings of Walt Whitman*.[24]

The offering of "Small Memoranda" is a rare instance of Whitman making explicit use of his government employment—in contrast with his memoranda based on volunteer work in the hospitals—for literary purposes. Curiously, out of all the ideas and policies among the "thousands lost" from his time in the Attorney General's office, in this article Whitman chose to give special emphasis to pardons granted former Confederate officers, in doing so implicitly endorsing President Andrew Johnson's approach to black suffrage and the restoration of the union. These emphases are remarkable both in their own right and because of what Whitman does not highlight: the highly commendable work he and his colleagues in the attorney general's office did, after Johnson left office, towards beating back the Ku Klux Klan.

It would be a mistake to see "Small Memoranda" as merely a neutral record—these pieces were shaped after the fact, as is illustrated by examination of the second of the three memoranda. This second item is based in

---

[23] Eldridge's remarks are quoted in Barbara Bair, "'A land of lovers and of friends': Whitman and the O'Connors," *Huntington Library Quarterly*, 73, no. 4 (2010), 671-72.

[24] Whitman, *Prose Works 1892* (New York: New York University Press), 2: 610-13.

part on a Whitman manuscript from 1865 that was apparently still in his possession (see Figure 5.3).[25] In the final published version, as is so often the case, Whitman's work exhibits what we might call multi-temporality. That is, he headlines it "*Washington, Sept. 8, 9 &c.* 1865" and refers to conditions "at present" (presumably meaning 1865), but because this item was first published in 1888, that is of course a second "present." The manuscript jotting is from the mid 1860s, while the more elaborated commentary blends experiences and ideas from the 1860s with the 1880s. A skeletal manuscript jotting with a distinctive date, "Sept 8-9-1865," seems to have set aflow Whitman's memory and imagination. This document says in its entirety:

> Memoranda
> Pardon applicants Sept 8-9-1865
> Also the negro-suffrage
> also position of the President

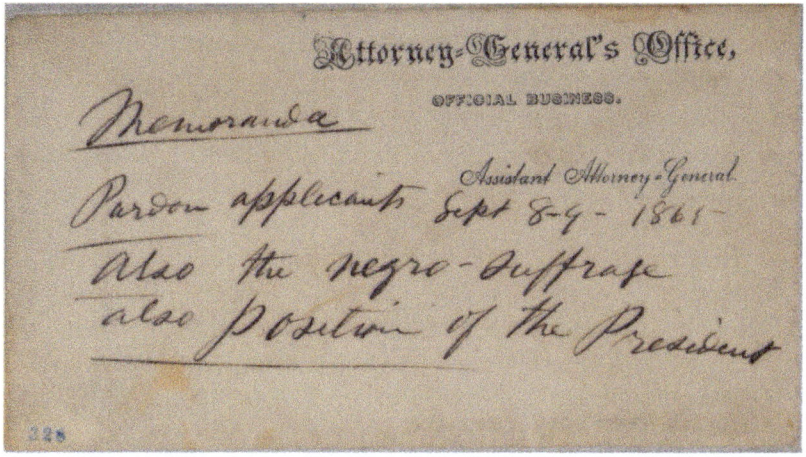

Figure 5.3. Courtesy Thomas Biggs Harned Collection of Walt Whitman Papers, 1842–1937, Library of Congress, Washington, DC.

---

[25] This is admittedly speculative, to some degree, though I assume the manuscript was in Whitman's possession for two reasons. First the dating in both the manuscript and the printed text is unusual and strikingly similar, suggesting that he worked from the manuscript in composing the printed text. Second, the manuscript is housed in Whitman's papers in the Library of Congress rather than in Department of Justice records in the National Archives, making it likely that the item was in his personal possession.

He expanded on this jotting in the 1880s:

> *Washington, Sept.* 8, 9, &c., 1865.—The arrivals, swarms, &c., of the $20,000 men[26] seeking pardons, still continue with increas'd numbers and pertinacity. I yesterday (I am a clerk in the U. S. Attorney General's office here) made out a long list from Alabama, nearly 200, recommended for pardon by the Provisional Governor. This list, in the shape of a requisition from the Attorney General, goes to the State Department. There the Pardon Warrants are made out, brought back here, and then sent to the President, where they await his signature. He is signing them very freely of late.
>
> The President, indeed, as at present appears, has fix'd his mind on a very generous and forgiving course toward the return'd secessionists. He will not countenance at all the demand of the extreme Philo-African element of the North, to make the right of negro voting at elections a condition and *sine qua non* of the reconstruction of the United States south, and of their resumption of co-equality in the Union.[27]

Of course, what was "generous and forgiving" for former secessionists was anything but fair for African Americans, since no past wrongs were addressed and future wrongs were enabled: as soon as the former Confederates resumed power in Southern state houses, they disenfranchised their fellow citizens.

Whitman's forgiving outlook here aligns with that of President Andrew Johnson, the "Tennessee tailor" and populist who began his career with primary loyalty to working-class whites and resentment toward the planter class. (He later changed and went from being hard on the planters to being too easy on them.) Disconcertingly, in favoring quick restoration of the equal status of white Southerners, Whitman seems to accommodate the dismantling of Reconstruction and to ignore black agency in the fight for civil rights. Or to frame the matter differently, in the debates between W. E. B. Du Bois and Booker T. Washington over suffrage and African American racial progress not long after *November Boughs*, Whitman

---

[26] Amnesty was granted to most Confederates in May 1865. However, high officials in the Confederacy and those who owned more than $20,000 in property had to apply to President Johnson for pardon.

[27] *Complete Prose*, 441–42.

inclined not toward Du Bois but toward Washington's gradualist approach to black voting rights. Even Whitman's phrase "extreme Philo-African" is dispiriting because it comes from a poet famous for his capacity to love—he applauded himself once as "the largest lover and sympathizer that has appeared in literature"—and because it implies that a strong love for African Americans is out of bounds, if not absurd.[28] It is all the more dispiriting through the implication that it requires an irrational love for African Americans in order merely to make imaginable the civic "right of negro voting at elections." It is, of course, not necessary to love a citizen at all to extend that right. In fact, extreme hatred across sectional bounds did not make it unimaginable that Southern planters could be pardoned and given the right to vote.

From "Blue Ontario's Shore" to *Democratic Vistas*

Whitman registered the profound changes of the postwar period, including pardoning Confederates and "negro suffrage," in the "extensive and ceaseless revision" of a poem known by its final title, "By Blue Ontario's Shore."[29] Large portions of this agenda-setting poem first appeared as prose in the 1855 Preface before being transfigured in 1856 into "Poem of Many In One." This evolving work displays Whitman's preoccupation with cohering forces, with the need for greater unity, even as the country fractured. Given the prewar political circumstances, he was more hopeful than accurate when his title of 1856 echoed the national motto of E Pluribus Unum.

Whitman continued to emphasize the significance of this work by using it to open the 1860 "Chants Democratic," one of the most vital poetic clusters in his edition of *Leaves* issued on the eve of the Civil War. The most significant change to the tone and meaning of the poem, however, came in the 1867 edition of *Leaves* where the poem appears in a coda-cluster, *Songs Before Parting*, that wrestles with the challenges of reunification (even as his book's format itself displayed little unity: there are separate books within the volume, each with separate pagination). The war, having exposed national unity as more wish than fact, has left the poet anguished, "solitary," and

---

[28] Unsigned review by Whitman, "Walt Whitman and His Poems," *The United States Review* 5 (September 1855): 210.

[29] *Leaves of Grass, Comprehensive Reader's Edition*, ed. Harold W. Blodgett and Sculley Bradley (New York: New York University Press, 1965), 340.

melancholic as he thinks of the "dead that return no more." But this poem then reaffirms the embrace of diversity Whitman had voiced in earlier editions of *Leaves*: in these states one still finds "not merely a nation, but a teeming nation of nations." He further asserts that here he encounters "the crowds, equality, diversity the Soul loves." Whitman credits "native and grand" bards with the ability to bring unity to this diversity, to make the whole cohere: "by them only can The States be fused into the compact organism of a nation." He contends that the poet is the "arbiter of the diverse" who settles disputes by being the "equalizer of his age and land." How a poet might settle disputes is not clarified, and Whitman's self-definition as an "equalizer" was beginning to fray in these years. Nonetheless, he boldly claims that the poet will bestow "on every object or quality its fit proportion, neither more nor less." Slavery, however, is nation-threatening and totally out of bounds:

> Slavery—the murderous, treacherous conspiracy to raise it upon the ruins of all the rest;
> On and on to the grapple with it—Assassin!—then your life or ours be the stake—and respite no more.

His idealized poet "cheers up slaves, and horrifies foreign despots." Whitman claims that the poet speaks not for a "coterie" but for the "whole people." Perhaps this reflects his role as a voice (or scribe) for the government, yet in 1867 he too often—by omitting any explicit discussion of African American rights at a time of historic civil rights legislation—speaks for a part rather than the whole, for whites rather than "every hue."[30]

Importantly, Whitman makes an uncharacteristic acknowledgment in this poem of wanting to purge his mind of the war: "The war—that war so bloody and grim—the war I wish to forget—was you and me." For Whitman, this is a rare but crucial expression of eagerness to forget. His wish to leave behind the pain of war made him far too ready to gain sectional reconciliation at the sacrifice of racial justice.[31]

It was, then, in the troubled aftermath of the war, in the late 1860s, when both Whitman and the nation were reckoning with events too painful to remember and too terrible to be forgotten that he wrote *Democratic Vistas*

---

[30] *LG* (1867), in the "Songs of Parting" appendix, 3–21.
[31] Folsom, in "'A yet more terrible and more deeply complicated problem,'" discusses how for Whitman "regional reconciliation trumped racial reconciliation" (554).

(1871), his most extensive prose commentary on the condition and prospects of the republic. Sections of the eventual book were initially developed as separate documents: "Democracy" appeared in *The Galaxy* in December 1867, "Personalism" appeared there in May 1868, and "Orbic Literature" was submitted to the same journal but not published. *The Galaxy*, a New York rival to *The Atlantic Monthly*, published various poems by Whitman and some important early criticism, including John Burroughs' "Walt Whitman and his 'Drum-Taps.'" Whitman's extended cultural criticism, so different from *Leaves of Grass* and its poetic language, was shaped by local circumstances in Washington, by national events that came before him in the attorney general's office, and by his engagement with international thinkers, particularly from Britain (Matthew Arnold and Thomas Carlyle most notably). Although Whitman often offered sweeping condemnations of British literature—dismissing it as "feudal" and ill-suited to the needs of democratic America—he was nonetheless intensely eager to compare himself favorably to the British poet laureate Alfred Tennyson (via an anonymous self-review and other writings). Just as he had long wished to surpass the most prestigious British poetry, he now also wished to challenge the British sages, that group of prose writers including Arnold, Carlyle, and John Stuart Mill. Whitman in *Democratic Vistas* saw an opportunity to offer a more optimistic theory of the capabilities of a republic based on ordinary, common citizens, his prized "divine average."

The first of Whitman's essays, "Democracy" constitutes much of the initial part of *Democratic Vistas* and defends democratic principles in broad strokes. In a draft advertisement or anonymous review, he explains that *Democratic Vistas* attempts to demonstrate how freedom and individualism rely on literature speaking to common people as "the life-blood of democracy."[32] Such literature provides them with "a basic model or portrait of personality for general use." He emphasizes that a democracy (and the ideals of a democratic literature) must balance personal liberty and communal bonding. Through what he calls "Personalism"—a vaguely defined term by which he seems to mean the transcendent essence of an individual realized through the blending of the individual with his or her society—the "democratic republican principle" and self-reliance can blend and harmonize.

[32] James Perrin Warren, "Reconstructing Language in *Democratic Vistas*," in Ed Folsom, ed., *Walt Whitman: The Centennial Essays* (Iowa City, IA: University of Iowa Press, 1994), 79.

Arnold's *Culture and Anarchy* (*Cornhill Magazine*, 1867–68; book publication 1869), with the elitism behind its emphasis on high culture, prompted Whitman's attempt to reconsider the basis and prospects of democratic culture. But he invoked even more directly Carlyle's essay "Shooting Niagara" (1867), which claimed that the extension of suffrage to newly emancipated blacks in the US was tantamount to going over Niagara Falls in a barrel—in effect, cultural suicide. The Scotsman had lamented that a "half million excellent White men... full of gifts and faculty, have torn and slashed one another into horrid death,... and three million absurd Blacks,... are completely 'emancipated;' launched into the career of improvement, likely to be 'improved off the face of the earth.'"[33] Although Whitman promised in the opening of *Democratic Vistas* to answer Carlyle, he never adequately did so but instead evaded the topic—another of his silences.[34] Only in the small notes at the back of the short volume does Whitman say: "As to general suffrage, after all, since we have gone so far, the more general it is, the better. I favor the widest opening of the doors. Let the ventilation and area be wide enough, and all is safe."[35] This is a curious affirmation. It holds promise for women and Native Americans, not just those formerly enslaved, but rather than the rhetoric of brotherly affection that appears in Whitman's poetry about democracy, the language of opening the doors and seeking "ventilation" invokes theories about illness as caused by poverty and crowding in such places as hospitals, urban tenements, and contraband camps. His point here—all can vote safely if the country is free from the disease-breeding conditions that are likely to infect these new voters—seems far from his own assertion in "Over the Carnage Rose Prophetic a Voice" where Whitman writes more vaguely if less conditionally, "Affection shall solve the problems of freedom."[36]

In other words, when Whitman dodged race, he could still speak the language of poetic and democratic universalism, of common adhesiveness. When he mentioned race specifically, he hedged. Whitman, from the start a reconciler of opposites, never saw the war and Reconstruction in terms of righting wrongs done to African Americans. Instead, for the poet, the War was primarily about the Union, and when he mourned the dead it was

---

[33] Thomas Carlyle, *Critical and Miscellaneous Essays* (New York: Scribner's 1899), 5: 7.
[34] Folsom, "The Vistas of *Democratic Vistas*," xxxv–xlii.
[35] *Democratic Vistas: The Original Edition in Facsimile*, 83.
[36] This idea was first articulated in "Calamus" number 5 (1860–61) and then reworked in the *Drum-Taps* poem "Over the Carnage Rose Prophetic a Voice."

Northern and Southern dead alike (though rarely, if ever, white and black dead alike). The difference is striking when Whitman is compared to a contemporary who also wrote about the condition and prospects of the post-war Republic. In a speech delivered immediately after Lincoln's death, Frederick Douglass declared: "Let us not forget that justice to the negro is safety to the nation."[37] In that same year, he made clear that "slavery is not abolished until the black man has the ballot."[38] He saw Reconstruction as a "continuation of the purpose of the war, a sacred responsibility to the Union dead and to 4 million freed slaves." For Douglass, the terrible conflict was a war of liberation. He was convinced that "crimes of treason and slavery" ought not be met with "amnesty and oblivion in behalf of men whose hands are red with the best blood of the land."[39]

Indeed, African American writers generally were much more alert than Whitman to the threats at hand. Frances Harper's "Words for the Hour" (1871), published in the same year as *Democratic Vistas*, highlights the very issues Whitman slights:

> Men of the North! it is no time
>   To quit the battle-field;
> When danger fronts your rear and van
>   It is no time to yield.
>
> No time to bend the battle's crest
>   Before the wily foe,
> And, ostrich-like, to hide your heads
>   From the impending blow.
>
> The minions of a baffled wrong
>   Are marshalling their clan,
> Rise up! Rise up, enchanted North!
>   And strike for God and man.

Harper argues that the foe has "only changed his base." It is up to Northerners to build common schools and "teach the Freedman how to wield / The ballot in his hand." Harper can detect a vista in view, too, and

---

[37] David Blight, *Frederick Douglass: Prophet of Freedom* (New York: Simon & Schuster, 2018), 462.
[38] Quoted in Blight, *Frederick Douglass: Prophet of Freedom*, 469.
[39] Blight, *Frederick Douglass: Prophet of Freedom*, 461.

she sees the "nation's golden hour": "To build on Justice, as a rock, /The future of the land."[40]

Andrew Johnson, the Klan, and Whitman's Postwar Vistas

Unlike Frederick Douglass, Whitman both before and after *Democratic Vistas* says surprisingly positive things about Andrew Johnson's states' rights-oriented and pro-Southern response to Reconstruction (what John Hope Franklin once called "Reconstruction, Confederate Style" because it led to so much violence against African Americans).[41] Early in Johnson's presidency, Whitman told Byron Sutherland, a soldier friend, "What I learn & know about him (the President), I think he is a *good man*."[42] The poet admired what he thought was an ordinary American unostentatiously exercising the powers of the presidency. He told his mother in May 1865, before Johnson's presidency hit the rocks:

> I saw the President several times, stood close by him, & took a good look at him—& like his expression much—he is very plain & substantial—it seemed wonderful that just that plain middling-sized ordinary man, dressed in black, without the least badge or ornament, should be the master of all these myriads of soldiers, the best that ever trod the earth, with forty or fifty Major-Generals, around him or riding by, with their broad yellow-satin belts around their waists—and of all the artillery & cavalry—to say nothing of all the Forts & Ships, &c, &c.[43]

Whitman clearly put too much faith in his ability to evaluate character based on physical appearance. He credited this president with "patriotic intentions" as late as 1884, even though Johnson's hostility toward blacks and leniency toward former Confederates was evident: "This is a country for white men," Johnson had been heard to say, "and by God, as long as I am president it shall be a government for white men."[44] If this is a form of patriotism, it is a debased and malign one.

---

[40] Frances Harper, *Poems* (Philadelphia, PA: Merrihew & Son, 1871), 32–33.
[41] Blight, *Frederick Douglass: Prophet of Freedom*, 473–75.
[42] Walt Whitman to Byron Sutherland, August 26, 1865 (*WWA*).
[43] Walt Whitman to Louisa Van Velsor Whitman, May 25, 1865 (*WWA*).
[44] In commenting on Johnson's "patriotic intentions," Whitman groups him with nativist Millard Fillmore and Democrat James Buchanan (interview with *The Philadelphia Press*,

Whitman's experience in the Attorney General's office under Johnson's successor, Ulysses S. Grant, exposed him to white vigilantism, but his encounter with it as a government clerk came after he had finished drafting *Democratic Vistas* in 1870. Although Whitman's work as a scribe documents the government's efforts to destroy the Klan, he remained silent in his poems, essays, and journalism about the dangers of Klan activity. As the national poet, as a bard of democracy, as the celebrant "of every hue and caste," as the spokesperson for a nation based on law and not soil, why did he not speak up? Whitman had an imagination and power with words few could equal, and it is a stubborn fact that he did not underscore the reality of Klan terrorism at a time when many suspected it was overblown if not an outright Republican fiction. Nor in these years did he turn his enormous talents to new writings to help Americans imagine their way toward greater tolerance and inclusiveness. This was a missed opportunity because, as he recognized in *Democratic Vistas*, to realize a democratic vista required not merely laws but the embrace of a people bolstered by the subtle and powerful ways of literature and myth. "Justice," he noted, "is not settled by legislators and laws—it is in the Soul."[45] And Whitman thought of himself as speaking for the spirit and the soul of America.

As noted, Whitman rarely commented directly on the policies of the attorney general's office, so it is not clear if he was wholeheartedly behind the anti-Klan work or, as a subordinate, he merely adhered to office policy.[46]

October 30, 1884: 8 available on the *WWA*). Johnson's phrase about the United States being a country for white men is quoted in Hans L. Trefousse, *Andrew Johnson: A Biography* (New York: Norton, 1997), 236. Whitman's opinion of President Johnson has been insufficiently studied by scholars. For example, there is no entry on President Andrew Johnson in the *Walt Whitman: An Encyclopedia* nor is there any article comparable to the many studies of Whitman and Lincoln or to the perceptive work on Whitman and Grant in Martin Buinicki, *Walt Whitman and Reconstruction: Between Memory and History* (Iowa City, IA: University of Iowa Press, 2011), 109–33. The best treatment of Johnson and Whitman is in David S. Reynolds's section "Undemocratic Vistas" in his Reconstruction chapter in *Walt Whitman's America* (New York: Knopf, 1995), 464–70. Reynolds examines Whitman's admiration for Johnson, reasons why Whitman supported him, and Whitman's hostility toward Johnson's Radical Republican foes.

[45] I quote from *LG* (1867), 293, though Whitman first articulated this view in the 1855 *Leaves*.
[46] In an email exchange, Sean Pears has pointed out a third possibility: that Whitman disagreed with Akerman's anti-Klan policy but adhered to it as a dutiful employee. I personally don't believe Whitman had it in him to be cruel and vicious in the way Klan activities were, so I discount this third possibility, even though I can't exclude it altogether. In fact, it is precisely Whitman's silence about the Klan *everywhere* in his writings that leaves this possibility troublingly open.

It is possible that the attorney general imposed restrictions on what employees could say in public about their anti-Klan work (I noted earlier that a clerk could be fired for divulging privileged information to a newspaper about pardons, perhaps explaining why Whitman waited until the late 1880s to make any direct and unmistakable literary use of his attorney general's office experience). Still, Klan activity was widely discussed in newspapers, and Whitman could have commented without providing information about specific cases. Moreover, Whitman didn't speak to Klan outrages even after he left government service, a glaring omission since he was perfectly positioned to give a ringing, detailed, and piercing critique of the Klan. Among other possibilities, he could have exercised the power of invective that he displayed in some of his journalism and in "The Eighteenth Presidency!"

Whitman, in "Origins of Attempted Secession," an essay included in *Specimen Days & Collect* (1882), though much of it was drafted earlier, says: "The slavery contest is settled—and the war is long over—yet do not those putrid conditions, too many of them, still exist? still result in diseases, fevers, wounds—not of war and army hospitals—but the wounds and diseases of peace?"[47] Given his experience as a scribe, he knew the conflict was not settled but continued as guerilla warfare, and the attempt to reinstitute slavery under a different name was well underway. Whitman's "diseases of peace" may point to the Klan fostering "putrid conditions" and committing atrocities or "wounds." But his vagueness allows readers to insert their own meaning; some readers might consider African American political participation a fever born of the peace. The Klan were white men, and apparently Whitman could not bring himself to name as a disease those he held to be the central constituents of his imagined democracy.

Whitman, especially in a forward-looking work of cultural criticism on the republic, wanted to think of the Civil War as closed. He needed to—he couldn't bear any more—and with the Union regarded as unified, he wished to foreground and secure the intrinsic nobility of ordinary white men. The Klan made this difficult. In assessing the Klan's hold and purposes in the South, Ulysses S. Grant was incisive: its goal was "by force and terror...to deprive colored citizens of the right to bear arms and of the right to a free ballot, to suppress schools in which colored children were taught, and to reduce the colored people to a condition closely akin to that of slavery."[48] On this topic, no statement of comparable

[47] *Complete Prose Works* (Philadelphia, PA: David McKay, 1892), 260.
[48] Chernow, *Grant*, 701.

clarity and force can be found in Whitman's writings. Grant's Attorney General Amos Akerman, following a single day in late November 1871 when 250 people in one South Carolina county confessed affiliation with the Klan, said: "I doubt whether from the beginning of the world until now, a community, nominally civilized, has been so fully under the domination of systematic and organized depravity."[49] By 1872, under the leadership of Grant and Akerman, the federal government temporarily beat back the Klan in the South (the twentieth-century Klan shared approaches with its earlier incarnation but was otherwise distinct).[50] As Grant's biographer Ron Chernow notes, "through the Justice Department, the federal government would emerge as the undisputed champion of civil liberties in the southern states, carving out a new role."[51] Whitman as a clerk in the attorney general's office inscribed over thirty letters treating the Ku Klux Klan alone as his office worked with remarkable early success to smash southern paramilitary groups.

In the attorney general's office, Whitman was positioned to see in lived experience, in policy, and in changing laws the prospects for a new and vibrant multi-racial society. The office treated a wide range of issues—not just pardons and civil rights, but plural marriage in Utah, the expansion of railroads onto Native American lands, international incidents, the governance of the western territories, and much else. He contributed to an attorney general's office that achieved a great deal in these years, though Attorney General Akerman was hindered by lack of adequate funding as he found himself on the front line of cases "running up into hundreds, and will soon reach thousands." He explained in another letter (according to a copy inscribed by Whitman): "The means that Congress has furnished for this

---

[49] Quoted in Chernow, *Grant*, 709. The attorney general's office, especially under the leadership of Amos Akerman (a native of Georgia appointed by President Grant), did praiseworthy work in support of civil rights. At considerable personal risk, Akerman travelled to South Carolina to take on the Klan directly. Lou Falkner Williams notes that "it was [in South Carolina] white supremacy versus black equality, vigilante justice versus the rule of law, constitutional liberty versus Republican superiority" (*The Great South Carolina Ku Klux Klan Trials*, 53). Whites in South Carolina were "either in complicity with the Ku-Klux conspiracy or intimidated by it." On another occasion, Akerman was equally blunt, denouncing the Klan as "the most atrocious organization that the civilized part of the world has ever known." Chernow, *Grant*, 709.

[50] Some historians question how successful the Department of Justice was in resisting the Klan. For an account stressing the limited nature of the success, see Lou Falkner Williams, *The Great South Carolina Ku Klux Klan Trials*, 40–84.

[51] Chernow, *Grant*, 703.

work are not sufficient for immediate operations everywhere."[52] When it came to Yorkville, South Carolina, a location of intense Klan depredations and where Akerman oversaw anti-Klan efforts at considerable personal risk, he had to resort to triage. In yet another Whitman-inscribed letter, Akerman lamented to D. T. Corbin, the US attorney in Yorkville, the "apparent impossibility of trying them all with the present judicial force." In light of the practical limitations he faced, the Attorney General focused on bringing to trial the "leaders in the conspiracies," though he thought those "whose criminality is inferior to that of the first class" should still require "some visitation from the law."[53] It would be nice if one could say that Whitman found in Georgians like Akerman the promise of ordinary white men, though he has very little to say about Akerman explicitly.

Adding to Akerman's problems was his recognition that Northerners were tired of Reconstruction. In a letter to a fellow Georgian and the Governor of that state, Benjamin Conley, Akerman wrote: "The Northern mind being active and full of what is called progress, runs away from the past."[54] Consistent with this observation by Akerman was the policy of the centennial exhibit in Philadelphia in 1876 that forbade paintings depicting the Civil War. By the end of 1871, Akerman reluctantly acknowledged the inadequacy of federal courts to protect citizens—especially blacks, though white Republicans, too—from Klan violence.[55] Whitman at this time had finished *Democratic Vistas* but was writing *Memoranda* and reflecting on the obligations and challenges of memory. However, the memory Whitman inscribed and wished to preserve, powerful and inspiring in many ways, was nevertheless a woefully partial one.

---

[52] Amos T. Akerman to John A. Minnis, November 11, 1871 and Amos T. Akerman to Charles Hooks, December 6, 1871. Copies of both letters are inscribed in Whitman's hand (*WWA*).

[53] Amos T. Akerman to D. T. Corbin, November 10, 1871. Akerman did not wish to "suspend the writ of *habeas corpus*, or to do any unusual thing in the suppression of crime, except where it is positively demonstrated that the ordinary process of law is insufficient." Class and racial bias hampered prosecutions. Those charged were always white and frequently prominent and admired members of the community. Their victims were typically black and almost always held less social status and wealth. Federal attorneys had to persuade jurors to believe the testimony of people thought to be inferior over that of respected community leaders. The only way convictions could be brought was to empanel juries made up entirely (or nearly so) of Republicans, leading to heated complaints that these prosecutions were a partisan vendetta.

[54] Quoted in Robert J. Kaczorowski, "Federal Enforcement of Civil Rights During the First Reconstruction," *Fordham Urban Law Journal* 23, no. 1 (1995), 178.

[55] Kaczorowski, "Federal Enforcement of Civil Rights During the First Reconstruction," 178.

Why Did He Ossify and Can We Learn from the Late Whitman?

Whitman wanted to be the poet of all Americans, a wish not limited by race, gender or even, paradoxically, national boundaries.[56] At times, however, he undermined his own attempts at inclusivity because of a belief in racial hierarchy.[57] For example, this passage from *Memoranda* on "Calhoun's Real Monument" is revealing:

> In one of the Hospital tents for special cases, as I sat to-day tending a new amputation, I heard a couple of neighboring soldiers talking to each other from their cots. One down with fever, but improving, had come up belated from Charleston not long before. The other was what we now call an "old veteran" (i. e., he was a Connecticut youth, probably of less than the age of twenty-five years, the four last of which he had spent in active service in the War in all parts of the country.) The two were chatting of one thing and another. The fever soldier spoke of John C. Calhoun's monument, which he had seen, and was describing it. The veteran said: "*I* have seen Calhoun's monument. *That* you saw is not the real monument. But I have seen it. It is the desolated, ruined South; nearly the whole generation of young men between seventeen and fifty destroyed or maim'd; all the old families used up—the rich impoverish'd, the plantations cover'd with weeds, the slaves unloos'd and become the masters, and the name of Southerner blacken'd with every shame—all *that* is Calhoun's *real* monument."[58]

African Americans in fact never made up more than twenty percent of elected representatives even during the height of Reconstruction. What is

---

[56] Whitman's phrase about the "Americans of all nations" being most full of poetical stuff can either mean 1) the Americans more than any other nation or 2) the Americans as a type of person—by virtue of outlook, predisposition, or democratic commitment—in whatever nation they happen to be in, have the most poetic nature.

[57] Whitman was by no means consistent in his views of racial hierarchy. Especially early in his career, he resisted arguments for white superiority. He marked an article on "The Slavonians and Eastern Europe" which argued that there are "three varieties of human beings" and that "up to the present moment, the destinies of the species appear to have been carried forward almost exclusively by its Caucasian variety." Whitman responded in the margin: "? yes of late centuries, but how about 5 or 10, or twenty thousand years ago?" See *Dear Brother Walt: The Letters of Thomas Jefferson Whitman*, ed. Dennis Berthold and Kenneth M. Price (Kent, OH: Kent State University Press, 1984), 92n.

[58] *MDW*, 54–55. Whitman's interest in the South and his reception there are vital areas of study. See in particular Matt Cohen, *Whitman's Drift: Imagining Literary Distribution* (Iowa City, IA: University of Iowa Press, 2017), 148–69.

striking, then, about the "old veteran" is his readiness to see African Americans having any role in multiracial governance as "blacks become the masters." Whitman's use of dialogue here may allow his own position to remain somewhat ambiguous. Although he doesn't speak these lines in his own voice, the rhetoric of the passage gives credit to the idea because Whitman includes it in the first place; because Whitman's own known skepticism about material monuments (as expressed, for example, in "Ah, Not This Granite Dead and Cold") aligns with the old veteran's views; and because Whitman grants the old veteran the all-important closing position in the anecdote. Elsewhere, Whitman's opinion regarding black participation in governance is made starkly clear in a note originally included in *Memoranda During the War* but not subsequently reprinted:

> The present condition of things (1875) in South Carolina, Mississippi, Louisiana, and other parts of the former Slave States—the utter change and overthrow of their whole social, and the greatest coloring feature of their political institutions—a horror and dismay, as of limitless sea and fire, sweeping over them, and substituting the confusion, chaos, and measureless degradation and insult of the present—the black domination, but little above the beasts—viewed as a temporary, deserv'd punishment for their Slavery and Secession sins, may perhaps be admissible; but as a permanency of course is not to be consider'd for a moment. (Did the vast mass of the blacks, in Slavery in the United States, present a terrible and deeply complicated problem through the just ending century? But how if the mass of the blacks in freedom in the U. S. all through the ensuing century, should present a yet more terrible and more deeply complicated problem?)[59]

As Folsom notes, this is an "unsettling mix of the reactionary and the prophetic," and it is disheartening to say the least.[60] Whitman's later decision not to reprint this note suggests that he doubted the suitability of such views for his published writings and recognized that they risked seriously undermining his life's work, and American democracy.

It will not do to deny, obfuscate, and look away from Whitman's, or the nation's, pattern of associating egalitarianism only with white men. In *Stony*

---

[59] *MDW*, 66.

[60] Ed Folsom, "'A yet more terrible and more deeply complicated problem': Walt Whitman, Race, Reconstruction, and American Democracy," *American Literary History* 30 (Fall 2018), 552.

the Road: Reconstruction, White Supremacy, and the Rise of Jim Crow, Henry Louis Gates analyzes racist images of African Americans. As Gates notes, we might prefer to ignore but we need to understand the failures of American culture as much as the successes. In the last chapter, I discussed a scribal document that included Whitman's own annotation: "This letter has been withdrawn and cancelled—is to be considered as never having been written. W.W." When there are failures of courage, generosity, clarity, and decency in even a revered cultural figure, we cannot allow ourselves to see them "as never having been written."[61]

The poet and critic Lavelle Porter has provocatively asked, "Should Walt Whitman Be #Cancelled?"[62] Porter's question is challenging, especially in an era newly sensitized to what some fear may be a belief in white supremacy hardwired into a significant portion of American society. Porter was responding to a 2013 incident involving a black, gay graduate student in music at Northwestern University, who refused to perform a piece of music based on Whitman's poetry because of Whitman's (not the composer's) racism. Porter says:

> I hope that we can celebrate [Whitman] while also telling the truth about his flaws—and America's flaws. As June Jordan says, "I too am a descendant of Walt Whitman. And I am not by myself struggling to tell the truth about this history of so much land and so much blood, of so much that should be sacred and so much that has been desecrated and annihilated boastfully."

Langston Hughes, who famously decided not to throw *Leaves of Grass* overboard on a journey to Africa (he discarded much else from western culture), urged us to remember the best in people, particularly in Whitman.[63] Yet in divisive, racially-charged times like the present, it is difficult to reckon honestly with the limitations of Whitman without killing off the expansive Whitman of hope and possibilities, the poet who has fueled progressive projects nationally and internationally. As Alan Trachtenberg has argued:

---

[61] Whitman's annotation on a document he inscribed, Matthew F. Pleasants to Benjamin Helm Smith, July 14, 1868 (*WWA*).

[62] https://daily.jstor.org/should-walt-whitman-be-cancelled/

[63] For a recent discussion of Hughes throwing his books overboard, see Ivy Wilson, "Introduction" *Whitman Noir: Black America and the Good Gray Poet* (Iowa City, IA: University of Iowa Press, 2014), x. For Hughes's forgiving attitude toward Whitman's shortcomings, see Martin Klammer, *Whitman, Slavery, and the Emergence of* Leaves of Grass (University Park, PA: Pennsylvania State University Press, 1995), 1–2.

The question is not whether Whitman was a racist. It's beyond debate that many of his random remarks were racist then just as they would be racist today. The more troubling question is the light this lurid feature of the Whitman landscape casts upon the meaning of equality, of democracy itself, in that landscape.... But it's predominantly white working-people that Whitman (the name derives from 'white man') celebrates, which raises the very disturbing question: is it the 'white republic,' Andrew Jackson's 'democracy,' of which Whitman sings and from which he derives his vision of equality, another twist on the crippling American paradox of slavery/freedom?[64]

At the same time, we should recognize and value (even if we sometimes puzzle over) how inspirational Whitman has been for progressive causes despite his own, complex, nuanced, contradictory, reactionary, and sometimes benighted views on an array of matters.

Relations between persona and person are vital in Whitman's case. One critic has remarked: "I continue to question if Whitman was using his poems to hide his true self or if his poems represented the person he wanted to be?"[65] Whitman seems to have grasped that in creating the "I" of *Leaves of Grass* he had forged an idealized version of himself distinct from his everyday life as Walt Whitman. Some commentators have seen the distance between person and persona as a sign of bad faith, hypocrisy, duplicity, or insincerity. But we should not regret that in his best writings he reached for more generous, more loving, and more tolerant views than those he imbibed and sometimes allowed himself to express in more hastily conceived journalism, in private jottings in notebooks, in correspondence with family members or working-class white soldiers, and (more rarely) blinkered moments in his poetry. To his credit, Whitman regularly strove, especially in his poetry, to rise above the biases of his culture.

The Paradoxes of a National Poet

Whitman gives voice to the contradictions of US society, highlighting its promise and achievements even as he perpetuates core failures. Whitman

---

[64] Alan Trachtenberg, review of Jerome Loving, *Walt Whitman: The Song of Himself*, in *Walt Whitman Quarterly Review* 17, no. 3 (Winter, 2000), 127.
[65] https://www.poetryfoundation.org/harriet/2015/06/from-whitman-to-walmart

asked for followers who would destroy the teacher and perhaps wanted "poets to come" to hold him to account. Because he presumed to speak for the country, he invited rigorous and demanding critique. Whitman speaks to both the tragedies and the potential of US experience. Whitman predicted that we'd work through his words and conceptualizations in forging a new way ahead:

> He that by me spreads a wider breast than my own proves the width of my own,
> He most honors my style who learns under it to destroy the teacher.
> The boy I love, the same becomes a man not through derived power but in his own right,
> ...
> I teach straying from me, yet who can stray from me?
> I follow you whoever you are from the present hour;
> My words itch at your ears till you understand them.

What did Washington, DC, have to do with Whitman's paradoxes? He became the national poet in the hospitals as soldiers from both North and South came to the capital. His humanitarian achievements in these years were heroic. Yet later he suffered a restriction of vision, a failure of love and affection. As clerk and kosmos he might have been positioned to be a national seer through his work in the attorney general's office, yet he failed to see that the battle needed to be continued after emancipation. Inclined toward forgiveness and reconciliation, he wanted to think—or kidded himself into believing—that the battle was over, freedom achieved, the goal realized. It is not a defense of Whitman but rather a sad fact that many former abolitionists did the same.

In "So Long!" (1860–61) Whitman calls for the day "when America does what was promised," and one wishes he could have more fully realized personally what he outlined, promised, and enabled for many followers. A book subtitled *Becoming the National Poet in the Federal City* does not mean to signal a fully celebratory assessment. He is the national poet because of both the magnitude of his achievements and the cultural ills he puts on display. Whitman's attempt to speak to and for the whole of the country was at once problematic, presumptuous, and necessary. We may need both myths and truths to sustain democracy. This book has tried to contribute to the not-always-flattering truth side of that formulation. Yet I don't want to dismiss the power of myth or the usefulness of the many "Whitmans" created in the poet's afterlife. Whitman has to some extent become his followers, and they have been on the whole a fascinating and forward-thinking lot. To understand, then, a cultural figure of Whitman's complexity, we need to avoid both worshipping and patronizing outlooks and to shun easy celebrations and equally easy dismissals. Whitman is complex, tricky, elusive:

> As if any man knew aught of my life;
> As if you, O cunning soul, did not keep your secret well.[66]

Whitman's lapses are serious and not mere "private liabilities."[67] Like much of late nineteenth-century American culture, he grew fatigued with the cause of African Americans during Reconstruction and beyond. Whitman, like *Leaves of Grass*, like the United States itself, was (and is) always a work in progress, and their developmental process resists simple formulations or descriptions.

Whitman is not beyond his culture but of it, for better and worse. He invited us to complete him or to defeat him. There is much work to be done.

---

[66] Lines are from 1867 version of "When I Read the Book."   [67] Trachtenberg, 127.

Works Cited

Aaron, Daniel. *The Unwritten War: American Writers and the Civil War*. New York: Knopf, 1973.

Allen, Gay Wilson. "Biblical Echoes in Whitman's Works." *American Literature*, 6 (November 1934), 302–15.

—— *The Solitary Singer: A Critical Biography of Walt Whitman*. 1955; reissued with revisions, New York: New York University Press, 1967.

Aron, Cindy Sondik. *Ladies and Gentlemen of the Civil Service: Middle-Class Workers in Victorian America*. Oxford: Oxford University Press, 1987.

Asch, Chris Myers and George Derek Musgrove. *Chocolate City: A History of Race and Democracy in the Nation's Capital*. Chapel Hill, NC: University of North Carolina Press, 2017.

Augst, Thomas. *The Clerk's Tale: Young Men and Moral Life in Nineteenth-Century America*. Chicago, IL: University of Chicago Press, 2003.

Bair, Barbara. "'A land of lovers and of friends': Whitman and the O'Connors." *Huntington Library Quarterly*, 73, no. 4 (2010), 659–77.

Barrett, Faith. "Addresses to a Divided Nation: Images of War in Emily Dickinson and Walt Whitman." *Arizona Quarterly*, 61, no. 4 (2005), 67–99.

—— *To Fight Aloud is Very Brave: American Poetry and the Civil War*. Amherst, MA: University of Massachusetts Press, 2012.

—— and Cristanne Miller, eds. *"Words for the Hour": A New Anthology of American Civil War Poetry*. Amherst, MA: University of Massachusetts Press, 2005.

Bauerlein, Mark. *Whitman and the American Idiom*. Baton Rouge, LA: Louisiana State University Press, 1991.

Bennett, Michael. "Anti-Pastoralism, Frederick Douglass, and the Nature of Slavery." In Karla Armbruster and Kathleen R. Wallace, eds., *Beyond Nature Writing: Expanding the Boundaries of Ecocriticism*. Charlottesville, VA: University Press of Virginia, 2001, 195–10.

Berthold, Dennis, and Kenneth M. Price, eds. *Dear Brother Walt: The Letters of Thomas Jefferson Whitman*. Kent, OH: Kent State University Press, 1984.

Blake, David Haven. "The American Revolution." In J.R. LeMaster and Donald D. Kummings, eds., *Walt Whitman: An Encyclopedia*. New York: Garland Publishing, 1998.

—— "Whitman's Ecclesiastes: The 1860 'Leaves of Grass' Cluster." *Huntington Library Quarterly*, 73 (2010), 613–27.

Blight, David. "Forgetting Why We Remember." *New York Times*, May 29, 2011. Online.

—— *Frederick Douglass: Prophet of Freedom*. New York: Simon & Schuster, 2018.

Blodgett, Harold, and Sculley Bradley, eds. *Leaves of Grass*. Comprehensive Reader's Edition. New York: New York University Press, 1965.
Boag, Peter. "Sexuality, Gender, and Identity in Great Plains History and Myth." *Great Plains Quarterly*, 18 (1998), 327–40.
Bohan, Ruth L. "*Vanity Fair*, Whitman, and the Counter Jumper." *Word & Image*, 33 no. 1 (2017), 57–69.
Borchert, James. *Alley Life in Washington: Family, Community, Religion, and Folklife in the City, 1850–1970*. Urbana, IL: University of Illinois Press, 1980.
Bradford, Adam. "Re-Collecting Soldiers: Walt Whitman and the Appreciation of Human Value." *Walt Whitman Quarterly Review*, 27 (Winter 2010), 127–52.
Bradford, Adam C. "Embodying the Book: Mourning for the Masses in Walt Whitman's *Drum-Taps*." *Mickle Street Review*, no. 21 (Spring 2016), micklestreet.rutgers.edu.
Brantlinger, Patrick. *Rule of Darkness: British Literature and Imperialism, 1830–1914*. Ithaca, NY: Cornell University Press, 1988.
Brooks, Joanna. *American Lazarus*. Oxford: Oxford University Press, 2007.
Brooks, Lisa. "'Every Swamp is a Castle': Navigating Native Spaces in the Connecticut River Valley, Winter 1675–1677 and 2005–2015." *Northeastern Naturalist*, 24 (2017), 45–80.
Buell, Lawrence. *The Environmental Imagination: Thoreau, Nature Writing, and the Formation of American Culture*. Cambridge, MA: Harvard University Press, 1996.
Buinicki, Martin. "The 'Need of Means Additional': Walt Whitman's Civil War Fundraising." *Walt Whitman Quarterly Review*, 31 (Spring 2014), 135–57.
―――― *Walt Whitman and Reconstruction: Between Memory and History*. Iowa City, IA: University of Iowa Press, 2011.
Burns, Sarah. *Pastoral Inventions: Rural Life in Nineteenth-Century American Art and Culture*. Philadelphia, PA: Temple University Press, 1989.
Burroughs, John. *Whitman: A Study*. Boston, MA: Houghton Mifflin, 1896.
Cahn, Susan K. Review of John Donald Gustav-Wrathall, *Take the Young Stranger by the Hand: Same-Sex Relations and the YMCA*. In *American Historical Review*, 104, no. 5 (December 1999), 1706–07.
Calder, Ellen M. "Personal Recollections of Walt Whitman." *Atlantic Monthly*, 99 (June 1907), 825–34.
Carlyle, Thomas. *Critical and Miscellaneous Essays*. New York: Scribner's 1899.
Chapman, J. Wilbur. *Life and Work of Dwight Moody*. London: James Nisbet, 1900.
Chernow, Ron. *Grant*. New York: Penguin Press, 2017.
Cohen, Matt. *Whitman's Drift: Imagining Literary Distribution*. Iowa City, IA: University of Iowa Press, 2017.
Connors, Judith. "Biography of Walt Whitman." In Harold Bloom, ed., *Walt Whitman*. Philadelphia, PA: Chelsea House, 2003, 5–54.
Cowan, Tynes. "The Slave in the Swamp: Affects of Uncultivated Regions on Plantation Life." In Grey Gundaker, ed., with the assistance of Tynes Cowan. *Keep Your Head to the Sky: Interpreting African American Home Ground*. Charlottesville, VA: University Press of Virginia, 1998, 193–207.

Davis, John. "Eastman Johnson's *Negro Life at the South* and Urban Slavery in Washington, D.C." *The Art Bulletin*, 80, no. 1 (March 1998), 67-92.

Day, Jared N. "Butchers, Tanners, and Tallow Chandlers: The Geography of Slaughtering in Early-Nineteenth-Century New York City." In Paula Young Lee, ed., *Meat, Modernity, and the Rise of the Slaughterhouse*. Durham, NH: University of New Hampshire Press; Lebanon, NH: published by University Press of New England, 2008, 178-97.

Donaldson, Thomas. *Walt Whitman the Man*. New York: Francis P. Harper, 1896.

Douglass, Frederick. "The Unknown Loyal Dead." In Philip S. Foner, ed.; abridged and adapted by Yuval Taylor, *Frederick Douglass: Selected Speeches and Writings*. Chicago, IL: Lawrence Hill Books, 1999, 609-10.

Dowden, Edward. "The Poetry of Democracy: Walt Whitman." *The Westminster Review*, 96 (July 1871), 33-68.

Eligon, John, and Michael Schwirtz. "In Rapes, Candidate Says, Body Can Block Pregnancy." *The New York Times*. August 20, 2012, A13.

Elliot, Charles N. *Walt Whitman as Man, Poet and Friend*. Boston, MA: R. G. Badger, Gorham Press, 1915.

Ely, M. Lynda. "Memorializing Lincoln: Whitman's 'Revision' of James Speed's Oration Upon the Inauguration of the Bust of Abraham Lincoln." *Walt Whitman Quarterly Review*, 14 (Spring 1997), 176-80.

Empson, William. *Some Versions of Pastoralism*. Rpt: New York: New Directions, 1950.

Erkkila, Betsy. *Whitman the Political Poet*. New York: Oxford University Press, 1989.

Eskridge, William N., Jr. *Dishonorable Passions: Sodomy Laws in America, 1861-2003*. New York: Viking, 2008.

Fahs, Alice. *The Imagined Civil War: Popular Literature of the North & South, 1861-1865*. Chapel Hill, NC: University of North Carolina Press, 2001.

Faust, Drew Gilpin. *This Republic of Suffering: Death and the American Civil War*. New York: Vintage, 2008.

Feehan, Michael. "Multiple Editorial Horizons of *Leaves of Grass*." *Resources for American Literary Study*, 20 (1994), 213-30.

Folsom, Ed. "'A spirt of my own seminal wet': Spermatoid Design in Walt Whitman's 1860 *Leaves of Grass*." *Huntington Library Quarterly*, 73 (2010), 585-600.

—— "Lucifer and Ethiopia: Whitman, Race, and Poetics before the Civil War and After." In David S. Reynolds, ed., *A Historical Guide to Walt Whitman*. New York: Oxford University Press, 2000, 45-95.

—— "The Vistas of *Democratic Vistas*." In *Democratic Vistas: The Original Edition in Facsimile*. Iowa City, IA: University of Iowa Press, 2010, xv-lxvii.

—— "Erasing Race: The Lost Black Presence in Whitman's Manuscripts." In Ivy G. Wilson, ed., *Whitman Noir: Black America and the Good Gray Poet*. Iowa City, IA: University of Iowa Press, 2014, 3-31.

—— "'A yet more terrible and more deeply complicated problem': Walt Whitman, Race, Reconstruction, and American Democracy." *American Literary History*, 30 (Fall 2018), 531-58.

Fone, Byrne R. S. "This Other Eden: Arcadia and the Homosexual Imagination." *The Journal of Homosexuality*, 8, nos. 3–4 (1983), 13–34.

Foner, Eric. *Reconstruction: America's Unfinished Revolution*. Updated Edition. New York: Harper Perennial, 2014.

Franklin, Wayne, and Michael Steiner, eds. *Mapping American Culture*. Iowa City, IA: University of Iowa Press, 1992.

French, R. W. "When Lilacs Last in the Dooryard Bloom'd." In J.R. LeMaster and Donald D. Kummings, eds., *Walt Whitman: An Encyclopedia*. New York: Garland Publishing, 1998, 770–73.

Fuller, Randall. *From Battlefields Rising: How the Civil War Transformed American Literature*. New York: Oxford University Press, 2011.

Gailey, Amanda. *Proofs of Genius: Collected Editions from the American Revolution to the Digital Age*. Ann Arbor, MI: University of Michigan Press, 2015.

Genoways, Ted. "'Memoranda of a year (1863)': Whitman in Washington, D.C." Mickle Street Review nos. 17–18 (2005), micklestreet.rutgers.edu

——— *Walt Whitman and the Civil War: America's Poet during the Lost Years of 1860–1862*. Berkeley, CA: University of California Press, 2009.

Glicksberg, Charles I. ed., *Walt Whitman and the Civil War*. 1933; rpt. New York: Barnes, 1963.

Golden, Arthur, ed. *Walt Whitman's Blue Book: The 1860-61* Leaves of Grass *Containing His Manuscript Additions and Revisions*. 2 vols. New York: New York Public Library, 1968, 1, 456 pp.; 2, 428 pp.

Gray, Nicole. "Toward an Embodied Poetics of Appraisal: Walt Whitman in the National Archives." *Archivaria*, 89 (Spring 2020), 104–25.

Grimké, Charlotte Forten. *The Journals of Charlotte Forten Grimké*. Ed. Brenda Stevenson. Oxford: Oxford University Press, 1988.

Gustav-Wrathall, John Donald. *Take the Young Stranger by the Hand: Same-Sex Relations and the YMCA*. Chicago, IL: University of Chicago Press, 1998.

Harper, Frances. *Poems*. Philadelphia, PA: Merrihew & Son, 1871.

Henry, James O. "History of the United States Christian Commission," PhD dissertation University of Maryland, 1959.

Hinton, Richard J [listed as H. J. R.]. "Washington Letter." *Cincinnati Commercial*. August 26, 1871, 1–2.

Hollis, C. Carroll. *Language and Style in* Leaves of Grass. Baton Rouge, LA: Louisiana State University Press, 1983.

Hoogenboom, Ari. *Outlawing the Spoils: A History of the Civil Service Reform Movement 1865–1883*. Urbana, IL: University of Illinois Press, 1968.

——— "Thomas A. Jenckes and Civil Service Reform." *The Mississippi Valley Historical Review*, 47, no. 4 (1961), 636–58.

Hopkins, C. Howard. *History of the YMCA in North America*. New York: Association Press, 1951.

Katz, Jonathan Ned. *Love Stories: Sex Between Men Before Homosexuality*. Chicago, IL: University of Chicago Press, 2001.

Kaczorowski, Robert J. "Federal Enforcement of Civil Rights During the First Reconstruction." *Fordham Urban Law Journal*, 23, no. 1 (1995), 155–86.

Killingsworth, M. Jimmie. "'As if the beasts spoke': The Animal/Animist/Animated Walt Whitman," *Walt Whitman Quarterly Review*, 28 (Summer/Fall 2010), 19–35.
—— *Whitman's Poetry of the Body: Sexuality, Politics, and the Text*. Chapel Hill, NC: University of North Carolina Press, 1989.
Lawrence, Susan C. "Military Hospitals in the Department of Washington." In Susan C. Lawrence, ed., *Civil War Washington: History, Place, and Digital Scholarship*. Lincoln, NE: University of Nebraska Press, 2015, 105–32.
Leech, Margaret. *Reveille in Washington*. New York: Harper and Brothers, 1941.
Lincoln, Abraham. "Second Inaugural Address." In Roy P. Basler, ed., *The Collected Works of Abraham Lincoln*. Volume 8. New Brunswick: Rutgers University Press, 1953, 332–33.
Loving, Jerome. *Walt Whitman: The Song of Himself*. Berkeley, CA: University of California Press, 1999.
—— *Walt Whitman's Champion: William Douglas O'Connor*. College Station, TX: Texas A&M University Press, 1978.
Lowenfels, Walter. *Walt Whitman's Civil War*. New York: Knopf, 1960.
Lybeer, Edward. "Whitman's War and the Status of Literature." *Arizona Quarterly*, 67 (2011), 23–40.
Mahoney, Timothy R. "Middle Class Experience in the Gilded Age, 1865–1900." *Journal of Urban History*, 31 (2005): 356–66.
Mancuso, Luke. "Civil War." In Donald D. Kummings, ed., *A Companion to Walt Whitman*. Malden, MA: Blackwell, 2006, 290–310.
Martin, Robert K. "Conversion and Identity: The 'Calamus' Poems." *Walt Whitman Review*, 25 (June 1979), 59–66.
Marrs, Cody. *Nineteenth-Century American Literature and the Long Civil War*. New York: Cambridge University Press, 2015.
Marvell, Andrew. "The Garden." In *The Poems of Andrew Marvell*. 2003; rptd. New York: Routledge, 2013.
Marx, Leo. "Pastoralism in America." In Sacvan Bercovitch and Myra Jehlen, eds., *Ideology and Classic American Literature*. Cambridge: Cambridge University Press, 1986, 36–69.
—— *The Machine in the Garden*. New York: Oxford University Press, 1964.
Masur, Kate. "Washington's Black Codes." *The New York Times*, December 7, 2011, online.
McDevitt, Theresa R. "Fighting for the Soul of America: A History of the United States Christian Commission," PhD dissertation Kent State University, 1997.
Miller, Andrew. "Taking Fire from the Bucolic: The Pastoral Tradition in Seven American War Poems." *Amerikastudien/American Studies*, 58, no. 1 (2013), 101–19.
Miller, Cristanne. *Reading in Time: Emily Dickinson in the Nineteenth Century*. Amherst, MA: University of Massachusetts Press, 2012.
Miller, David. *Dark Eden: The Swamp in Nineteenth-Century American Culture*. Cambridge: Cambridge University Press, 1989.
Morris, Roy, Jr. *The Better Angel: Walt Whitman in the Civil War*. New York: Oxford University Press, 2000.

Murray, Martin G. "Two Pieces of Uncollected Whitman Journalism: 'Washington as a Central Winter Residence' and 'The Authors of Washington.'" *Walt Whitman Quarterly Review*, 20 (Winter/Spring 2003), 151–76.

——— "Whitman Takes on D.C.'s Dailies." *Yale University Library Gazette*, 70 (October 1995), 47–57.

Nelson, Robert K. and Kenneth M. Price. "Debating Manliness: Thomas Wentworth Higginson, William Sloane Kennedy, and the Question of Whitman." *American Literature*, 73 (September 2001), 496–524.

O'Connor, Ellen M. *Myrtilla Miner: A Memoir*. Boston, MA: Houghton, Mifflin, 1885.

Ostriker, Alicia. "Loving Walt Whitman and the Problem of America." In Jim Perlman, Ed Folsom, and Dan Campion, eds., *Walt Whitman: The Measure of His Song*. Duluth, MN: Holy Cow! Press, 1998, 457–65.

Price, Kenneth M. "'Debris,' Creative Scatter, and the Challenges of Editing Whitman." In Michael Robertson and David Blake, eds., *Where the Future Becomes Present: Walt Whitman and* Leaves of Grass. Iowa City, IA: University of Iowa Press, 2008, pp. 59–80.

——— and Janel Cayer. "'It might be us speaking instead of him!': Individuality, Collaboration, and the Networked Forces Contributing to 'Whitman.'" *Walt Whitman Quarterly Review*, 33 (Fall 2015), 114–24.

——— "The Lost Negress of 'Song of Myself' and the Jolly Young Wenches of Civil War Washington." In Susan Belasco, Ed Folsom, and Kenneth M. Price, eds., *Leaves of Grass: The Sesquicentennial Essays*. Lincoln, NE: University of Nebraska Press, 2007, 224–43.

——— "'Many long dumb voices... clarified and transfigured': The Walt Whitman Archive and the Scholarly Edition in the Digital Age." *Nuovi Annali: Della Scuola Speciale per Archivisti e Bibliotecari* 28. Firenze, Italy: Leo S. Olschki, 2014, 241–56.

R. H. J. [Richard Hinton]. "A Reminiscence." *Cincinnati Commercial*, August 26, 1871, 2.

Rabasa, Jose. *Writing Violence on the Northern Frontier*. Durham, NC: Duke University Press, 2000.

Reeser, Todd W. "Queer Energy and the Indeterminate Object of Desire in Montaigne's 'On Some Verses of Virgil.'" *Journal for Early Modern Cultural Studies*, 16, no. 4 (2016), 38–71.

Report of the Secretary of the Navy in Relation to Armored Vessels. Washington: Government Printing Office, 1864.

Reynolds, David S. *Walt Whitman's America: A Cultural Biography*. New York: Knopf, 1995.

Richards, Eliza. "Weathering the News in US Civil War Poetry." In Kerry Larson, ed., *The Cambridge Companion to Nineteenth-Century American Poetry*. Cambridge: Cambridge University Press, 2011, 113–34.

Roberts, Kim. "A Corrected Map of Whitman's Washington Boarding Houses and Work Places." *Walt Whitman Quarterly Review*, 22 (Fall 2004/Winter 2005), 136–37.

―――― "A Map of Whitman's Washington Boarding Houses and Work Places." *Walt Whitman Quarterly Review*, 22 (Summer 2004), 23-28.

Roper, Robert. *Now the Drum of War: Walt Whitman and His Brothers in the Civil War.* New York: Walker, 2008.

Rosenberg, David M. *Oaten Reeds and Trumpets: Pastoral and Epic in Virgil, Spenser, and Milton.* Lewisburg, PA: Bucknell University Press, 1981.

St. Armand, Barton Levi. *Emily Dickinson and Her Culture: The Soul's Society.* Cambridge: Cambridge University Press, 1986.

Sanborn, Franklin Benjamin. "Reminiscent of Whitman." In Joel Myerson, ed., *Whitman in His Own Time.* Iowa City, IA: University of Iowa Press, 2000, 142-50.

Savage, Kirk. "The Self-Made Monument: George Washington and the Fight to Erect a National Memorial." *Winterthur Portfolio*, 22, No. 4 (Winter, 1987), 225-42.

Schmidgall, Gary. *Containing Multitudes: Walt Whitman and the British Literary Tradition.* New York: Oxford University Press, 2014.

―――― *Walt Whitman: A Gay Life.* New York: William Abrahams; Dutton, 1997.

Shepard, Rob. "Historical Geography, GIS, and Civil War Washington." In Susan Lawrence, ed., *Civil War Washington: The City and the Site.* Lincoln, NE: University of Nebraska Press, 2015.

Smith, Sherwood. "Constantin Volney." In J. R. LeMaster and Donald D. Kummings, eds., *Walt Whitman: An Encyclopedia.* New York: Garland, 755.

Stacy, Jason. "Introduction." *Leaves of Grass, 1860: The 150th Anniversary Facsimile Edition.* Iowa City, IA: University of Iowa Press, 2009.

Stiles, T. J. "The Constitutional Amendment that Reinvented Freedom" *The New York Times*, July 26, 2018. Online.

Stovall, Floyd. *The Foreground of Leaves of Grass.* Charlottesville, VA: University Press of Virginia, 1974.

Sumner, Charles. *Charles Sumner: His Complete Works.* 20 vols. Boston, MA: Lee and Shepard, 1900.

Sweet, Timothy. *Traces of War: Poetry, Photography, and the Crisis of the Union.* Baltimore, MD: Johns Hopkins University Press, 1990.

Tabor, Charles R. "Editorial Essay: Mission, Missions, Missionary—The Words We Use." *Leaven*, 7 (1999), 4.

Thomas, M. Wynn. "Weathering the Storm: Walt Whitman and the Civil War." *Walt Whitman Quarterly Review* 15 (Fall 1997/Winter 1998), 87-109.

Tidei, James A. "Healing the Wounded: The United States Christian Commission During the Civil War," MA thesis University of Nebraska-Kearney, 2015.

Tinker, George E. *Missionary Conquest: The Gospel and Native American Cultural Genocide.* Minneapolis, MN: Fortress Press, 1993.

Tolson, M[elvi]n B. Review of *Selected Poems of Claude McKay. Poetry* 83, no. 5 (February 1954), 287-90.

Trachtenberg, Alan. Review of Jerome Loving, *Walt Whitman: The Song of Himself.* In *Walt Whitman Quarterly Review*, 17, no. 3 (Winter, 2000), 124-28.

Trefousse, Hans L. *Andrew Johnson: A Biography.* New York: Norton, 1997.

Trowbridge, John Townsend. "Reminiscences of Walt Whitman." *Atlantic Monthly* 89 (February 1902), 163-75.

Tuggle, Lindsay. *The Afterlives of Specimens: Science Mourning, and Whitman's Civil War*. Iowa City, IA: University of Iowa Press, 2017.

Twain, *Pudd'nhead Wilson and Those Extraordinary Twins* (1894; New York: Norton, 1980), 105.

Unglaub, Jonathan. "The *Concert Champêtre*: The Crises of History and the Limits of Pastoral." *Arion: A Journal of Humanities and the Classics*, Third Series, 5, no. 1 (Spring–Summer, 1997), 46–91, 93–96.

Vendler, Helen. "Poetry and the Mediation of Value: Whitman on Lincoln." In *The Tanner Lectures on Human Values*, vol. 22. Salt Lake City: University of Utah Press, 2001, 141–58.

Wachtell, Cynthia. "The Civil War: Post-9/11," *American Literary History*, 26 (Fall 2014), 627–38.

——— *War No More: The Antiwar Impulse in American Literature, 1861–1914*. Baton Rouge, LA: Louisiana State University Press, 2010.

Wagner-McCoy, Sarah. "Transatlantic Pastoral and the Realist Novel," PhD dissertation, Harvard University, 2011.

——— "Virgilian Chesnutt: Eclogues of Slavery and Georgics of Reconstruction." *ELH*, 80, no. 1 (2013), 199–220.

Warren, James Perrin. "Reconstructing Language in *Democratic Vistas*." In Ed Folsom, ed., *Walt Whitman: The Centennial Essays*. Iowa City, IA: University of Iowa Press, 1994, 79–87.

Wecter, Dixon. "Walt Whitman as Civil Servant." *PMLA*, 58 (December 1943), 1094–09.

Whitley, Edward. "Networked Literary History and the Bohemians of Antebellum New York." *American Literary History*, 29 (Summer 2017), 287–306.

Whitman, Walt. *Daybooks and Notebooks*. Ed. William White. Volume 1: *Daybooks, 1876–November 1881*; Volume II: *Daybooks, December 1881–1891*; Volume III: *Diary in Canada: Notebooks, Index*. New York: New York University Press, 1978.

——— *The Journalism*. Volume 1: 1834–1846. Ed. Herbert Bergman; Douglas A. Noverr, and Edward J. Recchia, Associate Editors. New York: Peter Lang, 1998.

——— "Talbot's Pictures." *American Phrenological Journal* (February 1853), 45.

Wilkenfeld, Jacob. "Re-Scripting Southern Poetic Discourse in Whitman's 'Longings for Home.'" *Walt Whitman Quarterly Review*, 29 (Fall 2011/Winter 2012), 47–65.

Williams, Lou Falkner. *The Great South Carolina Ku Klux Klan Trials 1871–1872*. Athens, GA: University of Georgia Press, 1996.

Williams, Megan Rowley. *Through the Negative: The Photographic Image and the Written Word in Nineteenth-Century American Literature*. New York: Routledge, 2003.

Williams, Raymond. *The Country and the City*. New York: Oxford University Press, 1973.

Winkle, Kenneth J. *Lincoln's Citadel: The Civil War in Washington, DC*. New York: W. W. Norton, 2013.

Wood, Peter H. *Near Andersonville: Winslow Homer's Civil War*. Cambridge, MA: Harvard University Press, 2010.

―――― and Karen C. C. Dalton, *Winslow Homer's Images of Blacks*. Austin, TX: University of Texas Press, 1988.

Wordsworth, William. "Home at Grasmere." In *William Wordsworth: The Major Works*, ed. Stephen Gill. Oxford: Oxford University Press, 1984, 174–98.

Ziparo, Jessica. *This Grand Experiment: When Women Entered the Federal Workforce in Civil War-Era Washington, D.C.* Chapel Hill, NC: University of North Carolina Press, 2017.

Index

African Americans:
   civil rights 121, 124
   and pastoralism 86–7
   role in emancipation 8–9
   as soldiers 15–16, 51, 52–3
   suffrage 124, **147–51**, *150*, 155, 162, 163
   visual depictions of **84–99**, *86*, *89*, *91*, *92*, *96*, *97*, 149, *150*
   in Washington, DC 8, 13, **146–9**
   see also black emancipation, contraband camps; enslaved persons; Reconstruction; slavery; Whitman, Walt, and African Americans; Whitman, Walt, and black civil rights; Whitman, Walt, and black emancipation; Whitman, Walt, and black female sexuality; Whitman, Walt, and black male sexuality; Whitman, Walt, and slavery
Akerman, Amos 116, **167–8**
Akin, Todd 135–6
Alcott, Louisa May 24
Allen, Gay Wilson 27, 111, 140–1
Andersonville, *see* Camp Sumpter
animal slaughter 82
antipastoralism, *see* Whitman, Walt, and antipastoralism
Appomattox 18
April Fool's Day 10
Arcadia 60, **62**
Arnold, Matthew 161, 162
Aron, Cindy Sondik 105, 106, 111
Asch, Chris Myers 149
Ashton, J. Hubley 106, 125, 127
Attorney General, Office of the 38; *see also* Whitman, Walt, in Attorney General's office
Augst, Thomas 112

Barrett, Faith 57
Barton, Clara 40
Bauerlein, Mark 130
Bellows, Henry Whitney 24, *25*, 40

Benedict, Mrs. Newton 119
Bennett, Michael 85–6
Bible 83; *see also* Christianity; Whitman, Walt, and Christianity
Binckley, John M. 119–21, 125
Bing, Julius 122
Brigham, Johnson 127
black emancipation 8, 9, 15, 146, 148, 149, 155, 163
Blake, David Haven 132
Blight, David 53, 163
Bliss, D. Willard 40
Bloom, Nathaniel 4
Bonds, Margaret 89
Bowen, Sayles J. 147–8
Bradford, Adam 39, 78
Bristow, Benjamin Helm 121
Brooklyn Daily Eagle 41
Brooklyn Standard 65–6
Brown, John 17, 18
Brown, Lewy 101
Browning, Orville 126
Browning, Robert 118
Bruff, J. Goldsborough 113
   rebus letter 113, *114*
Buchanan, James 164
Bureau of Indian Affairs 38; *see also* Whitman, Walt, in Bureau of Indian Affairs
Buell, Lawrence 64
Buinicki, Martin 38, 165
Burleigh, Harry T. 89
Burns, Sarah 72
Burroughs, John 74, 101, 111, 161

Calhoun, John C. 169
Camp Sumpter 133–4
Carlyle, Thomas 12, 161, 162
Carpenter, Matthew 135–6, 138
cattle, *see* enslaved persons, and cattle; Washington, DC, cattle in; Whitman, Walt and cattle
Chambers, Robert 84

Charleston, attack on 15
Chase, Salmon P. 111
Chernow, Ron 121, 167
Christian Commission, US 26
  and evangelism 24, 29
  foundation of 24–5
  mission and policies of 31, 34, 36, 37
  vs. Sanitary Commission 24, **29–31**, 36
  see also Whitman, Walt, and Christian Commission
Christianity:
  and the Civil War 23
  and masculinity 27
  see also Bible; Christian Commission, US; Whitman, Walt, and Christianity
Church, William Conant 121
Cohen, Matt 169
Coleridge, Samuel Taylor 151
Coleridge-Taylor, Samuel 89
Compensated Emancipation Act v–vi, 8–9, 148–9
comradeship 2, 19, 58, 60, 117, 143; *see also* Whitman, Walt, and adhesiveness
Concert Champêtre 60, *61*
Conley, Benjamin 168
Connors, Judith 82
contraband camps 8, 14, 52, 84, 162
Corbin, D. T. 168
Cowan, Tynes 75
Cui, Yaxiao 140
Cunningham, Oscar 72–3

Daily Globe, The 41–2
Darwin, Charles 84
Davis, Jefferson 116
Day, Jared N. 82
Decoration Day, *see* Memorial Day
Dickens, Charles 41
Dickinson, Emily 45
Dismal Swamp 88
Douglass, Frederick v, xii, 13, 53–4, 85–6, 146, 163, 164
Dowden, Edward 57
Doyle, Peter 72, 74, 110, 125, 132, 136–7
Du Bois, W. E. B. 158–9
Dubois, Jesse K. 156

Eakins, Thomas, *Arcadia* 60, *62*
Eldridge, Charles 112, 151, 155–6

Emancipation Proclamation, *see* black emancipation
Emerson, Ralph Waldo 2, 34–5, 67, 84, 110, 118
Empson, William 63
enslaved persons 75
  and cattle 84–5
  and property 99
  see also black emancipation; Whitman, Walt, and enslaved persons
Eskridge, William 133–4
Evarts, William M. 127
Evening Star, The 147

Fahs, Alice xi, 46
Father Damien 41, 42
federal bureaucracy 104–5, 106, 111
  women in 111, 119, 121
  racial minorities in 111, 121
  see also Whitman, Walt, as government employee
Fillmore, Millard 164
First Bull Run, Battle of 78
Folsom, Ed 9, 48, 89–90, 95, 116, 131–2, 149, 151, 152, 160, 170
Franklin, John Hope 164
Frayer, Samuel 51–3
Fredericksburg, Battle of 5
French, R. W. 73
Fugitive Slave Law 9

Gates, Henry Louis 171
Gettysburg, Battle of vi, 17, 82
Gilchrist, Anne 75
Given, John T. 147
Golden, Arthur 129, 131–2, 140, 141
Grant, Ulysses S. 17, 116, 120, 165, 166–7
Gray, Nicole 138
Grimké, Charlotte Forten 155
Gross, Hattie 119

Hale, John 148
Hapgood, Lyman 52
Harlan, James 119, 127, 133, 156
Harper, Frances 163–4
Harper's Weekly 85, 86, *86*, 88, 90–3, *91*, *92*, 94, 97, *150*
Harper's Monthly 88, 89
Harris, W. C. 38

INDEX 187

Hawthorne, Nathaniel 118
Hegel, Georg Wilhelm Friedrich 84
Higginson, Thomas Wentworth 36
Hinton, Richard 43
Homer, Winslow 95, 97
   Near Andersonville 84, **95-7**, *96*, 98, 99
homosexuality:
   anti-sodomy laws 133-4
   in the works of Montaigne 60
   in the works of Virgil 59
   see also Whitman, Walt, and homosexuality
homosociality:
   in pastoral literature 59-60
   and YMCA 25-6, 29
   see also Whitman, Walt, and adhesiveness
Hoogenboom, Ari 120, 122
hospitals:
   Armory Square 1, 6, 34, 40
   churches used as 46-7
   see also Whitman, Walt, hospital visits by
Hubbard, Albion 50
Hughes, Langston 89, 93, 171
Hugo, Victor 118
Humboldt, Wilhelm von 84

Ingersoll, Robert Green 44

Jackson, Jane 95
Jackson, Stonewall 17
Jenckes, T. A. 119-21, 125
Johnson, Andrew 106, 116, 124, 127, 133, 158, 164-5
Johnson, Eastman, *Union Soldiers Accepting a Drink* 84, *97*, **97-9**
Johnston, Alma 75
Jordan, Edward 7
Jordan, Mary 7
Julian, George 147

Kaczorowski, Robert J. 168
Keckly, Elizabeth 149
Kerr, Andrew 133
Killingsworth, Jimmie 85, 140-1
King, Preston 110
Klammer, Martin 171
Ku Klux Klan v, 116, 156, 165-8

Lafayette 155
Lee, Robert E. vi, x, 17
letter writing conventions 114

Lincoln, Abraham vi, 8, 14, 19-20, 29, 73, 75-7, 83, 156
   bust of 125
   on causes of Civil War 17
   Melville on 17-18
   Second Inaugural Address 17, 83
   see also Compensated Emancipation Act; Whitman, Walt, on Abraham Lincoln
Lincoln, Willie 14
Lion, Oscar 131
Loving, Jerome 133

Mahay, John 78
Mahoney, Timothy 105
Manassas, Battle of 17
Mann, Horace 84
Marvell, Andrew 80
Marx, Leo 62-4, 67
masculinity:
   and Christianity 27
   and nursing 36
   see also Whitman, Walt, and masculinity
Masur, Kate 148
Melville, Herman 17, 41
Memorial Day:
   African American origins of 53
   and co-option by whites 54
Mill, John Stuart 161
Miller, David 87
Mills, William H. 126
Milton, John vii, 145
Miner, Myrtilla 13
Moody, Dwight 37
Mormons 29
Murray, Martin 74, 110, 119
Musgrove, George Derek 149

Native Americans 87; *see also* Whitman, Walt, and Native Americans
New York Sunday Dispatch 66
New-York Times 37, 45
New-York Tribune 42
New York Weekly Graphic 40
Nightingale, Florence 40
Noah, Mordecai Manuel 152

O'Connor, Ellen 6, 13, 14, 60, 104, 151
O'Connor, William Douglas 6, 104, 106, 112, 118, 121-2, 126-7, 151, 152-3, *154*
Olmsted, Frederick Law 36

Ostriker, Alicia 2
Otto, William T. 106

Parker, Erastus Otis 124
pastoralism:
   and the Bible 61
   and class 63–4
   and comradeship 58
   and the natural world 63, 64–5
   and nostalgia 64, 72
   and property 58
   and race 64
   and shepherding 58, 61–2, 81, 83
   and slavery 58, 83
   and US identity 63–4
   see also Whitman, Walt, and pastoralism
Pears, Sean 165
Pleasants, Matthew F. 126–7
   letter from *123*
Porter, Lavelle 171
Price, Abby H. 124, 125, 126, 133
Price, Helen 101

rape 135–6, 138
Reconstruction vii, xii–xiii, 87, 98, 127, 155, **163-8**, 169–70
   land redistribution 94–5
   reactions against 53, 119–20, 121, 124, 127, 158
   see also Ku Klux Klan; Whitman, Walt, and postwar reconciliation; Whitman, Walt, and property
Redpath, James 34–6, 53
Reeser, Todd 60
Reid, Whitelaw 42
Reynolds, David S. 165
Richards, Eliza 57
Roberts, Kim 74
Roberts, Milton 46–7, 51
Robinson, Winnie 119
Roper, Robert 21
Rosenberg, David M. 64
Rossetti, William Michael 111–12, 118
Rowland, John 125

Sanitary Commission, US 24, *25*
   see also Christian Commission, US; Whitman, Walt, and Sanitary Commission
Sawyer, Thomas 101, 109–10, 117
Seward, William 110

sexuality 35–6
Shakers 29
Sherman, William Tecumseh 17, 90, 91, 94
Shiloh, Battle of 17
Shugerman, Jed Handelsman 121
slavery:
   as cause of Civil War 17, 53–4, 83
   and pastoralism 83
   see also black emancipation; enslaved persons; Whitman, Walt, and slavery
Smith, Robert Pearsall 41
soldiers *see* African Americans, as soldiers; Whitman, Walt, hospital visits by; Whitman, Walt, and soldiers
Southey, Robert 151
Speed, James 125, 126
Stafford, Harry 44
Stanbery, Henry 116, 124, 126
Stiles, T. J. 149–50
store clerks 108–9, *109*
Strother, David Hunter 88–9
Stuart, George 36
Sumner, Charles 110, 146
Sutherland, Byron 164
swamps 67, 74–6, 87–8
Swedenborgianism 27–8, 84
Sweet, Timothy 57
Swinburne, Charles Algernon 118

Talbot, Jesse 27
Tennyson, Alfred 118, 161
Thayer and Eldridge 38, 129
Theocritus 58, 64–5, 79
Tolson, Melvin 89
Trachtenberg, Alan 171–2, 174
Traubel, Horace 27, 31, 41, 43, 49, 51, 52, 59, 107, 116 124, 130–1, 135–6, 147, 152
Trefousse, Hans L. 165
Trowbridge, John 34, 111, 151
Tuggle, Lindsay 50
Turner, Nat 88
Twain, Mark 10

Vaughan, Fred 137
Vedder, Elihu 95
Virgil 58–61, 65, 67, 69, 73, 79, 87, 99
Volney, Constantin 43

Wachtell, Cynthia 81
Wade, Benjamin Franklin 133
Wagner-McCoy, Sarah 58

INDEX 189

Walker, F. A. 122
Washington, Booker T. 158–9
Washington Daily National Intelligencer 99–100
Washington, DC:
  cattle in 80
  emancipation in 146–9
  prostitution in 14
  sewage system 10, 14
  unpaved streets in 10, 14
  water system in 6, 14
  Whitman inscription in Metro station 20–1
  see also African Americans, in Washington, DC; Whitman, Walt, Washington, DC, residence in
Washington Weekly Chronicle, The 147
Wecter, Dixon 107
Wheatley, Phyllis 94
Whitley, Ed 123
Whitman, George 5, 16, 126
Whitman, Louisa Van Velsor 100–2, 125–6
  Walt Whitman's letters to 14, 37–8, 72, 82, 100–1, 102, 112, 116, 125–6, 130, 148, 155, 164
Whitman, Thomas Jefferson 110
Whitman, Walt 5
  and abolition movement 156
  on Abraham Lincoln 19–20, 73–6, 77, 156
  and adhesiveness 2, 4, 19, 21, 38, 45, 78, 110, 117–19, 132, 136–7, 143–5, 162
  and African Americans 7–17, 52, 84–99, 119, 124, 146–74
  and animals 44, 99–100
  and antipastoralism 57–**103**
  in Army Paymaster's office 7, 106
  in Attorney General's office 105, 106, 112, 115–16, 118, 119–27, 136, 138, 146, 156–9, 165–7, 173
  and black civil rights 9, 16, 17, **146–74**
  and black emancipation 9, 15, 17, 90, 93, 148, 155
  and black female sexuality 11–12, 16
  and black male sexuality 16
  and the body 2–4, 104, 105
  in Bureau of Indian Affairs 106, 119, 127, 132, 138–9
  in Camden, NJ 102
  and cattle 76, 78–9
  on causes of Civil War 17, 162
  and children 7–14

  and Christian Commission 27, **29–38**
  and Christianity 23, 27–9, 34, **38–49**, 75, 84
  and cities 58, 67, 101–2, 103
  and classical literature 58–61
  and collaboration 122–5
  on death 71–3, 75–7, 79, 81–3, 102–3
  on death penalty 116
  and decorum 113–16, 140
  diction 1–2, 38–9, 43, 93–4, 114–15, 140–5, 153
  and egalitarianism 58, 151, 154–5, 159–63, 170–1
  and enslaved persons 3, 78, 113
  and evangelism 38, 39, 41–2
  and the gaze 12
  and genre paintings 10
  as government employee 7, 38, 104–29, 132–6, 138–40, 146, 156, 158, 165–7
  and homosexuality 136–8, 143
  hospital visits by 1, 3, 4–7, 14, 20, 21, 23, 31, 37–40, 46–53, 169, 173
  independence, importance of 37–8, 100–2
  journalism of 37, 41, 65–6, 105, 109, 116
  and Ku Klux Klan 165–8
  as liberating force 2
  and masculinity 138–9
  and Memorial Day 53–5
  and Mormon polygamy 167
  and Native Americans 138–9, 151, 162, 167
  and nature 44, 54–6, 65, 67, 70–1, 73, 76, 78, 80, 87, 99, 103
  in New York 1, 67, 82, 95
  and pastoralism 57–63, 64, 67, 69–71, 73, 74, 82–3, 84, 103
  and pensiveness 79, 141–5
  at Pfaff's beer hall 4, 95, 108, 110
  poetic treatment of Civil War 16, 17–22, 46–8, 54–6, 66–7, 69–77, 88–90, 93–9, 130–1, 140–5, 160
  and postwar reconciliation 54–6, 77, 116, 143–5, 156–60, 162–3, 166, 173
  and property 65–6, 67, 68–9, 99–103
  and Quaker thought 39
  and racial hierarchy 169
  religious language 38–44, 54–6, 59
  and Sanitary Commission 24, 29–31, 36

Whitman, Walt (*cont.*)
  as scribe for soldiers **49–53**, 71–2, 113, 139
  and sexuality 2, 105, 131–2, 133–6, 141–3
  and slavery 3, 69, 73, 83, 86–7, 90, 160
  and social hierarchy 73–5, 77, 81, 100, 113–14, 151, 152
  and soldiers 15–16, 52, 101
  and the South 73, 86–7
  and sympathy 13–15
  tomb of *102*, 102–3
  and transnationalism 169
  and ventriloquism 16, 50–1, 113, 139
  Washington, DC, residence in 5–6, 67, 82, 104–6, 119, 123, 128
  and wilderness 65, 67, 74–5, 101
  works:
    "Ah, Not This Granite Dead and Cold" 170
    "As I Lay with My Head in your Lap, Camerado" 45, 46
    "Ashes of Roses" 39, 54–6, 77
    Banner at Day-Break, The 129
    "Bathed in War's Perfume" 72
    "Behold This Swarthy Face" 15
    Blue Book 60, 72–3, 105, 127–32, *128*, 139–45, *142*
    "Broadway Pageant, A" 67
    "By Blue Ontario's Shore" 73, 159
    "Calamus 19" 15
    "Calamus" cluster 2, 60, 132, 136–7
    "Calhoun's Real Monument" 169
    "Carol of Harvest, A" 121
    "Cattle Droves About Washington" 78–9
    "Chants Democratic 1" 73, 159
    "Chants Democratic 13" 108
    "Children of Adam" 16, 136
    "City of Ships" 67
    Collected Writings of Walt Whitman 156
    "Come Up from the Fields Father" 66–7, 68, **69–72**
    Complete Poems and Prose 103
    "Debris" 76–7
    "Democracy" 161
    Democratic Vistas vii, 12, 105, 113, 115, 146, 153, 160–2, 163, 164, 165
    Drum-Taps 17–18, 39, 46, 50, 66–8, 78, 90, 131–2, 162
    "Drum-Taps" cluster 16, 90
    "Eighteenth Presidency!, The" 166
    "Ethiopia Saluting the Colors" 16, 17, 88–90, **93–9**, 139, 152
    "Farm Picture, A" 66
    "First O Songs for a Prelude" 67
    Galaxy, The 112, 121, 161
    "Give Me the Splendid Silent Sun" 67, 68, 86
    "Great Army of the Sick, The" 37
    "Great Washington Hospitals, The" 49
    "Hospital Perplexity" 79–80
    "I Sing the Body Electric" 3, 10, 68
    "Indian Bureau Reminiscence, An" 138
    "Laws for Creations" 109
    Leaves of Grass (1855) 1–2, 3, 139, 140, 141, 153–5
    Leaves of Grass (1856) 4, 139, 141, 159
    Leaves of Grass (1860–61) 2, 4, 15, 34, 38–9, 45, 60, 73, 76, 86, 88, 90, 108, 127–32, 140, 141, 143, 159, 162, 173
    Leaves of Grass (1867) 76, 131, 159–60, 165, 174
    Leaves of Grass (1871–72) 72
    Leaves of Grass (1881–82) 16
    Life and Adventures of Jack Engle: An Auto-Biography 107
    "Longings for Home" 86, 87–8
    "Manly Health and Training" 27, 136, 139
    "March in the Ranks Hard-Prest, and the Road Unknown, A" 46, 51, 71
    Memoranda During the War 12, 17, 36, 45, 46, 49, 52, 58, **77–83**, 168, 169–70
    "Million Dead, too, summ'd up—The Unknown, The" 79, 82–3
    "New Army Organization Fit for America Needed, A" 81
    November Boughs 138, 156, 158
    "O Magnet-South" 86, 87–8
    "O Tan-Faced Prairie Boy" 16
    "Orbic Literature" 161
    "Origins of Attempted Secession" 166
    "Osceola" 139
    "Over the Carnage Rose Prophetic a Voice" 162
    "Personalism" 161
    "Pioneers! O Pioneers!" 66
    "Poem of Many In One" 159
    "Poetry To-Day in America— Shakspere—the Future" 143
    "Prayer of Columbus" 139
    Preface to *Leaves of Grass* (1855) 28, 44, 159

"Proto-Leaf" 143
"Proud Music of the Sea-Storm" 122
"Return of the Heroes, The" 68
"Rev. Mr. Jacobus's Church.—Foreign Missions" 41
"Sleepers, The" 10, 113
"Small Memoranda" 156–8
"So Long!" 173
"Song of Myself" 2, 10, 67, 79, 113, 139–40, 142
Songs Before Parting 159
"Spanish Element in Our Nationality, The" 152
Specimen Days & Collect 77, 78, 166
"'Tis But Ten Years Since" 40
"To Think of Time" 10
"Travelling Bachelor, A" 65, 66, 107
"Vigil Strange I Kept on the Field One Night" 18–19
"Warble for Lilac-Time" 112
"When I Read the Book" 174
"When Lilacs Last in the Dooryard Bloom'd" 20, 73–6
"Wound Dresser, The" 20–1
"Wounded at Chancellorsville, The" 80–1
Wigglesworth, Michael 107–8
Wilber, Oscar F. 44–5
Wilkenfield, Jacob 86
Williams, Lou Falkner 167
Williams, Megan Rowley 95
Wilson, Ivy 171
Wilson, Woodrow 111
Wirz, Henry 133
letter regarding *134*
Wood, Peter H. 95
Woolf, Virginia 140
Wordsworth, William 62–3, 151

YMCA (Young Men's Christian Association):
and abolition movement 25
foundation of 24
and homosociality 25–6, 29
and job training 27

Ziparo, Jessica 105, 111